THE ORIGIN OF

PAUL'S RELIGION

The Origin of Paul's Religion

THE JAMES SPRUNT LECTURES
DELIVERED AT UNION THEOLOGICAL SEMINARY
IN VIRGINIA

BY

J. GRESHAM MACHEN, D.D.

ASSISTANT PROFESSOR OF NEW TESTAMENT LITERATURE AND
EXECESIS IN PRINCETON THEOLOGICAL SEMINARY

WM. B. EERDMANS PUBLISHING COMPANY
GRAND RAPIDS   MICHIGAN

ISBN 0-8028-1123-X

Reprinted, April 1970
Reprinted, June 1973
Reprinted, August 1976

PHOTOLITHOPRINTED BY EERDMANS PRINTING COMPANY
GRAND RAPIDS, MICHIGAN, UNITED STATES OF AMERICA

TO

WILLIAM PARK ARMSTRONG
MY GUIDE
IN THE STUDY OF THE NEW TESTAMENT
AND IN ALL GOOD THINGS

THE JAMES SPRUNT LECTURES

In 1911 Mr. James Sprunt of Wilmington, North Carolina, gave to The Trustees of Union Theological Seminary in Virginia the sum of thirty thousand dollars, since increased by his generosity to fifty thousand dollars, for the purpose of establishing a perpetual lectureship, which would enable the institution to secure from time to time the services of distinguished ministers and authoritative scholars, outside the regular Faculty, as special lecturers on subjects connected with various departments of Christian thought and Christian work. The lecturers are chosen by the Faculty of the Seminary and a committee of the Board of Trustees, and the lectures are published after their delivery in accordance with a contract between the lecturer and these representatives of the institution. The ninth series of lectures on this foundation is presented in this volume.

W. W. MOORE, *President.*

TABLE OF CONTENTS

CHAPTER I
INTRODUCTION

THE
ORIGIN OF PAUL'S RELIGION

CHAPTER I

INTRODUCTION

THE following discussion is intended to deal, from one particular point of view, with the problem of the origin of Christianity. That problem is an important historical problem, and also an important practical problem. It is an important historical problem not only because of the large place which Christianity has occupied in the medieval and modern world, but also because of certain unique features which even the most unsympathetic and superficial examination must detect in the beginnings of the Christian movement. The problem of the origin of Christianity is also an important practical problem. Rightly or wrongly, Christian experience has ordinarily been connected with one particular view of the origin of the Christian movement; where that view has been abandoned, the experience has ceased.

This dependence of Christianity upon a particular conception of its origin and of its Founder is now indeed being made the object of vigorous attack. There are many who maintain that Christianity is the same no matter what its origin was, and that therefore the problem of origin should be kept entirely separate from the present religious interests of the Church. Obviously, however, this indifference to the question as to what the origin of Christianity was depends upon a particular conception of what Christianity now is; it depends upon the conception which makes of Christianity simply a manner of life. That conception is indeed widespread, but it is by no means universal; there are still hosts of earnest Christians who regard Christianity, not simply as a manner of life, but as a manner of life founded upon a message —upon a message with regard to the Founder of the Christian

3

movement. For such persons the question of the origin of Christianity is rather to be called the question of the truth of Christianity, and that question is to them the most important practical question of their lives. Even if these persons are wrong, the refutation of their supposed error naturally proceeds, and has in recent years almost always proceeded, primarily by means of that very discussion of the origin of the Christian movement which is finally to be shorn of its practical interest. The most important practical question for the modern Church is still the question how Christianity came into being.

In recent years it has become customary to base discussions of the origin of Christianity upon the apostle Paul. Jesus Himself, the author of the Christian movement, wrote nothing —at least no writings of His have been preserved. The record of His words and deeds is the work of others, and the date and authorship and historical value of the documents in which that record is contained are the subject of persistent debate. With regard to the genuineness of the principal epistles of Paul, on the other hand, and with regard to the value of at least part of the outline of his life which is contained in the Book of Acts, all serious historians are agreed. The testimony of Paul, therefore, forms a fixed starting-point in all controversy.

Obviously that testimony has an important bearing upon the question of the origin of Christianity. Paul was a contemporary of Jesus. He attached himself to Jesus' disciples only a very few years after Jesus' death; according to his own words, in one of the universally accepted epistles, he came into early contact with the leader among Jesus' associates; throughout his life he was deeply interested (for one reason or another) in the affairs of the primitive Jerusalem Church; both before his conversion and after it he must have had abundant opportunity for acquainting himself with the facts about Jesus' life and death. His testimony is not, however, limited to what he says in detail about the words and deeds of the Founder of the Christian movement. More important still is the testimony of his experience as a whole. The religion of Paul is a fact which stands in the full light of history. How is it to be explained? What were its presuppositions? Upon what sort of Jesus was it founded? These questions lead into the very heart of the historical problem. Explain the origin of the religion of Paul, and you have solved the problem of the origin of Christianity.

That problem may thus be approached through the gateway of the testimony of Paul. But that is not the only way to approach it. Another way is offered by the Gospel picture of the person of Jesus. Quite independent of questions of date and authorship and literary relationships of the documents, the total picture which the Gospels present bears unmistakable marks of being the picture of a real historical person. Internal evidence here reaches the point of certainty. If the Jesus who in the Gospels is represented as rebuking the Pharisees and as speaking the parables is not a real historical person living at a definite point in the world's history, then there is no way of distinguishing history from fiction. Even the evidence for the genuineness of the Pauline Epistles is no stronger than this. But if the Jesus of the Gospels is a real person, certain puzzling questions arise. The Jesus of the Gospels is a supernatural person; He is represented as possessing sovereign power over the forces of nature. What shall be done with this supernatural element in the picture? It is certainly very difficult to separate it from the rest. Moreover the Jesus of the Gospels is represented as advancing some lofty claims. He regarded Himself as being destined to come with the clouds of heaven and be the instrument in judging the world. What shall be done with this element in His consciousness? How does it agree with the indelible impression of calmness and sanity which has always been made by His character? These questions again lead into the heart of the problem. Yet they cannot be ignored. They are presented inevitably by what every serious historian admits.

The fundamental evidence with regard to the origin of Christianity is therefore twofold. Two facts need to be explained—the Jesus of the Gospels and the religion of Paul. The problem of early Christianity may be approached in either of these two ways. It should finally be approached in both ways. And if it is approached in both ways the investigator will discover, to his amazement, that the two ways lead to the same result. But the present discussion is more limited in scope. It seeks to deal merely with one of the two ways of approach to the problem of Christianity. What was the origin of the religion of Paul?

In discussing the apostle Paul the historian is dealing
with a subject important for its own sake, even aside from the
importance of what it presupposes about Jesus. Unquestionably Paul was a notable man, whose influence has been felt
throughout all subsequent history. The fact itself cannot be
called in question. But since there is wide difference of opinion
about details, it may be well, in a brief preliminary word, to
define a little more closely the nature and extent of the influence of Paul.

That influence has been exerted in two ways. It was
exerted, in the first place, during the lifetime of Paul; and
it has been exerted, in the second place, upon subsequent generations through the medium of the Pauline Epistles.

With regard to the second kind of influence, general considerations would make a high estimate natural. The Pauline
Epistles form a large proportion of the New Testament, which
has been regarded as fundamental and authoritative in all ages
of the Church. The use of the Pauline Epistles as normative
for Christian thought and practice can be traced back to
very early times, and has been continuous ever since. Yet
certain considerations have been urged on the other side as
indicating that the influence of Paul has not been so great as
might have been expected. For example, the Christianity of
the Old Catholic Church at the close of the second century
displays a strange lack of understanding for the deeper elements in the Pauline doctrine of salvation, and something of
the same state of affairs may be detected in the scanty remains of the so-called "Apostolic Fathers" of the beginning
of the century. The divergence from Paul was not conscious;
the writers of the close of the second century all quote the
Pauline Epistles with the utmost reverence. But the fact of
the divergence cannot altogether be denied.

Various explanations of this divergence have been proposed. Baur explained the un-Pauline character of the Old
Catholic Church as due to a compromise with a legalistic Jewish Christianity; Ritschl explained it as due to a natural
process of degeneration on purely Gentile Christian ground;
Von Harnack explains it as due to the intrusion, after the
time of Paul, of Greek habits of thought. The devout believer,
on the other hand, might simply say that the Pauline doctrine

of grace was too wonderful and too divine to be understood fully by the human mind and heart.[1]

Whatever the explanation, however, the fact, even after exaggerations have been avoided, remains significant. It remains true that the Church of the second century failed to understand fully the Pauline doctrine of the way of salvation. The same lack of understanding has been observable only too frequently throughout subsequent generations. It was therefore with some plausibility that Von Harnack advanced his dictum to the effect that Paulinism has established itself as a ferment, but never as a foundation, in the history of doctrine.[2]

In the first place, however, it may be doubted whether the dictum of Von Harnack is true; for in that line of development of theology which runs from Augustine through the Reformation to the Reformed Churches, Paulinism may fairly be regarded as a true foundation. But in the second place, even if Von Harnack's dictum were true, the importance of Paul's influence would not be destroyed. A ferment is sometimes as important as a foundation. As Von Harnack himself says, "the Pauline reactions mark the critical epochs of theology and of the Church. . . . The history of doctrine could be written as a history of the Pauline reactions in the Church." [3] As a matter of fact the influence of Paul upon the entire life of the Church is simply measureless. Who can measure the influence of the eighth chapter of Romans?

The influence of Paul was also exerted, however, in his own lifetime, by his spoken words as well as by his letters. To estimate the full extent of that influence one would have to write the entire history of early Christianity. It may be well, however, to consider briefly at least one outstanding aspect of that influence—an aspect which must appeal even to the most unsympathetic observer. The Christian movement began in the midst of a very peculiar people; in 35 A.D. it would have appeared to a superficial observer to be a Jewish sect. Thirty years later it was plainly a world religion.

[1] Compare "Jesus and Paul," in *Biblical and Theological Studies* by Members of the Faculty of Princeton Theological Seminary, 1912, pp. 553 f.

[2] Harnack, *Lehrbuch der Dogmengeschichte*, 4te Aufl., i, 1909, p. 155. (English Translation, *History of Dogma*, i, 1895, p. 136.)

[3] Harnack, *loc. cit.*

True, the number of its adherents was still small. But the really important steps had been taken. The conquest of the world was now a mere matter of time. This establishment of Christianity as a world religion, to almost as great an extent as any great historical movement can be ascribed to one man, was the work of Paul.

This assertion needs to be defended against various objections, and at the same time freed from misinterpretations and exaggerations.

In the first place, it might be said, the Gentile mission of Paul was really only a part of a mighty historical process—the march of the oriental religions throughout the western world. Christianity was not the only religion which was filling the void left by the decay of the native religions of Greece and Rome. The Phrygian religion of Cybele had been established officially at Rome since 204 B.C., and after leading a somewhat secluded and confined existence for several centuries, was at the time of Paul beginning to make its influence felt in the life of the capital. The Greco-Egyptian religion of Isis was preparing for the triumphal march which it began in earnest in the second century. The Persian religion of Mithras was destined to share with Isis the possession of a large part of the Greco-Roman world. Was not the Christianity of Paul merely one division of a mighty army which would have conquered even without his help?

With regard to this objection a number of things may be said. In the first place, the apostle Paul, as over against the priests of Isis and of Cybele, has perhaps at least the merit of priority; the really serious attempt at world-conquest was made by those religions (and still more clearly by the religion of Mithras) only after the time of Paul. In the second place, the question may well be asked whether it is at all justifiable to class the Christianity of Paul along with those other cults under the head of Hellenized oriental religion. This question will form the subject of a considerable part of the discussion which follows, and it will be answered with an emphatic negative. The Christianity of Paul will be found to be totally different from the oriental religions. The threat of conquest made by those religions, therefore, only places in sharper relief the achievement of Paul, by showing the calamities from which the world was saved by his energetic mission.

If except for the Pauline mission the world would have become devoted to Isis or Mithras, then Paul was certainly one of the supreme benefactors of the human race.

Even apart from any detailed investigation, however, one difference between the religion of Paul and the oriental religions is perfectly obvious. The oriental religions were tolerant of other faiths; the religion of Paul, like the ancient religion of Israel, demanded an absolutely exclusive devotion. A man could become initiated into the mysteries of Isis or Mithras without at all giving up his former beliefs; but if he were to be received into the Church, according to the preaching of Paul, he must forsake all other Saviours for the Lord Jesus Christ. The difference places the achievement of Paul upon an entirely different plane from the successes of the oriental mystery religions. It was one thing to offer a new faith and a new cult as simply one additional way of obtaining contact with the Divine, and it was another thing, and a far more difficult thing (and in the ancient world outside of Israel an unheard-of thing), to require a man to renounce all existing religious beliefs and practices in order to place his whole reliance upon a single Saviour. Amid the prevailing syncretism of the Greco-Roman world, the religion of Paul, with the religion of Israel, stands absolutely alone. The successes of the oriental religions, therefore, only place in clearer light the uniqueness of the achievement of Paul. They do indeed indicate the need and longing of the ancient world for redemption; but that is only part of the preparation for the coming of the gospel which has always been celebrated by devout Christians as part of the divine economy, as one indication that "the fullness of the time" was come. But the wide prevalence of the need does not at all detract from the achievement of satisfying the need. Paul's way of satisfying the need, as it is hoped the later chapters will show, was unique; but what should now be noticed is that the way of Paul, because of its exclusiveness, was at least far more difficult than that of any of his rivals or successors. His achievement was therefore immeasurably greater than theirs.

But if the successes of the oriental religions do not detract from the achievement of Paul, what shall be said of the successes of pre-Christian Judaism? It must always be remembered that Judaism, in the first century, was an active missionary religion. Even Palestinian Judaism was imbued with the missionary spirit; Jesus said to the Pharisees that they compassed sea and land to make one proselyte. The Judaism of the Dispersion was no doubt even more zealous for winning adherents. The numberless synagogues scattered throughout the cities of the Greco-Roman world were not attended, as Jewish synagogues are attended to-day, only by Jews, but were also filled with hosts of Gentiles, some of whom had accepted circumcision and become full Jews, but others of whom, forming the class called in the Book of Acts "God-fearers" or "God-worshipers," had accepted the monotheism of the Jews and the lofty morality of the Old Testament without definitely uniting themselves with the people of Israel. In addition to this propaganda in the synagogues, an elaborate literary propaganda, of which important remnants have been preserved, helped to carry on the misionary work. The question therefore arises whether the preaching of Paul was anything more than a continuation, though in any case a noteworthy continuation, of this pre-Christian Jewish mission.

Here again, as in the case of the longing for redemption which is attested by the successes of the oriental religions, an important element in the preparation for the gospel must certainly be detected. It is hard to exaggerate the service which was rendered to the Pauline mission by the Jewish synagogue. One of the most important problems for every missionary is the problem of gaining a hearing. The problem may be solved in various ways. Sometimes the missionary may hire a place of meeting and advertise; sometimes he may talk on the street corners to passers-by. But for Paul the problem was solved. All that he needed to do was to enter the synagogue and exercise the privilege of speaking, which was accorded with remarkable liberality to visiting teachers. In the synagogue, moreover, Paul found an audience not only of Jews but also of Gentiles; everywhere the "God-fearers" were to be found. These Gentile attendants upon the synagogues formed not only an audience but a picked audience; they were just the class of persons who were most likely to be won by the gospel preaching. In their case much of the preliminary work had been accomplished; they were already acquainted with the doctrine of the one true God; they had already, through the lofty ethical teaching of the Old Testament, come to connect religion with morality in a way which is to us matter-of-course but was very exceptional in the ancient world. Where, as in the market-place at Athens, Paul had to begin at the very beginning, without presupposing this previous instruction on the part of his hearers, his task was rendered far more difficult.

Undoubtedly, in the case of many of his converts he did have to begin in that way; the First Epistle to the Thessalonians, for example, presupposes, perhaps, converts who turned directly from idols to serve the living and true God. But even in such cases the God-fearers formed a nucleus; their manifold social relationships provided points of contact with the rest of the Gentile population. The debt which the Christian Church owes to the Jewish synagogue is simply measureless.

This acknowledgment, however, does not mean that the Pauline mission was only a continuation of the pre-Christian missionary activity of the Jews. On the contrary, the very earnestness of the effort made by the Jews to convert their Gentile neighbors serves to demonstrate all the more clearly the hopelessness of their task. One thing that was fundamental in the religion of the Jews was its exclusiveness. The people of Israel, according to the Old Testament, was the chosen people of God; the notion of a covenant between God and His chosen people was absolutely central in all ages of the Jewish Church. The Old Testament did indeed clearly provide a method by which strangers could be received into the covenant; they could be received whenever, by becoming circumcised and undertaking the observance of the Mosaic Law, they should relinquish their own nationality and become part of the nation of Israel. But this method seemed hopelessly burdensome. Even before the time of Paul it had become evident that the Gentile world as a whole would never submit to such terms. The terms were therefore sometimes relaxed. Covenant privileges were offered by individual Jewish teachers to individual Gentiles without requiring what was most offensive, like circumcision; merit was sought by some of the Gentiles by observance of only certain parts of the Law, such as the requirements about the Sabbath or the provisions about food. Apparently widespread also was the attitude of those persons who seem to have accepted what may be called the spiritual, as distinguished from the ceremonial, aspects of Judaism. But all such compromises were affected by a deadly weakness. The strict requirements of the Law were set forth plainly in the

Old Testament. To cast them aside, in the interests of missionary activity, meant a sacrifice of principle to practice; it meant a sacrifice of the zeal and the good conscience of the missionaries and of the true satisfaction of the converts. One of the chief attractions of Judaism to the world of that day was the possession of an ancient and authoritative Book; the world was eagerly searching for authority in religion. Yet if the privileges of the Old Testament were to be secured, the authority of the Book had to be set aside. The character of a national religion was therefore too indelibly stamped upon the religion of Israel; the Gentile converts could at best only be admitted into an outer circle around the true household of God. What pre-Christian Judaism had to offer was therefore obviously insufficient. Perhaps the tide of the Jewish mission had already begun to ebb before the time of Paul; perhaps the process of the withdrawal of Judaism into its age-long seclusion had already begun. Undoubtedly that process was hastened by the rivalry of Christianity, which offered far more than Judaism had offered and offered it on far more acceptable terms. But the process sooner or later would inevitably have made itself felt. Whether or not Renan was correct in supposing that had it not been for Christianity the world would have been Mithraic, one thing is certain—the world apart from Christianity would never have become Jewish.

But was not the preaching of Paul itself one manifestation of that liberalizing tendency among the Jews to which allusion has just been made and of which the powerlessness has just been asserted? Was not the attitude of Paul in remitting the requirement of circumcision, while he retained the moral and spiritual part of the Old Testament Law— especially if, as the Book of Acts asserts, he assented upon occasion to the imposition of certain of the less burdensome parts even of the ceremonial Law—very similar to the action of a teacher like that Ananias who was willing to receive king Izates of Adiabene without requiring him to be circumcised? These questions in recent years have occasionally been answered in the affirmative, especially by Kirsopp Lake.[1] But despite the plausibility of Lake's representation

---

[1] *The Earlier Epistles of St. Paul*, 1911, pp. 16-28, especially p. 24. Compare Lake and Jackson, *The Beginnings of Christianity*, Part I, vol. i, 1920, p. 166.

he has thereby introduced a root error into his reconstruction of the apostolic age. For whatever the teaching of Paul was, it certainly was not "liberalism." The background of Paul is not to be sought in liberal Judaism, but in the strictest sect of the Pharisees. And Paul's remission of the requirement of circumcision was similar only in form, at the most, to the action of the Ananias who has just been mentioned. In motive and in principle it was diametrically opposite. Gentile freedom according to Paul was not something permitted; it was something absolutely required. And it was required just by the strictest interpretation of the Old Testament Law. If Paul had been a liberal Jew, he would never have been the apostle to the Gentiles; for he would never have developed his doctrine of the Cross. Gentile freedom, in other words, was not, according to Paul, a relaxing of strict requirements in the interests of practical missionary work; it was a matter of principle. For the first time the religion of Israel could go forth (or rather was compelled to go forth) with a really good conscience to the spiritual conquest of the world.

Thus the Pauline mission was not merely one manifestation of the progress of oriental religion, and it was not merely a continuation of the pre-Christian mission of the Jews; it was something new. But if it was new in comparison with what was outside of Christianity, was it not anticipated within Christianity itself? Was it not anticipated by the Founder of Christianity, by Jesus Himself?

At this point careful definition is necessary. If all that is meant is that the Gentile mission of Paul was founded altogether upon Jesus, then there ought to be no dispute. A different view, which makes Paul rather than Jesus the true founder of Christianity, will be combated in the following pages. Paul himself, at any rate, bases his doctrine of Gentile freedom altogether upon Jesus. But he bases it upon what Jesus had done, not upon what Jesus, at least during His earthly life, had said. The true state of the case may therefore be that Jesus by His redeeming work really made possible the Gentile mission, but that the discovery of the true significance of that work was left to Paul. The achievement of Paul, whether it be regarded as a discovery made by him or a divine revelation made to him, would thus remain intact. What did Jesus say or imply, during His earthly ministry, about the universal-

ism of the gospel? Did He make superfluous the teaching of
Paul?

The latter question must be answered in the negative; attempts at finding, clearly expressed, in the words of Jesus
the full doctrine of Gentile freedom have failed. It is often
said that Jesus, though He addressed His teaching to Jews,
addressed it to them not as Jews but as men. But the discovery of that fact (whenever it was made) was no mean
achievement. Certainly it was not made by the modern writers
who lightly repeat the assertion, for they have the benefit of
the teaching of Paul and of nineteen centuries of Christian
experience based upon that teaching. Even if Jesus did address not the Jew as a Jew, but the man in the Jew, the achievement of Paul in the establishment of the Gentile Church was
not thereby made a matter of course. The plain man would
be more likely to stick at the fact that however Jesus addressed
the Jew He did address the Jew and not the Gentile, and He
commanded His disciples to do the same. Instances in which
He extended His ministry to Gentiles are expressly designated
in the Gospels as exceptional.

But did He not definitely command His disciples to engage
in the Gentile work after His departure? Certainly He did
not do so according to the modern critical view of the Gospels.
But even if the great commission of Matt. xxviii. 19, 20 be
accepted as an utterance of Jesus, it is by no means clear that
the question of Gentile liberty was settled. In the great commission, the apostles are commanded to make disciples of all
the nations. But on what terms were the new disciples to be
received? There was nothing startling, from the Jewish point
of view, in winning Gentile converts; the non-Christian Jews,
as has just been observed, were busily engaged in doing that.
The only difficulty arose when the terms of reception of the new
converts were changed. Were the new converts to be received
as disciples of Jesus without being circumcised and thus without becoming members of the covenant people of God? The
great commission does not answer that question. It does indeed mention only baptism and not circumcision. But might
that not be because circumcision, for those who were to enter
into God's people, was a matter of course?

In a number of His utterances, it is true, Jesus did
adopt an attitude toward the ceremonial Law, at least toward

the interpretation of it by the scribes, very different from what was customary in the Judaism of His day. "There is nothing from without the man," He said, "that entering into him can defile him: but the things which come out of him, those are they that defile the man" (Mark vii. 15). No doubt these words were revolutionary in their ultimate implications. But there is no evidence that they resulted in revolutionary practice on the part of Jesus. On the contrary, there is definite reason to suppose that He observed the ceremonial Law as it was contained in the Old Testament, and definite utterances of His in support of the authority of the Law have been preserved in the Gospels.

The disciples, therefore, were not obviously unfaithful to the teachings of Jesus if after He had been taken from them they continued to minister only to the lost sheep of the house of Israel. If He had told them to make disciples of all the nations, He had not told them upon what terms the disciples were to be received or at what moment of time the specifically Gentile work should begin. Perhaps the divine economy required that Israel should first be brought to an acknowledgment of her Lord, or at least her obduracy established beyond peradventure, in accordance with the mysterious prophecy of Jesus in the parable of the Wicked Husbandmen,[1] before the Gentiles should be gathered in. At any rate, there is evidence that whatever was revolutionary in the life and teaching of Jesus was less evident among His disciples, in the early days of the Jerusalem Church. Even the Pharisees, and at any rate the people as a whole, could find nothing to object to in the attitude of the apostles and their followers. The disciples continued to observe the Jewish fasts and feasts. Outwardly they were simply loyal Jews. Evidently Gentile freedom, and the abolition of special Jewish privileges, had not been clearly established by the words of the Master. There was therefore still need for the epoch-making work of Paul.

But if the achievement of Paul was not clearly anticipated in the teaching of Jesus Himself, was it not anticipated or at any rate shared by others in the Church? According to

[1] Matt. xxi. 41, and parallels. This verse can perhaps hardly be held to refer exclusively to the rejection of Jesus by the rulers; it seems also to apply to a rejection by the people as a whole. But the full implications of so mysterious an utterance may well have been lost sight of in the early Jerusalem Church.

the Book of Acts, a Gentile, Cornelius, and his household were baptized, without requirement of circumcision, by Peter himself, the leader of the original apostles; and a free attitude toward the Temple and the Law was adopted by Stephen. The latter instance, at least, has ordinarily been accepted as historical by modern criticism. Even in founding the churches which are usually designated as Pauline, moreover, Barnabas and Silas and others had an important part; and in the founding of many churches Paul himself was not concerned. It is an interesting fact that of the churches in the three most important cities of the Roman Empire not one was founded by Paul. The Church at Alexandria does not appear upon the pages of the New Testament; the Church at Rome appears fully formed when Paul was only preparing for his coming by the Epistle to the Romans; the Church at Antioch, at least in its Gentile form, was founded by certain unnamed Jews of Cyprus and Cyrene. Evidently, therefore, Paul was not the only missionary who carried the gospel to the Gentile world. If the Gentile work consisted merely in the geographical extension of the frontiers of the Church, then Paul did not by any means stand alone.

Even in the geographical sphere, however, his achievements must not be underestimated; even in that sphere he labored far more abundantly than any other one man. His desire to plant the gospel in places where it had never been heard led him into an adventurous life which may well excite the astonishment of the modern man. The catalogue of hardships which Paul himself gives incidentally in the Second Epistle to the Corinthians shows that the Book of Acts has been very conservative in its account of the hardships and perils which the apostle endured; evidently the half has not been told. The results, moreover, were commensurate with the hardships that they cost. Despite the labors of others, it was Paul who planted the gospel in a real chain of the great cities; it was he who conceived most clearly the thought of a mighty Church universal which should embrace both Jew and Gentile, barbarian, Scythian, bond and free in a common faith and a common life. When he addressed himself to the Church at Rome, in a tone of authority, as the apostle to the Gentiles who was ready to preach the gospel to those who were at Rome also, his lofty claim was supported, despite the fact that the Church at

Rome had itself been founded by others, by the mere extent of his labors.

The really distinctive achievement of Paul, however, does not consist in the mere geographical extension of the frontiers of the Church, important as that work was; it lies in a totally different sphere—in the hidden realm of thought.[1] What was really standing in the way of the Gentile mission was not the physical barriers presented by sea and mountain, it was rather the great barrier of religious principle. Particularism was written plain upon the pages of the Old Testament; in emphatic language the Scriptures imposed upon the true Israelite the duty of separateness from the Gentile world. Gentiles might indeed be brought in, but only when they acknowledged the prerogatives of Israel and united themselves with the Jewish nation. If premonitions of a different doctrine were to be found, they were couched in the mysterious language of prophecy; what seemed to be fundamental for the present was the doctrine of the special covenant between Jehovah and His chosen people.

This particularism of the Old Testament might have been overcome by practical considerations, especially by the consideration that since as a matter of fact the Gentiles would never accept circumcision and submit to the Law the only way to carry on the broader work was quietly to keep the more burdensome requirements of the Law in abeyance. This method would have been the method of "liberalism." And it would have been utterly futile. It would have meant an irreparable injury to the religious conscience; it would have sacrificed the good conscience of the missionary and the authoritativeness of his proclamation. Liberalism would never have conquered the world.

Fortunately liberalism was not the method of Paul. Paul was not a practical Christian who regarded life as superior to doctrine, and practice as superior to principle. On the contrary, he overcame the principle of Jewish particularism in the only way in which it could be overcome; he overcame principle by principle. It was not Paul the practical missionary, but Paul the theologian, who was the real apostle to the Gentiles.

[1] For what follows, compare the article cited in *Biblical and Theological Studies,* pp. 555-557.

In his theology he avoided certain errors which lay near at hand. He avoided the error of Marcion, who in the middle of the second century combated Jewish particularism by representing the whole of the Old Testament economy as evil and as the work of a being hostile to the good God. That error would have deprived the Church of the prestige which it derived from the possession of an ancient and authoritative Book; as a merely new religion Christianity never could have appealed to the Gentile world. Paul avoided also the error of the so-called "Epistle of Barnabas," which, while it accepted the Old Testament, rejected the entire Jewish interpretation of it; the Old Testament Law, according to the Epistle of Barnabas, was never intended to require literal sacrifices and circumcision, in the way in which it was interpreted by the Jews. That error, also, would have been disastrous; it would have introduced such boundless absurdity into the Christian use of the Scriptures that all truth and soberness would have fled.

Avoiding all such errors, Paul was able with a perfectly good conscience to accept the priceless support of the Old Testament Scriptures in his missionary work while at the same time he rejected for his Gentile converts the ceremonial requirements which the Old Testament imposed. The solution of the problem is set forth clearly in the Epistle to the Galatians. The Old Testament Law, according to Paul, was truly authoritative and truly divine. But it was temporary; it was authoritative only until the fulfillment of the promise should come. It was a schoolmaster to bring the Jews to Christ; and (such is the implication, according to the Epistle tc the Romans) it could also be a schoolmaster to bring every one to Christ, since it was intended to produce the necessary consciousness of sin.

This treatment of the Old Testament was the only practical solution of the difficulty. But Paul did not adopt it because it was practical; he adopted it because it was true. It never occurred to him to hold principle in abeyance even for the welfare of the souls of men. The deadening blight of pragmatism had never fallen upon his soul.

The Pauline grounding of the Gentile mission is not to be limited, however, to his specific answer to the question,

"What then is the law?" It extends rather to his entire un-
folding of the significance of the Cross of Christ. He exhibited the temporary character of the Old Testament dispensation by showing that a new era had begun, by exhibiting
positively the epoch-making significance of the Cross.

At this point undoubtedly he had precursors. The significance of the Cross of Christ was by no means entirely
unknown to those who had been disciples before him; he himself places the assertion that Christ "died for our sins according to the Scriptures" as one of the things that he had "received." But unless all indications fail Paul did bring an
unparalleled enrichment of the understanding of the Cross.
For the first time the death of Christ was viewed in its full
historical and logical relationships. And thereby Gentile freedom, and the freedom of the entire Christian Church for all
time, was assured.

Inwardly, indeed, the early Jerusalem disciples were already free from the Law; they were really trusting for their
salvation not to their observance of the Law but to what
Christ had done for them. But apparently they did not fully
know that they were free; or rather they did not know exactly
why they were free. The case of Cornelius, according to the
Book of Acts, was exceptional; Cornelius had been received
into the Church without being circumcised, but only by direct
command of the Spirit. Similar direct and unexplained guidance was apparently to be waited for if the case was to be
repeated. Even Stephen had not really advocated the immediate abolition of the Temple or the abandonment of Jewish
prerogatives in the presence of Gentiles.

The freedom of the early Jerusalem Church, in other
words, was not fully grounded in a comprehensive view
of the meaning of Jesus' work. Such freedom could not
be permanent. It was open to argumentative attacks, and
as a matter of fact such attacks were not long absent. The
very life of the Gentile mission at Antioch was threatened
by the Judaizers who came down from Jerusalem and said,
"Except ye be circumcised after the manner of Moses, ye
cannot be saved." Practical considerations, considerations
of church polity, were quite powerless before such attacks;
freedom was held by but a precarious tenure until its under-

lying principles were established. Christianity, in other words, could not live without theology. And the first great Christian theologian was Paul.

It was Paul, then, who established the principles of the Gentile mission. Others labored in detail, but it was he who was at the heart of the movement. It was he, far more than any other one man, who carried the gospel out from Judaism into the Gentile world.

The importance of the achievement must be apparent to every historian, no matter how unsympathetic his attitude toward the content of Christianity may be. The modern European world, what may be called "western civilization," is descended from the civilization of Greece and Rome. Our languages are either derived directly from the Latin, or at any rate connected with the same great family. Our literature and art are inspired by the great classical models. Our law and government have never been independent of the principles enunciated by the statesmen of Greece, and put into practice by the statesmen of Rome. Our philosophies are obliged to return ever anew to the questions which were put, if not answered, by Plato and Aristotle.

Yet there has entered into this current of Indo-European civilization an element from a very diverse and very unexpected source. How comes it that a thoroughly Semitic book like the Bible has been accorded a place in medieval and modern life to which the glories of Greek literature can never by any possibility aspire? How comes it that the words of that book have not only made political history—moved armies and built empires—but also have entered into the very fabric of men's souls? The intrinsic value of the Book would not alone have been sufficient to break down the barriers which opposed its acceptance by the Indo-European race. The race from which the Bible came was despised in ancient times and it is despised to-day. How comes it then that a product of that race has been granted such boundless influence? How comes it that the barriers which have always separated Jew from Gentile, Semite from Aryan, have at one point been broken through, so that the current of Semitic life has been allowed to flow unchecked over the rich fields of our modern civilization?

The answer to these questions, to the large extent which the preceding outline has attempted to define, must be sought in the inner life of a Jew of Tarsus. In dealing with the apostle Paul we are dealing with one of the moving factors of the world's history.

That conclusion might at first sight seem to affect unfavorably the special use to which it is proposed, in the present discussion, to put the examination of Paul. The more important Paul was as a man, it might be said, the less important he becomes as a witness to the origin of Christianity. If his mind had been a blank tablet prepared to receive impressions, then the historian could be sure that what is found in Paul's Epistles about Jesus is a true reflection of what Jesus really was. But as a matter of fact Paul was a genius. It is of the nature of genius to be creative. May not what Paul says about Jesus and the origin of Christianity, therefore, be no mere reflection of the facts, but the creation of his own mind?

The difficulty is not so serious as it seems. Genius is not incompatible with honesty—certainly not the genius of Paul. When, therefore, Paul sets himself to give information about certain plain matters of fact that came under his observation, as in the first two chapters of Galatians, there are not many historians who are inclined to refuse him credence. But the witness of Paul depends not so much upon details as upon the total fact of his religious life. It is that fact which is to be explained. To say merely that Paul was a genius and therefore unaccountable is no explanation. Certainly it is not an explanation satisfactory to modern historians. During the progress of modern criticism, students of the origin of Christianity have accepted the challenge presented by the fact of Paul's religious life; they have felt obliged to account for the emergence of that fact at just the point when it actually appeared. But the explanations which they have offered, as the following discussion may show, are insufficient; and it is just the greatness of Paul for which the explanations do not account. The religion of Paul is too large a building to have been erected upon a pin-point.

Moreover, the greater a man is, the wider is the area of his contact with his environment, and the deeper is his penetration into the spiritual realm. The "man in the street" is not so good an observer as is sometimes supposed; he observes only what lies on the surface. Paul, on the other hand, was able to sound the depths. It is, on the whole, certainly no disadvantage to the student of early Christianity that that particular member of the early Church whose inner life stands clearest in the light of history was no mere nonentity, but one of the commanding figures in the history of the world.

But what, in essence, is the fact of which the historical implications are here to be studied? What was the religion of Paul? No attempt will now be made to answer the question in detail; no attempt will be made to add to the long list of expositions of the Pauline theology. But what is really essential is abundantly plain, and may be put in a word—the religión of Paul was a religion of redemption. It was founded not upon what had always been true, but upon what had recently happened; not upon right ideas about God and His relations to the world, but upon one thing that God had done; not upon an eternal truth of the fatherhood of God, but upon the fact that God had chosen to become the Father of those who should accept the redemption offered by Christ. The religion of Paul was rooted altogether in the redeeming work of Jesus Christ. Jesus for Paul was primarily not a Revealer, but a Saviour.

The character of Paulinism as a redemptive religion involved a certain conception of the Redeemer, which is perfectly plain on the pages of the Pauline Epistles. Jesus Christ, Paul believed, was a heavenly being; Paul placed Him clearly on the side of God and not on the side of men. "Not by man but by Jesus Christ," he says at the beginning of Galatians, and the same contrast is implied everywhere in the Epistles. This heavenly Redeemer existed before His earthly life; came then to earth, where He lived a true human life of humiliation; suffered on the cross for the sins of those upon whom the curse of the Law justly rested; then rose again from the dead by a mighty act of God's power; and is present always with His Church through His Spirit.

That representation has become familiar to the devout Christian, but to the modern historian it seems very strange. For to the modern historian, on the basis of the modern view of Jesus, the procedure of Paul seems to be nothing else than the deification by Paul of a man who had lived but a few years before and had died a shameful death.[1] It is not necessary to

[1] H. J. Holtzmann (in *Protestantische Monatshefte*, iv, 1900, pp. 465f., and in *Christliche Welt*, xxiv, 1910, column 153) admitted that for the rapid apotheosis of Jesus as it is attested by the epistles of Paul he could cite no parallel in the religious history of the race.

argue the question whether in Rom. ix. 5 Paul actually applies the term "God" to Jesus—certainly he does so according to the only natural interpretation of his words as they stand—what is ,really important is that everywhere the relationship in which Paul stands toward Jesus is not the mere relationship of disciple to master, but is a truly religious relationship. Jesus is to Paul everywhere the object of religious faith.

That fact would not be quite so surprising if Paul had been of polytheistic training, if he had grown up in a spiritual environment where the distinction between divine and human was being broken down. Even in such an environment, indeed, the religion of Paul would have been quite without parallel. The deification of the eastern rulers or of the emperors differs *in toto* from the Pauline attitude toward Jesus. It differs in seriousness and fervor; above all it differs in its complete lack of exclusiveness. The lordship of the ruler admitted freely, and was indeed always accompanied by, the lordship of other gods; the lordship of Jesus, in the religion of Paul, was absolutely exclusive. For Paul, there was one Lord and one Lord only. When any parallel for such a religious relationship of a notable man to one of his contemporaries with whose most intimate friends he had come into close contact can be cited in the religious annals of the race, then it will be time for the historian to lose his wonder at the phenomenon of Paul.

But the wonder of the historian reaches its climax when he remembers that Paul was not a polytheist or a pantheist, but a Jew, to whom monotheism was the very breath of life.[1] The Judaism of Paul's day was certainly nothing if not monotheistic. But in the intensity of his monotheism Paul was not different from his countrymen. No one can possibly show a deeper scorn for the many gods of the heathen than can Paul. "For though there be that are called gods," he says, "whether in heaven or in earth, (as there be gods many, and lords many,) But to us there is but one God, the Father, of whom are all things, and we unto him; and one Lord Jesus Christ, by whom are all things, and we by him." (I Cor. viii. 5, 6.) Yet it was this monotheist sprung of a race of monotheists, who stood in a full religious relation to a man who had died but a few years before; it was this monotheist who designated that man, as a matter of course, by the supreme religious term "Lord," and did not hesitate to apply to Him the passages

[1] Compare R. Seeberg, *Der Ursprung des Christusglaubens*, 1914, pp. 1f.

in the Greek Old Testament where that term was used to translate the most awful name of the God of Israel! The religion of Paul is a phenomenon well worthy of the attention of the historian.

In recent years that phenomenon has been explained in four different ways. The four ways have not always been clearly defined; they have sometimes entered into combination with one another. But they are logically distinct, and to a certain extent they may be treated separately.

There is first of all the supernaturalistic explanation, which simply accepts at its face value what Paul presupposes about Jesus. According to this explanation, Jesus was really a heavenly being, who in order to redeem sinful man came voluntarily to earth, suffered for the sins of others on the cross, rose from the dead, ascended to the right hand of God, from whence He shall come to judge the quick and the dead. If this representation be correct, then there is really nothing to explain; the religious attitude of Paul toward Jesus was not an apotheosis of a man, but recognition as divine of one who really was divine.

The other three explanations are alike in that they all reject supernaturalism, they all deny the entrance into human history of any creative act of God, unless indeed all the course of nature be regarded as creative. They all agree, therefore, in explaining the religion of Paul as a phenomenon which emerged in the course of history under the operation of natural causes.

The most widespread of these naturalistic explanations of the religion of Paul is what may be called the "liberal" view. The name is highly unsatisfactory; it has been used and misused until it has often come to mean almost nothing. But no other term is ready to hand. "Ritschlian" might possibly describe the phenomenon that is meant, but that term is perhaps too narrow, and would imply a degree of logical connection with the Ritschlian theology which would not fit all forms of the phenomenon. The best that can be done, therefore, is to define the term "liberal" in a narrower way than is sometimes customary and then use it in distinction not only from traditional and supernaturalistic views, but also from various "radical" views, which will demand separate consideration.

The numerous forms of the liberal view differ from other naturalistic hypotheses in that they attribute supreme importance in the formation of the religion of Paul to the influence of the real historic person, Jesus of Nazareth, and to the experience which Paul had near Damascus when he thought he saw that person risen from the dead. Jesus of Nazareth, according to the liberal view, was the greatest of the children of men. His greatness centered in His consciousness of standing toward God in the relation of son to Father. That consciousness of sonship, at least in its purity, Jesus discovered, was not shared by others. Some category was therefore needed to designate the uniqueness of His sonship. The category which He adopted, though with reluctance, and probably toward the end of His ministry, was the category of Messiahship. His Messianic consciousness was thus not fundamental in His conception of His mission; certainly it did not mean that He put His own person into His gospel. He urged men, not to take Him as the object of their faith, but only to take Him as an example for their faith; not to have faith in Him, but to have faith in God like His faith. Such was the impression of His personality, however, that after His death the love and reverence of His disciples for Him not only induced the hallucinations in which they thought they saw Him risen from the dead but also led them to attribute to His person a kind of religious importance which He had never claimed. They began to make Him not only an example for faith but also the object of faith. The Messianic element in His life began now to assume an importance which He had never attributed to it; the disciples began to ascribe to Him divine attributes. This process was somewhat hindered in the case of His intimate friends by the fact that they had seen Him under all the limitations of ordinary human life. But in the case of the apostle Paul, who had never seen Him, the process of deification could go on unchecked. What was fundamental, however, even for Paul, was an impression of the real person of Jesus of Nazareth; that impression was conveyed to Paul in various ways—especially by the brave and pure lives of Jesus' disciples, which had impressed him, against his will, even when he was still a persecutor. But Paul was a child of his time. He was obliged, therefore, to express that which he had received from Jesus in the categories that were ready to hand. Those categories as applied to Jesus constitute the Pauline theology. Thus Paul was really the truest disciple of Jesus in the depths of his inner life, but his theology was the outer and perishable shell for the precious kernel. His theology was the product of his time, and may now be abandoned; his religion was derived from Jesus of Nazareth and is a permanent possession of the human race.

Such in bare outline is the liberal view of the origin of Paulinism and of Christianity. It has been set forth in so many brilliant treatises that no one may be singled out as clearly representative Perhaps Von Harnack's "What is Christianity?" [1], among the popular expositions, may still serve as well as any other. The liberal view of the origin of Christianity seemed at one time likely to dominate the religious life of the modern world; it found expression in countless sermons and books of devotion as well as in scientific treatises. Now, however, there are some indications that it is beginning to fall; it is being attacked by radicalism of various kinds. With some of these attacks it will not now be worth while to deal; it will not be worth while to deal with those forms of radicalism which reject what have been designated as the two starting-points for an investigation of the origin of Christianity—the historicity of Jesus and the genuineness of the major epistles of Paul. These hypotheses are some of them ·interesting on the negative side, they are interesting for their criticism of the dominant liberal view; but when it comes to their own attempts at reconstruction they have never advanced beyond the purest dilettantism. Attention will now be confined to the work of historians who have really attempted seriously to grapple with the historical problems, and specifically to those who have given attention to the problem of Paul.

Two lines of explanation have been followed in recent years by those who reject, in the interest of more radical views, the liberal account of the origin of Paulinism. But these two lines run to a certain point together; they both reject the liberal emphasis upon the historic person of Jesus as accounting for the origin of Paul's religion. The criticism of the customary view was put sharply by W. Wrede in 1904[2], when he declared

---

[1] Harnack, *Das Wesen des Christentums*, 1900. (English Translation, *What is Christianity?*, 1901.)
[2] Wrede, *Paulus*, 1904. (English Translation, *Paul*, 1907.)

that Paul was no disciple of Jesus, but a second founder of Christianity. The religious life of Paul, Wrede insisted, was not really derived from Jesus of Nazareth. What was fundamental for Paul was not the example of Jesus, but His redeeming work as embraced in the death and resurrection, which were regarded as events of a cosmic significance. The theology of Paul—his interpretation of the death and resurrection of Jesus—cannot, therefore, be separated from his religion; on the contrary, it is in connection with the theology, and not in connection with any impression of the character of Jesus, that the fervor of Paul's religious life runs full and free. Theology and religion in Paul, therefore, must stand or fall together; if one was derived from extra-Christian sources, probably the other must be so derived also. And such, as a matter of fact, Wrede concludes is the case. The religion of Paul is not based at all upon Jesus of Nazareth.

Such, in true import, though not in word or in detail, was the startling criticism which Wrede directed against the liberal account of the origin of Paulinism. He had really only made explicit a type of criticism which had gradually been becoming inevitable for some time before. Hence the importance of his little book. The current reconstruction of the origin of Christianity had produced a Jesus and a Paul who really had little in common with each other. Wrede, in his incomparably succinct and incisive way, had the courage to say so.

But if Paulinism was not derived from Jesus of Nazareth, whence was it derived? Here the two lines of radical opinion begin to diverge. According to Wrede, who was supported by M. Brückner,[1] working contemporaneously, the Pauline conception of Christ, which was fundamental in Paul's religious thought and life, was derived from the pre-Christian conception of the Messiah which Paul already had before his conversion. The Messiah, in the thought of the Jews, was not always conceived of merely as a king of David's line; sometimes he was regarded rather as a mysterious, preëxistent, heavenly being who was to come suddenly with the clouds of heaven and be the judge of all the earth. This transcendent conception which

[1] *Die Entstehung der paulinischen Christologie,* 1903; "Zum Thema Jesus und Paulus," in *Zeitschrift für die neutestamentliche Wissenschaft,* vii, 1906, pp. 112-119; "Der Apostel Paulus als Zeuge wider das Christusbild der Evangelien," in *Protestantische Monatshefte,* x, 1906, pp. 352-364.

is attested by the Jewish apocalypses like the Ethiopic Book of Enoch, was, Wrede maintained, the conception of the Jew, Saul of Tarsus. When, therefore, Paul in his Epistles represents Christ as preëxistent, and as standing close to the Supreme Being in rulership and judgment, the phenomenon, though it may seem strange to us, is not really unique; it is exactly what is found in the apocalypses. What was new in Paul, as over against pre-Christian Judaism, was the belief that the heavenly Messiah had already come to earth and carried out a work of redemption. This belief was not derived, Wrede maintained, from any impression of the exalted moral character of Jesus; on the contrary, if Paul had really come into any close contact with the historical Jesus, he might have had difficulty in identifying Him so completely with the heavenly Messiah; the impression of the truly human character of Jesus and of His subjection to all the ordinary limits of earthly life would have hindered the ascription to Him of the transcendent attributes. Jesus, for Paul, merely provided the one fact that the Messiah had already come to earth and died and risen again. Operating with that fact, interpreting the coming of the Messiah as an act of redemption undertaken out of love for men, Paul was able to develop all the fervor of his Christ-religion.

In very recent years, another account of the origin of Paulinism is becoming increasingly prevalent. This account agrees with Wrede in rejecting the liberal derivation of the religion of Paul from an impression of the historical person of Jesus. But it differs from Wrede in its view of the source from which the religion of Paul is actually to be derived. According to this latest hypothesis, Paulinism was based not upon the pre-Christian Jewish conception of the Messiah, but upon contemporary pagan religion.

This hypothesis represents the application to the problem of Paulinism of the method of modern comparative religion. About twenty years ago that method began to be extended resolutely into the New Testament field, and it has been becoming increasingly prevalent ever since. Despite the prevalence of the method, however, and the variety of its application, one great comprehensive work may now fairly lay claim to be taken as summing up the results. That work is the book of W. Bousset, entitled "Kyrios Christos," which appeared in

1913.[1] It is perhaps too early as yet to estimate the full importance of Bousset's work. But unless all indications fail, the
work is really destined to mark an epoch in the history of New
Testament criticism. Since the days of F. C. Baur, in the
former half of the nineteenth century, there has been no such
original, comprehensive, and grandly conceived rewriting of
early Christian history as has now appeared in Bousset's
"Kyrios Christos." The only question is whether originality,
in this historical sphere, is always compatible with truth.

According to Bousset, the historicity of Jesus is to be
maintained; Jesus was really a religious teacher of incom-
parable power. But Bousset rejects much more of the Gospel
account of Jesus' life than is rejected in the ordinary "liberal"
view; Bousset seems even to be doubtful as to whether
Jesus ever presented Himself to His disciples as the Messiah,
the Messianic element in the Gospels being regarded for the
most part as a mere reflection of the later convictions of the
disciples. After the crucifixion, the disciples in Jerusalem,
Bousset continues, were convinced that Jesus had risen from
the dead, and that He was truly the Messiah. They conceived
of His Messiahship chiefly under the category of the "Son of
Man"; Jesus, they believed, was the heavenly being who in
their interpretation of the Book of Daniel and in the apocalypses appears in the presence of the supreme God as the one
who is to judge the world. This heavenly Son of Man was
taken from them for a time, but they looked with passionate
eagerness for His speedy return. The piety of the early Jerusalem Church was therefore distinctly eschatological; it was
founded not upon any conviction of a present vital relation to
Jesus, but on the hope of His future coming. In the Greek-
speaking Christian communities of such cities as Antioch and
Tarsus, Bousset continues, an important additional step was
taken; Jesus there began to be not only hoped for as the future
judge but also adored as the present Lord. He came to be
regarded as present in the meetings of the Church. The term
"Lord," with the conception that it represents, was never, according to Bousset, applied to Jesus in the primitive Palestinian Church; it was first applied to Him in Hellenistic
Christian communities like the one at Antioch. And it was
there derived distinctly from the prevalent pagan religion. In

[1] Compare also Bousset, *Jesus der Herr*, 1916.

the type of religion familiar to the disciples at Antioch, the term "Lord" was used to denote the cult-god, especially in the so-called "mystery religions"; and the Antioch disciples naturally used the same term to designate the object of their own adoration. But with the term went the idea; Jesus was now considered to be present in the meetings of the Church, just as the cult-gods of the pagan religions were considered to be present in the worship practiced by those religions. An important step had been taken beyond the purely eschatological piety of the Jerusalem disciples.

But how about Paul? Here is to be found one of the boldest elements in all the bold reconstruction of Bousset. Paul, Bousset believes, was not connected in any intimate way with the primitive Christianity in Palestine; what he "received" he received rather from the Hellenistic Christianity, just described, of cities like Antioch. He received, therefore, the Hellenistic conception of Jesus as Lord. But he added to that conception by connecting the "Lord" with the "Spirit." The "Lord" thus became present not only in the meetings of the Church for worship but also in the individual lives of the believers. Paulinism as it appears in the Epistles was thus complete. But this distinctly Pauline contribution, like the conception of the Lordship of Jesus to which it was added, was of pagan origin; it was derived from the mystical piety of the time, with its sharp dualism between a material and a spiritual realm and its notion of the transformation of man by immediate contact with the divine. Paulinism, therefore, according to Bousset, was a religion of redemption. But as such it was derived not at all from the historical Jesus (whose optimistic teaching contained no thought of redemption) but from the pessimistic dualism of the pagan world. The "liberal" distinction between Pauline religion and Pauline theology, the attempt at saving Paul's religion by the sacrifice of his theology, is here abandoned, and all that is most clearly distinctive of Paulinism (though of course some account is taken of the contribution of his Jewish inheritance and of his own genius) is derived from pagan sources.

The hypothesis of Bousset, together with the rival reconstructions which have just been outlined, will be examined in the following discussion. But before they can be examined it will be necessary to say a word about the sources of information with regard to the life of Paul. No discussion of the literary questions can indeed here be undertaken. Almost all that can be done is to set forth very briefly the measure of agreement which has been attained in this field, and the bearing of the points that are still disputed upon the subject of the present investigation.

The sources of information about Paul are contained almost exclusively in the New Testament. They are, first, the Pauline Epistles, and, second, the Book of Acts.

Four of the Pauline Epistles—Galatians, 1 and 2 Corinthians, and Romans—were accepted as certainly genuine by F. C. Baur, the founder of the "Tübingen School" of criticism in the former half of the nineteenth century. This favorable estimate of the "major epistles" has never been abandoned by any number of really serious historians, and three of the other epistles—1 Thessalonians, Philippians, and Philemon—have now been added to the "homologoumena." Seven epistles, therefore, are accepted as genuine to-day by all historians except a few extremists. Of the remaining epistles, Colossians is accepted by the majority of investigators of all shades of opinion, and even in the case of 2 Thessalonians and Ephesians, the acceptance of the hypothesis of genuineness is no longer regarded as a clear mark of "conservatism," these two epistles being regarded as genuine letters of Paul by some even of those who are not in general favorable to the traditional view of the New Testament.

With regard to the Pastoral Epistles—1 and 2 Timothy and Titus—the issue is more clearly drawn. These epistles, at least in their entirety, are seldom regarded as genuine except by those who adopt in general the traditional view of the New Testament and the supernaturalistic conception of the origin of Christianity. That does not mean that the case of the Pastoral Epistles is desperate—certainly the present writer is firmly convinced that the epistles are genuine and that a denial of their genuineness really impoverishes in important respects our conception of the work of Paul—but it does mean that with regard to these epistles the two great contending views concerning the New Testament come into sharp conflict; common ground, in other words, cannot here be found, as in the case of the major epistles, between those who hold widely divergent views as to the origin of Christianity.

It would be out of place in the present connection to discuss the question of the genuineness of the Pastorals. That question is indeed enormously important. It is important for the view which is to be held concerning the New Testament canon; it is important for any estimate of Christian tradition; it is important even for a complete estimate of the work of Paul. But it is not directly important for the question as to the origin of Paulinism; for all the essential features of Paulinism, certainly all those features which make Paulinism, upon naturalistic principles, most difficult of explanation, appear plainly in the accepted epistles.

The question of the Book of Acts, on the other hand, is of vital importance even for the present investigation. Even that question, however, must here be dismissed with a word, though it is hoped that light may be shed upon it by the whole of the following discussion.

Literary evidence of peculiar strength may be adduced in favor of the view that the Book of Acts was really written, as tradition affirms, by a companion of Paul. This evidence is based primarily upon the presence in the book of certain sections where the narrative is carried on in the first person instead of the third. It is generally or even universally admitted that these "we-sections" are the work of an eyewitness, an actual traveling companion of Paul. But according to the common-sense view—according to the first impression made upon every ordinary reader—the author of the we-sections was also the author of the whole book, who when he came in his narrative to those parts of the missionary journeys of Paul where he had actually been present with the apostolic company naturally dropped into the use of the first person instead of the third. If this common-sense view be incorrect, then a later author who produced the completed book has in the we-sections simply made use of an eyewitness source. But this hypothesis is fraught with the most serious difficulty. If the author of the completed book, writing at a time long after the time of Paul, was in the we-sections using the work of a companion of Paul, why did he not either say that he was quoting or else change the "we" of the source to "they." The first person plural, used without explanation by a writer of, say, 100 A.D. in a narrative of the journeys of Paul, would be preposterous.

What could be the explanation of so extraordinary a procedure?

Only two explanations are possible. In the first place, the author may have retained the "we" with deceitful intent, with the intent of producing the false impression that he himself was a companion of Paul. This hypothesis is fraught with insuperable difficulty and is generally rejected. In the second place, the author may have retained the "we" because he was a mere compiler, copying out his sources with mechanical accuracy, and so unable to make the simple editorial change of "we" to "they." This hypothesis is excluded by the striking similarity of language and style between the we-sections and the rest of Luke-Acts, which shows that if the author of the completed double work is in the we-sections making use of a source written by some one else, he has revised the source so as to make it conform to his own style. But if he revised the source, he was no mere compiler, and therefore could not have retained the first person plural which in the completed book produced nonsense. The whole hypothesis therefore breaks down.

Such considerations have led a number of recent scholars— even of those who are unable to accept the supernaturalistic account which the Book of Acts gives of the origin of Christianity—to return to the traditional view that the book was actually written by Luke the physician, a companion of Paul. The argument for Lucan authorship has been developed with great acumen especially by Von Harnack[1] And on the basis of purely literary criticism the argument is certainly irrefutable. It can be refuted, if at all, only through a consideration of the historical contents of the book.

Such attempts at refutation have not been lacking; the Lucan authorship of Acts is still rejected by the great majority of those who maintain the naturalistic view of the origin of Christianity. The objections may be subsumed under two main heads. The Book of Acts, it is said, is not the kind of book that could have been written by a companion of Paul, in the first place because it contains an account of miracles,

[1] *Lukas der Arzt*, 1906 (English Translation, *Luke the Physician*, 1907); *Die Apostelgeschichte*, 1908 (English Translation, *The Acts of the Apostles*, 1909); *Neue Untersuchungen zur Apostelgeschichte und zur Abfassungszeit der synoptischen Evangelien*, 1911 (English Translation, *The Date of the Acts and of the Synoptic Gospels*, 1911).

and in the second place, because it contradicts the Pauline Epistles, particularly in the account which it gives of the relations between Paul and the Jerusalem Church.

The former objection is entirely valid on the basis of any naturalistic account of the origin of Christianity. Efforts have indeed been made by Von Harnack, C. C. Torrey, and others, to overcome the objection. Belief in miracles, it is said, was very general in the ancient world; a miraculous interpretation could therefore be placed upon happenings for which the modern man would have no difficulty in discovering a natural cause. Luke was a child of his time; even in the we-sections, Von Harnack insists, where the work of an eyewitness is universally recognized, a supernaturalistic interpretation is placed upon natural events—as, for example, when Paul excites the wonder of his companions by shaking off into the fire a viper that was no doubt perfectly harmless. Why, then, should the presence of the supernatural in the rest of the book be used to refute the hypothesis of the Lucan authorship, if it is not so used in the we-sections? [1]

This method of refuting the objection drawn from the presence of the supernatural in Luke-Acts has sometimes led to a curious return to the rationalizing method of interpretation which was prevalent one hundred years ago. By that method of interpretation even the details of the New Testament miracles were accepted as historical, but it was thought that the writers were wrong in regarding those details as miraculous. Great ingenuity was displayed by such rationalists as Paulus and many others in exhibiting the true natural causes of details which to the first observers seemed to be supernatural. Such rationalizing has usually been thought to have received its death-blow at the hands of Strauss, who showed that the New Testament narratives were either to be accepted as a whole—miracles and all—or else regarded as myths, that is, as the clothing of religious ideas in historical forms. But now, under the impulsion of literary criticism, which has led away from the position of Baur and Strauss and back to the traditional view of the authorship and date of the New Testament books, the expedients of the rationalizers have in some cases been revived.

[1] Harnack, *Die Apostelgeschichte*, 1908, pp. 111-130 (English Translation, *The Acts of the Apostles*, 1909, pp. 133-161).

The entire effort of Von Harnack is, however, quite hopeless. The objection to the Lucan authorship of Acts which is drawn from the supernatural element in the narrative is irrefutable on the basis of any naturalistic view of the origin of Christianity. The trouble is that the supernatural element in Acts does not concern merely details; it lies, rather, at the root of the whole representation. The origin of the Church, according to the modern naturalistic reconstruction, was due to the belief of the early disciples in the resurrection of Jesus; that belief in turn was founded upon certain hallucinations in which they thought they saw Jesus alive after His passion. In such experiences, the optic nerve is affected not by an external object but by the condition of the subject himself. But there are limitations to what is possible in experiences of that sort, especially where numbers of persons are affected and at different times. It cannot be supposed, therefore, that the disciples of Jesus thought they had any extended intercourse with Him after His passion; momentary appearances, with possibly a few spoken words, were all that they could have experienced. This view of the origin of the Church is thought to be in accord with the all-important testimony of Paul, especially in 1 Cor. xv. 3-8 where he is reproducing a primitive tradition. Thus desperate efforts are made to show that the reference by Paul to the burial of Jesus does not by any means confirm the accounts given in the Gospels of events connected with the empty tomb. Sometimes, indeed, in recent criticism, the fact of the empty tomb is accepted, and then explained in some naturalistic way. But at any rate, the cardinal feature of the modern reconstruction is that the early Church, including Paul, had a spiritual rather than a physical conception of the risen body of Jesus; there was no extended intercourse, it is supposed; Jesus appeared to His disciples momentarily, in heavenly glory.

But this entire representation is diametrically opposed to the representation in the Gospel of Luke and in the Book of Acts. If there is any one writer who emphasizes the plain, physical character of the contact between the disciples and their risen Lord, it is the author of Luke-Acts. In proof, it is only necessary to point to Acts x. 41, where it is said that the risen Jesus held table-companionship with His disciples after

He was risen from the dead! But that is only one detail. The author of Acts is firmly convinced that the contact of the risen Jesus with His disciples, though not devoid of mysterious features, involved the absence of the body of Jesus from the tomb and an intercourse (intermittent, it is true, but including physical proofs of the most definite kind) extending over a period of forty days. Nothing could possibly be more directly contrary to what the current critical view regards as the real account given in the primitive Jerusalem Church and by the apostle Paul.

Yet on the basis of that modern critical view, Von Harnack and others have maintained that the book in which so false an account is given of the origin of the Church was actually the work of a man of the apostolic age. It is no wonder that Von Harnack's conclusions have evoked an emphatic protest from other naturalistic historians. Luke was a close associate of Paul. Could he possibly have given an account of things absolutely fundamental in Paul's gospel (1 Cor. xv. 1-8) which was so diametrically opposed to what Paul taught? He was in Jerusalem in 58 A.D. or earlier, and during years of his life was in close touch with Palestinian disciples. Could he possibly have given an account of the origin of the Jerusalem Church so totally at variance with the account which that church itself maintained? These questions constitute a complete refutation of Von Harnack's view, when that view is taken as a whole. But they do not at all constitute a refutation of the conclusions of Von Harnack in the sphere of literary criticism. On the contrary, by showing how inconsistent those conclusions are with other elements in the thinking of the investigator, they make only the more impressive the strength of the argument which has overcome such obstacles. The objection points out the antinomy which exists between the literary criticism of Von Harnack and his naturalistic account of the origin of Christianity. What that antinomy means is merely that the testimony of Acts to the supernatural origin of Christianity, far from being removed by literary criticism, is strongly supported by it. A companion of Paul could not have been egregiously mistaken about the origin of the Church; but literary criticism establishes Luke-Acts as the work of a companion of Paul. Hence there is some reason for supposing that the account given in this book is essentially correct, and that the naturalistic reconstruction of the origin of Christianity must be abandoned.

The second objection to the Lucan authorship of Acts is based upon the contradiction which is thought to exist between the Book of Acts and the Epistles of Paul.[1] The way to test the value of a historical work, it is said, is to compare it with some recognized authority. With regard to most of the narrative in Acts, no such comparison is possible, since there is no account parallel to Acts by which it may be tested. But in certain places the Book of Acts provides an account of events which are also narrated in the isolated biographical parts of the Pauline Epistles—notably in the first two chapters of Galatians. Here at last is found the long-sought opportunity for comparison. And the comparison, it is said, results unfavorably to the Book of Acts, which is found to contradict the Epistle to the Galatians, not merely in details, but in the whole account which it gives of the relation between Paul and the Jerusalem Church. But if the Book of Acts fails to approve itself in the one place where it can be tested by comparison with a recognized authority, the presumption is that it may be wrong elsewhere as well; in particular, it is quite impossible that a book which so completely misrepresents what happened at a most important crisis of Paul's life could have been written by a close friend of the apostle.

This argument was developed particularly by Baur and Zeller and their associates in the "Tübingen School." According to Baur, the major epistles of Paul constitute the primary source of information about the apostolic age; they should therefore be interpreted without reference to any other source. When they are so interpreted, they show that the fundamental fact of apostolic history was a conflict between Paul on one side and the original apostles on the other. The conflict, Baur maintained further, is particularly plain in the Epistles to the Galatians and Corinthians, which emphasize the complete independence of Paul with reference to the pillars of the Jerusa-

[1] For what follows, compare "Jesus and Paul," in *Biblical and Theological Studies* by the Members of the Faculty of Princeton Theological Seminary, 1912, pp. 553f.; "Recent Criticism of the Book of Acts," in *Princeton Theological Review*, xvii, 1919, pp. 593-597.

lem Church, and his continued opposition to the efforts of Jewish Christians to bring the Gentiles into subjection to the Jewish Law—efforts which must have been supported to some extent by the attitude of the original apostles. This conflict, Baur supposed further, continued up to the middle of the second century; there was a Gentile Christian party appealing to Paul and a Jewish Christian party appealing to Peter. Finally however, Baur continued, a compromise was effected; the Pauline party gave up what was really most distinctive in the Pauline doctrine of justification, while the Petrine party relinquished the demand of circumcision. The New Testament documents, according to Baur, are to be dated in accordance with the position that they assume in the conflict; those documents which take sides—which are strongly anti-Pauline or strongly anti-Petrine—are to be placed early, while those which display a tendency toward compromise are to be placed late, at the time when the conflict was being settled. Such was the "tendency-criticism" of Baur. By that criticism the Book of Acts was dated well on in the second century, because it was thought to display a tendency toward compromise—an "irenic tendency." This tendency, Baur supposed, manifested itself in the Book of Acts in a deliberate falsification of history; in order to bring about peace between the Petrine and the Pauline parties in the Church, the author of Acts attempted to show by a new account of the apostolic age that Peter and Paul really were in perfect agreement. To that end, in the Book of Acts, Paul is Petrinized, and Peter is Paulinized; the sturdy independence of Paul, which actually kept him long away from Jerusalem after his conversion, gives place, in Acts, to a desire of contact with the Jerusalem Church, which brought him early to Jerusalem and finally led him even to accept for his Gentile converts, at the "Apostolic Council," a portion of the ceremonial law. Peter, on the other hand, is represented in Acts as giving expression at the Apostolic Council to Pauline sentiments about the Law; and all through the book there is an elaborate and unhistorical parallelism between Peter and Paul.

The theory of Baur did not long maintain itself in its entirety. It received a searching criticism particularly from A. Ritschl. The conflict of the apostolic age, Ritschl pointed out, was not a conflict between Paul and the original apostles, but between all the apostles (including both Paul and Peter) on the one side, and an extreme Judaizing party on the other; that conflict did not continue throughout the second century; on the contrary, specifically Jewish Christianity soon ceased to be influential, and the legalistic character of the Old Catholic Church of the end of the second century, in which Christianity was conceived of as a new law, was due not to any compromise with the legalism of the Judaizers but to a natural process of degeneration from Paulinism on purely Gentile Christian ground.

The Tübingen dating of the New Testament documents, moreover, has been abandoned under a more thorough investigation of early Christian literature. A study of patristics soon rendered it impossible to string out the New Testament books anywhere throughout the second century in the interest of a plausible theory of development. External evidence has led to a much earlier dating of most of the books than Baur's theory required. The Tübingen estimate of the Book of Acts, in particular, has for the most part been modified; the book is dated much earlier, and it is no longer thought to be a party document written in the interests of a deliberate falsification of history.

Nevertheless, the criticism of Baur and Zeller, though no longer accepted as a whole, is still influential; the comparison of Acts and Galatians, particularly in that which concerns the Apostolic Council of Acts xv, is still often thought to result unfavorably to the Book of Acts. Even at this point, however, a more favorable estimate of Acts has been gaining ground. The cardinal principle of Baur, to the effect that the major epistles of Paul should be interpreted entirely without reference to the Book of Acts, is being called in question. Such a method of interpretation, it may well be urged, is likely to result in one-sidedness. If the Book of Acts commends itself at all as containing trustworthy information, it should be allowed to cast light upon the Epistles. The account which Paul gives in Galatians is not so complete as to render superfluous any assistance which may be derived from an independent narrative. And as a matter of fact, no matter what principles of interpretation are held, the Book of Acts simply must be used in interpreting the Epistles; without the outline given in Acts the Epistles would be unintelligible.[1]   Perhaps it may turn out, therefore, that Baur produced his imposing reconstruction of the apostolic age by neglecting all sources except Galatians and the Corinthian Epistles—and then by misinterpreting these.

The comparison of Acts and the Pauline Epistles will be reserved for the chapters that deal with the outline of Paul's life.   It will there be necessary to deal with the vexed question of the Apostolic Council.   The question is vital for the present discussion; for if it can really be shown that Paul was in fundamental disagreement with the intimate friends of Jesus of Nazareth, then the way is opened for supposing that he was in disagreement with Jesus Himself.   The question raised by Baur with regard to the Book of Acts has a most important bearing upon the question of the origin of Paulinism.

All that can now be done, however, is to point out that the tendency at the present time is toward a higher and higher estimate of the Book of Acts.   A more careful study of the Pauline Epistles themselves is exhibiting elements in Paul's thinking which justify more and more clearly the account which the Book of Acts gives of the relations of Paul to Judaism and to Jewish Christianity.

[1] J. Weiss, *Urchristentum,* 1914, p. 107: "It is simply impossible for us to erase it [the Book of Acts] so completely from our memory as to read the Epistle to the Galatians as though we had never known Acts; without the Book of Acts we should simply not be able to understand Galatians at all."

CHAPTER II
THE EARLY YEARS

CHAPTER II

BEFORE examining the various hypotheses which have been advanced to account for the origin of Paulinism, the investigator must consider first the outline of Paul's life, at least so far as the formative years are concerned. Paulinism has been explained by the influence upon Paul of various features of his environment. It is important, therefore, to determine at what points Paul came into contact with his environment. What, in view of the outline of his life, were his probable opportunities for acquainting himself with the historical Jesus and with the primitive Jerusalem Church? Whence did he derive his Judaism? Where, if at all, could he naturally have been influenced by contemporary paganism? Such questions, it is hoped, may be answered by the two following chapters.

In these chapters, the outline of Paul's life will be considered not for its own sake, but merely for the light that it may shed upon the origin of his thought and experience. Many questions, therefore, may be ignored. For example, it would here be entirely aside from the point to discuss such intricate matters as the history of Paul's journeys to Corinth attested by the Corinthian Epistles. The present discussion is concerned only with those events in the life of Paul which determined the nature of his contact with the surrounding world, both Jewish and pagan, and particularly the nature of his contact with Jesus and the earliest disciples of Jesus.

Paul was born at Tarsus, the chief city of Cilicia. This fact is attested only by the Book of Acts, and formerly it did not escape unchallenged. It was called in question, for example, in 1890 by Krenkel, in an elaborate argument.[1] But Krenkel's argument is now completely antiquated, not merely because of the rising credit of the Book of Acts, but also be-

[1] Krenkel, *Beiträge zur Aufhellung der Geschichte und der Briefe des Apostels Paulus,* 1890, pp. 1-17.

cause the birth of Paul in a Greek city like Tarsus is in harmony with modern reconstructions. Krenkel argued, for example, that the apostle shows little a⁀quaintance with Greek
culture, and therefore could not have spent his youth in a
Greek university city. Such assertions appear very strange
to-day. Recent philological investigation of the Pauline
Epistles has proved that the author uses the Greek language
in such masterly fashion that he must have become familiar
with it very early in life; the language of the Epistles is certainly no Jewish-Greek jargon. With regard to the origin of
the ideas, also, the tendency of recent criticism is directly
contrary to Krenkel; Paulinism is now often explained as
being based either upon paganism or else upon a Hellenized
Judaism. To such reconstructions it is a highly welcome piece
of information when the Book of Acts makes Paul a native
not of Jerusalem but of Tarsus. The author of Acts, it is
said, is here preserving a bit of genuine tradition, which is
the more trustworthy because it runs counter to the tendency,
thought to be otherwise in evidence in Acts, which brings Paul
into the closest possible relation to Palestine. Thus, whether
for good or for bad reasons, the birth of Paul in Tarsus is
now universally accepted, and does not require defense.

A very interesting tradition preserved by Jerome does indeed make Paul a native of Gischala in Galilee; but no one
to-day would be inclined to follow Krenkel in giving credence
to Jerome rather than to Acts. The Gischala tradition does
not look like a pure fiction, but it is evident that Jerome has
at any rate exercised his peculiar talent for bringing things
into confusion. Zahn [1] has suggested, with considerable
plausibility, that the shorter reference to Gischala in the
treatise "De viris illustribus" [2] is a confused abridgment of
the longer reference in the "Commentary on Philemon." [3] The
latter passage asserts not that Paul himself but only that the
parents of Paul came from Gischala. That assertion may
possibly be correct. It would explain the Aramaic and Palestinian tradition which undoubtedly was preserved in the boyhood home of Paul.

---

[1] *Einleitung in das Neue Testament*, 3te Aufl., i, 1906, pp. 48-50 (English
Translation, *Introduction to the New Testament*, 2nd ed., 1909, i, pp. 68-70).
[2] *De vir. ill.* 5 (ed. Vall. ii, 836).
[3] *Comm. in Philem.* 23 (ed. Vall. vii, 762).

Tarsus was an important city. Its commercial importance, though of course inferior to that of places like Antioch or Corinth, was considerable; and it was also well known as a center of intellectual life. Although the dramatic possibilities of representing the future Christian missionary growing up unknown under the shadow of a Greek university may sometimes have led to an exaggeration of the academic fame of Tarsus, still it remains true that Tarsus was a real university city, and could boast of great names like that of Athenodorus, the Stoic philosopher, and others. The life of Tarsus has recently been made the subject of two elaborate monographs, by Ramsay [1] and by Böhlig,[2] who have collected a mass of information about the birthplace of Paul. The nature of the pagan religious atmosphere which surrounded the future apostle is of peculiar interest; but the amount of direct information which has come down to us should not be exaggerated.

The social position of Paul's family in Tarsus must not be regarded as very humble; for according to the Book of Acts not only Paul himself, but his father before him, possessed the Roman citizenship, which in the provinces was still in the first century a highly prized privilege from which the great masses of the people were excluded. The Roman citizenship of Paul is not attested by the Pauline Epistles, but the representation of Acts is at this point universally, or almost universally, accepted. Only one objection might be urged against it. If Paul was a Roman citizen, how could he have been subjected three times to the Roman punishment of beating with rods (2 Cor. xi. 25), from which citizens were exempted by law? The difficulty is not insuperable. Paul may on some occasions have been unwilling to appeal to a privilege which separated him from his Jewish countrymen; or he may have wanted to avoid the delay which an appeal to his privilege, with the subsequent investigation and trial, might have caused. At any rate, the difficulty, whether easily removable or not, is quite inadequate to overthrow the abundant evidence for the fact of Paul's Roman citizenship. That fact is absolutely necessary to account for the entire representation which the Book of Acts gives of the journey of Paul as a prisoner to Rome, which representation, it will be remembered,

[1] *The Cities of St. Paul*, 1908, pp.. 85-244.
[2] *Die Geisteskultur von Tarsos*, 1913.

is contained in the we-sections. The whole account of the relation between Paul and Roman authorities, which is contained in the Pauline Epistles, the Book of Acts, and trustworthy Christian tradition, is explicable only if Paul possessed the rights of citizenship.[1]

Birth in a Greek university city and Roman citizenship constitute the two facts which bring Paul into early connection with the larger Gentile world of his day. Other facts, equally well-attested, separate him just as clearly from the Gentile world and represent him as being from childhood a strict Jew. These facts might have been called in question, in view of the present tendency of criticism, if they had been attested only by the Book of Acts. But fortunately it is just these facts which are attested also by the epistles of Paul.

In 2 Cor. xi. 22, Paul is declared to be a "Hebrew," and in Phil. iii. 5 he appears as a "Hebrew of Hebrews." The word "Hebrew" in these passages cannot indicate merely Israelitish descent or general adherence to the Jews' religion. If it did so it would be a meaningless repetition of the other terms used in the same passages. Obviously it is used in some narrower sense. The key to its meaning is found in Acts vi. 1, where, within Judaism, the "Hellenists" are distinguished from the "Hebrews," the Hellenists being the Jews of the Dispersion who spoke Greek, and the Hebrews the Jews of Palestine who spoke Aramaic. In Phil. iii. 5, therefore, Paul declares that he was an Aramaic-speaking Jew and descended from Aramaic-speaking Jews; Aramaic was used in his boyhood home, and the Palestinian tradition was preserved. This testimony is not contrary to what was said above about Paul's use of the Greek language—not improbably Paul used both Aramaic and Greek in childhood—but it does contradict all those modern representations which make Paul fundamentally a Jew of the Dispersion. Though he was born in Tarsus, he was, in the essential character of his family tradition, a Jew of Palestine.

Even more important is the assertion, found in the same verse in Philippians, that Paul was "as touching the law a Pharisee." Conceivably, indeed, it might be argued that his Pharisaism was not derived from his boyhood home, but was acquired later. But surely it requires no excessively favorable estimate of Acts to give credence to the assertion in Acts

[1] Compare Mommsen, "Die Rechtsverhältnisse des Apostels Paulus," in *Zeitschrift für die neutestamentliche Wissenschaft,* ii, 1901, pp. 88-96.

xxiii. 6 that Paul was not only a Pharisee but the "son of Pharisees"; and it is exceedingly unlikely that this phrase refers, as Lightfoot [1] suggested, to teachers rather than to ancestors. For when Paul says in Gal. i. 14 that he advanced in the Jews' religion beyond many of his contemporaries, being more exceedingly zealous for his paternal traditions, it is surely natural, whatever interpretation may be given to the word "paternal," to find a reference to the Pharisaic traditions cultivated in his boyhood home.

There is not the slightest evidence, therefore, for supposing that Paul spent his early years in an atmosphere of "liberal Judaism"—a Judaism really though unconsciously hospitable to pagan notions and predisposed to relax the strict requirements of the Law and break down the barrier that separated Israel from the Gentile world. Whether such a liberal Judaism even existed in Tarsus we do not know. At any rate, if it did exist, the household of Paul's father was not in sympathy with it. Surely the definite testimony of Paul himself is here worth more than all modern conjectures. And Paul himself declares that he was in language and in spirit a Jew of Palestine rather than of the Dispersion, and as touching the Law a Pharisee.

According to the Book of Acts, Paul went at an early age to Jerusalem, received instruction there from Gamaliel, the famous rabbi, and finally, just before his conversion, persecuted the Jerusalem Church (Acts xxii. 3; vii. 58-viii. 1; ix. 1, etc.). In recent years, this entire representation has been questioned. It has been maintained by Mommsen,[2] Bousset[3], Heitmüller,[4] and Loisy [5] that Paul never was in Jerusalem before his conversion. That he persecuted the Church is, of course, attested unequivocally by his own Epistles, but the persecution, it is said, really took place only in such cities as Damascus, and not at all in Palestine.

This elimination of the early residence of Paul in Jerusalem

[1] On Phil. iii. 5.
[2] *Op. cit.,* pp. 85f.
[3] *Kyrios Christos,* 1913, p. 92. Bousset's doubt with regard to the early Jerusalem residence of Paul extended, explicitly at least, only to the persecution in Jerusalem, and it was a doubt merely, not a positive denial. In his supplementary work he has admitted that his doubt was unjustified (*Jesus der Herr,* 1916, p. 31).
[4] "Zum Problem Paulus und Jesus," in *Zeitschrift für die neutestamentliche Wissenschaft,* xiii, 1912, pp. 320-337.
[5] *L'épître aux Galates,* 1916, pp. 68-73; *Les mystères païens et le .mystère chrétien,* 1919, pp. 317-320.

is no mere by-product of a generally skeptical attitude toward the Book of Acts, but is important for the entire reconstruction of early Christian history which Bousset and Heitmüller and Loisy propose; it is made to assist in explaining the origin of the Pauline Christology. Paul regarded Jesus Christ as a supernatural person, come to earth for the redemption of men; and toward this divine Christ he assumed a distinctly religious attitude. How could he have formed such a conception of a human being who had died but a few years before? If he had been separated from Jesus by several generations, so that the nimbus of distance and mystery would have had time to form about the figure of the Galilean prophet, then his lofty conception of Jesus might be explained. But as a matter of fact he was actually a contemporary of the Jesus whose simple human traits he obscured. How could the "smell of earth" have been so completely removed from the figure of the Galilean teacher that He could actually be regarded by one of His contemporaries as a divine Redeemer? The question could perhaps be more easily answered if Paul, before his lofty conception of Christ was fully formed, never came into any connection with those who had seen Jesus subject to the petty limitations of human life. Thus the elimination of the early Jerusalem residence of Paul, by putting a geographical if not a temporal gulf between Jesus and Paul, is thought to make the formation of the Pauline Christology more comprehensible. Peter and the original disciples, it is thought, never could have separated Jesus so completely from the limitations of ordinary humanity; the simple memory of Galilean days would in their case have been an effective barrier against Christological speculation. But Paul was subject to no such limitation; having lived far away from Palestine, in the company, for the most part, of those who like himself had never seen Jesus, he was free to transpose to the Galilean teacher attributes which to those who had known the real Jesus would have seemed excessive or absurd.

Before examining the grounds upon which this elimination of Paul's early Jerusalem residence is based, it may first be observed that even such heroic measures do not really bring about the desired result; even this radical rewriting of the story of Paul's boyhood and youth will not serve to explain on naturalistic principles the origin of the Pauline Christology.

Even if before his conversion Paul got no nearer to Jerusalem than Damascus, it still remains true that after his conversion he conferred with Peter and lived in more or less extended intercourse with Palestinian disciples. The total lack of any evidence of a conflict between the Christology of Paul and the views of those who had walked and talked with Jesus of Nazareth remains, for any naturalistic reconstruction, a puzzling fact. Even without the early Jerusalem residence, Paul remains too near to Jesus both temporally and geographically to have formed a conception of Him entirely without reference to the historical person. Even with their radical treatment of the Book of Acts, therefore, Bousset and Heitmüller have not succeeded at all in explaining how the Pauline Christology ever came to be attached to the Galilean prophet.

But is the elimination of the early Jerusalem residence of Paul historically justifiable? Mere congruity with a plausible theory of development will not serve to justify it. For the Jerusalem residence is strongly attested by the Book of Acts. The testimony of Acts can no longer be ruled out except for very weighty reasons; the history of recent criticism has on the whole exhibited the rise of a more and more favorable estimate of the book. And in the case of the early Jerusalem residence of Paul the testimony is so insistent and so closely connected with lifelike details that the discrediting of it involves an exceedingly radical skepticism. The presence of Paul at the stoning of Stephen is narrated in the Book of Acts in a concrete way which bears every mark of trustworthiness; the connection of Paul with Gamaliel is what might have been expected in view of the self-testimony of the apostle; the account of Paul's vision in the Temple (Acts xxii. 17-21) is based, in a manner which is psychologically very natural, upon the fact of Paul's persecuting activity in Jerusalem; the presence of Paul's sister's son in Jerusalem, attested in a part of the narrative of which the essential historicity must be universally admitted (Acts xxiii. 16-22), suggests that family connections may have facilitated Paul's residence in the city. Finally, the geographical details of the three narratives of the conversion, which place the event on a journey of Paul from Jerusalem to Damascus, certainly look as though they were founded upon genuine tradition. One of the details— the place of the conversion itself—is confirmed in a purely incidental way by the Epistle to the Galatians, and the reader has the impression that if Paul had happened to introduce other details in the Epistles the rest of the narrative in Acts would have been similarly confirmed. Except for Paul's incidental reference to Damascus in Gal. i. 17, the conversion might have been put by Heitmüller and others in a place even more conveniently remote than Damascus from the scene of Jesus' earthly labors. But the incidental confirmation of Acts at this point raises a distinct presumption in favor of the account as a whole. The main trend of modern criticism has been favorable on the whole to the tradition embodied in the accounts of the conversion; it is a very extreme form of skepticism which rejects the whole framework of the tradition by eliminating the journey from Jerusalem to Damascus.

Enough has been said to show that the early Jerusalem residence of Paul stood absolutely firm in the tradition used by the author of Acts; the author has taken it as a matter of course and woven it in with his narrative at many points. Such a tradition certainly cannot be lightly rejected; the burden of proof clearly rests upon those who would deny its truthworthiness.

The only definite proof which is forthcoming is found in Gal. i. 22, where Paul says that after his departure for Syria and Cilicia, three years after his conversion, he was "unknown by face to the churches of Judæa which are in Christ." If he had engaged in active persecution of those churches, it is argued, how could he have been personally unknown to them?

By this argument a tremendous weight is hung upon one verse. And, rightly interpreted, the verse will not bear the weight at all. In Gal. i. 22, Paul is not speaking so much of what took place before the departure for Syria and Cilicia, as of the condition which prevailed at the time of that departure and during the immediately ensuing period; he is simply drawing attention to the significance for his argument of the departure from Jerusalem. Certainly he would not have been able to speak as he does if before he left Jerusalem he had had extended intercourse with the Judæan churches, but when he says that the knowledge of the Judæan churches about him in the period just succeeding his departure from Jerusalem was a hearsay knowledge merely, it would have been pedantic for him to think about the question whether some of the members of those churches had or had not seen him years before as a persecutor.

Furthermore, it is by no means clear that the word "Judæa" in Gal. i. 22 includes Jerusalem at all. In Mark iii. 7, 8, for example, "Jerusalem" is clearly not included in "Judæa," but is distinguished from it; "Judæa" means the country outside of the capital. It may well be so also in Gal. i. 22; and if so, then the verse does not exclude a personal acquaintance of Paul with the Jerusalem Church. But even if "Judæa" is not used so as to exclude the capital, still Paul's words would be natural enough. That the Jerusalem Church formed an exception to the general assertion was suggested by the account of the visit in Jerusalem immediately preceding, and was probably well known to his Galatian readers. All that Paul means is that he went away to Syria and Cilicia without becoming acquainted generally with the churches of Judæa. It is indeed often said that since the whole point of Paul's argument in Galatians was to show his lack of contact with the pillars of the Jerusalem Church, his acquaintance or lack of acquaintance with the churches of Judæa outside of Jerusalem was unworthy of mention, so that he must at least be including Jerusalem when he speaks of Judæa. But this argument is not decisive. If, as is altogether probable, the apostles except Peter were out of the city at the time of Paul's visit, and were engaging in missionary work in Judæan churches, then acquaintance with the Judæan churches would have meant intercourse with the apostles, so that it was very much to the point for Paul to deny that he had had such acquaintance. Of course, this whole argument against the early Jerusalem residence of Paul, based on Gal. i. 22, involves a rejection of the account which the Book of Acts gives of the visit of Paul to Jerusalem three years after his conversion. If Gal. i. 22 means that Paul was unknown by sight to the Jerusalem Church, then he could not have gone in and out among the disciples at Jerusalem as Acts ix. 28 represents, but must have been in strict hiding when he was in the city. Such is the account of the matter which is widely prevalent in recent years. Not even so much correction of Acts is at all required by a correct understanding of Gal. i. 22. But it is a still more unjustifiable use of that verse when it is made to exclude even the persecuting activity of Paul in Jerusalem.

If, however, the words of Galatians are really to be taken in the strictest and most literal sense, what is to be done with Gal. i. 23, where (immediately after the words which have just been discussed) Paul says that the churches of Judæa were receiving the report, "He that persecuted us formerly is now preaching as a gospel the faith which formerly he laid waste"? What is meant by the pronoun "us" in this verse? Conceivably it might be taken in a broad sense, as referring to all disciples wherever found; conceivably, therefore, the persecution referred to by the Judæan disciples might be persecution of their brethren in the faith in Tarsus or Damascus. But that is not the kind of interpretation which has just been applied to the preceding verse, and upon which such a vast structure has been reared. It may well be urged against Heitmüller and those like him that if Paul's words are to be taken so strictly in one verse they should be taken in the same way in the other; if the "Judæa" and "unknown by face" of verse 22 are to be taken so strictly, then the "us" of verse 23 should also be taken strictly, and in that case Paul is made to contradict himself, which of course is absurd. Verse 23 certainly does not fully confirm the representation of Acts about the persecuting activity of Paul in Judæa, but at any rate it tends to confirm that representation at least as strongly as verse 22 tends to discredit it.[1]

Thus the early Jerusalem residence of Paul is strongly attested by the Book of Acts, and is thoroughly in harmony with everything that Paul says about his Pharisaic past. It is not surprising that Bousset has now receded from his original position and admits that Paul was in Jerusalem before his conversion and engaged in persecution of the Jerusalem Church.

That admission does not necessarily carry with it an acceptance of all that the Book of Acts says about the Jerusalem period in Paul's life, particularly all that it says about his having been a disciple of Gamaliel. But the decisive point has been gained. If the entire account of the early Jerusalem residence of Paul is not ruled out by the testimony of his own Epistles, then there is at least no decisive objection against the testimony of Acts with regard to the details. Certainly

[1] Compare Wellhausen, *Kritische Analyse der Apostelgeschichte.* 1914, p. 16.

the common opinion to the effect that Paul went to Jerusalem
to receive rabbinical training is admirably in accord with
everything that he says in his Epistles about his zeal for the
Law. It is also in accord with his habits of thought and expression, which were transformed and glorified, rather than
destroyed, by his Christian experience. The decision about
every detail of course depends ultimately upon the particular
conclusion which the investigator may have reached with regard to the Book of Acts. If that book was written by a
companion of Paul—an opinion which is gaining ground even
in circles which were formerly hostile—then there is every
reason to suppose that Paul was brought up in Jerusalem at
the feet of Gamaliel (Acts xxii. 3). Some important questions
indeed still remain unanswered, even with full acceptance of
the Lucan testimony. It can never be determined, for example, at exactly what age Paul went to Jerusalem. The
words, "brought up in this city," in Acts xxii. 3 might seem
to suggest that Paul went to Jerusalem in early childhood, in
which case his birthplace would be of comparatively little
importance in his preparation for his lifework, and all the
elaborate investigations of Tarsus, so far as they are intended
to shed light upon the environment of the apostle in his formative years, would become valueless. But the Greek word
"brought up" or "nourished" might be used figuratively in
a somewhat flexible way; it remains, therefore, perfectly possible that Paul's Jerusalem training began, not in childhood,
but in early youth. At any rate, an early residence in Jerusalem is not excluded by the masterly way in which the apostle
uses the Greek language. It must always be remembered that
Palestine in the first century was a bilingual country; [1] the
presence of hosts of Greek-speaking Jews even in Jerusalem
is amply attested, for example, by the early chapters of Acts.
Moreover, even after Paul's Jerusalem studies had begun, his
connection with Tarsus need not have been broken off. The
distance between the two cities was considerable (some four
or five hundred miles), but travel in those days was safe and
easy. A period of training in Jerusalem may have been followed by a long residence at Tarsus.

[1] See Zahn, *Einleitung in das Neue Testament*, 3te Aufl., i, 1906, pp.
24-32, 39-47 (English Translation, *Introduction to the New Testament*,
2nd Ed., 1917, i, pp. 34-46, 57-66).

At this point, an interesting question arises, which, however, can never be answered with any certainty. Did Paul ever see Jesus before the crucifixion? In the light of what has just been established about the outline of Paul's life, an affirmative answer might seem to be natural. Paul was in Jerusalem both before and after the public ministry of Jesus—before it when he was being "brought up" in Jerusalem, and after it when he was engaged in persecution of the Jerusalem Church. Where was he during the interval? Where was he on those occasions when Jesus visited Jerusalem—especially at the time of that last Passover? If he was in Jerusalem, it seems probable that he would have seen the great prophet, whose coming caused such a stir among the people. And that he was in the city at Passover time would seem natural in view of his devotion to the Law. But the matter is by no means certain. He may have returned to Tarsus, in the manner which has just been suggested.

The question could only be decided on the basis of actual testimony either in Acts or in the Epistles. One verse has often been thought to provide such testimony. In 2 Cor. v. 16, Paul says, "Even if we have known Christ after the flesh, yet now we know him so no longer." Knowledge of Christ after the flesh can only mean, it is said, knowledge of Him by the ordinary use of the senses, in the manner in which one man in ordinary human intercourse knows another. That kind of knowledge, Paul says, has ceased to have significance for the Christian in his relation to other men; it has also ceased to have significance for him in his relation to Christ. But it is that kind of knowledge which Paul seems to predicate of himself, as having existed in a previous period of his life. He does not use the unreal form of condition; he does not say, "Even if we had known Christ after the flesh (though as a matter of fact we never knew Him so at all), yet now we should know Him so no longer." Apparently, then, when he says "if" he means "although"; he means to say, "Although we have known Christ after the flesh, yet now we know Him so no longer." The knowledge of Christ after the flesh is thus put as an actual fact in Paul's experience, and that can only mean that he knew Him in the way in which His contemporaries knew Him in Galilee and in Jerusalem, a way which in itself, Paul says, was altogether without spiritual significance.

One objection to this interpretation of the passage is that it proves too much. If it means anything, it means that Paul had extended personal acquaintance with Jesus before the crucifixion; for if Paul merely saw Him for a few moments—for example, when the crowds were surging about Him at the time of the last Passover—he could hardly be said to have "known" Him. But, for obvious reasons, any extended intercourse between Paul and Jesus in Palestine is exceedingly improbable. It is natural, therefore, to look for some other interpretation.

Other interpretations undoubtedly are possible. Some of the interpretations that have been proposed must indeed be eliminated. For example, Paul cannot possibly be contrasting a former immature stage of his Christian experience with the present mature stage; he cannot possibly mean, "Even if in the first period after my conversion I had a low view of Christ, which made of Him merely the son of David and the Jewish Messiah, yet now I have come to a higher conception of His divine nature." For the whole point of the passage is found in the sharp break which comes in a man's experience when he appropriates the death and resurrection of Christ. Any consciousness of a subsequent revolution in the thinking of the Christian is not only unsupported anywhere in the Pauline Epistles, but is absolutely excluded by the present passage. Another interpretation also must be eliminated. Paul cannot possibly be contrasting his pre-Christian notions about the Messiah with the higher knowledge which came to him with his conversion; he cannot possibly mean, "Even if before I knew the fulfillment of the Messianic promise I cherished carnal notions of what the Messiah was to be, even if I thought of Him merely as an earthly ruler who was to conquer the enemies of Israel, yet now I have come to have a loftier, more spiritual conception of Him." For the word "Christ," especially without the article, can hardly here be anything other than a proper name, and must refer not to the conception of Messiahship but to the concrete person of Jesus. But another interpretation remains. The key to it is found in the flexible use of the first person plural in the Pauline Epistles. Undoubtedly, the "we" of the whole passage in which 2 Cor. v. 16 is contained refers primarily to Paul himself. But, especially in 2 Cor. v. 16, it may include also all true ambassadors for

Christ whose principles are the same as Paul's. Among such true ambassadors there were no doubt to be found some who had known Christ by way of ordinary intercourse in Palestine. "But," says Paul, "even if some of us have known Christ in that way, we know him so no longer." This interpretation is linguistically more satisfactory, perhaps, than that which explains the sentence as simply a more vivid way of presenting a condition contrary to fact. "Granted," Paul would say according to this interpretation, "even that we have known Christ according to the flesh (which as a matter of fact we have not), yet now we know him so no longer." But our interpretation really amounts to almost the same thing so far as Paul is concerned. At any rate, the passage is not so clear as to justify any certain conclusions about Paul's life in Palestine; it does not clearly imply any acquaintance of Paul with Jesus before the passion.

If such acquaintance is to be established, therefore, it must be established on the basis of other evidence. J. Weiss [1] seeks to establish it by the very fact of Paul's conversion. Paul, Weiss believes, saw a vision of the risen Christ. How did he know that the figure which appeared to him in the vision was Jesus? Why did he not think, for example, merely that it was the Messiah, who according to one strain of Jewish Messianic expectation was already existent in heaven? Apparently he recognized the person who appeared to him as Jesus of Nazareth. But how could he have recognized Him as Jesus unless he had seen Jesus before?

This argument depends, of course, altogether upon the naturalistic conception of the conversion of Paul, which regards the experience as an hallucination. In the account of the conversion given in the Book of Acts, on the contrary, it is distinctly said that far from recognizing the person who appeared to him, Paul was obliged to ask the question, "Who art thou, Lord?" and then received the answer, "I am Jesus." Such a conversation between Paul and the One who appeared to him is perfectly possible if there was a real appearance of the risen Christ, but it exceeds the ordinary limits of hallucinations. Weiss has therefore merely pointed out an additional psychological difficulty in explaining the experience of Paul

[1] *Paulus und Jesus*, 1909, pp. 22, 23. Compare Ramsay, *The Teaching of Paul in Terms of the Present Day*, 1914, pp. 21-30.

as an hallucination, a difficulty which, on naturalistic principles, may have to be removed by the assumption that Paul
had seen Jesus before the passion.   But if Jesus really appeared to Paul in such a way as to be able to answer his
questions, then it is not necessary to suppose that Paul recognized Him.   The failure of Paul to recognize Jesus (according
to the narrative in Acts) does not indeed positively exclude
such previous acquaintance; the two disciples on the road to
Emmaus, for example, also failed to recognize the Lord, though
they had been acquainted with Him before.   But, at any rate,
if the supernaturalistic view of Paul's conversion be accepted,
the experience sheds no light whatever upon any previous personal acquaintance with Jesus.

Thus there is no clear evidence for supposing that Paul
saw Jesus before the passion.   At the same time there is no
evidence to the contrary, except the evidence that is to be
found in the silence of the Epistles.

The argument from silence, precarious as it is, must here
be allowed a certain amount of weight.   If Paul had seen
Jesus before the crucifixion, would not so important a fact
have been mentioned somewhere in the Epistles?   The matter
is by no means absolutely clear; a brief glimpse of Jesus in
the days of His flesh would perhaps not have seemed so important to Paul, in view of the richer knowledge which came
afterwards, as it would seem to us.   The silence of the Epistles
does, however, render improbable any extended contact between
Paul and Jesus, particularly any active opposition of the
youthful Paul toward Jesus.   Paul was deeply penitent for
having persecuted the Church; if he had committed the more
terrible sin of having helped bring the Lord Himself to the
shameful cross, the fact would naturally have appeared in
his expressions of penitence.   Even if Paul did see Jesus in
Palestine, then, it is highly improbable that he was one of
those who cried out to Pilate, "Crucify him, crucify him!"

One thing, however, is certain.   If Paul never saw Jesus
in Palestine, he certainly heard about Him.   The ministry of
Jesus caused considerable stir both in Galilee and in Jerusalem.
These things were not done in a corner.   The appearance of
Jesus at the last Passover aroused the passions of the multitude, and evidently caused the deepest concern to the authorities.   Even one who was indifferent to the whole matter

could hardly have helped learning something of the content of Jesus' teaching, and the main outline of the story of His death. But Paul, at least at a time only a very few years after the crucifixion, was not indifferent; for he was an active persecutor. If he was in Palestine at all during the previous period, his interest probably began then. The outlines of Jesus' life and death were known to friend and foe alike, and certainly were not unknown to Paul before his conversion, at the time when he was persecuting the Church. It is only a woeful lack of historical imagination which can attribute to Paul, even before his conversion, a total ignorance of the earthly life of Jesus.

The opposite error, however, is even more serious. If Paul before his conversion was not totally ignorant of Jesus, on the other hand his knowledge only increased his opposition to Jesus and Jesus' followers. It is not true that before the conversion Paul was gradually coming nearer to Christianity. Against any such supposition stands the explicit testimony of the Epistles.

Despite that testimony, various attempts have been made to trace a psychological development in Paul which could have led to the conversion. Paul was converted through a vision of the risen Christ. According to the supernaturalistic view that vision was a "vision," not in any specialized meaning of the word, but in its original etymological meaning; Paul actually "saw" the risen Lord. According to the modern naturalistic view, which rejects any direct creative interposition of God in the course of nature, different in kind from His works of providence, the vision was produced by the internal condition of the subject, accompanied perhaps by favorable conditions without—the heat of the sun or a thunder storm or the like. But was the condition of the subject, in the case of Paul, really favorable to a vision of the risen Christ? If the vision of Christ was an hallucination, as it is held to be by modern naturalistic historians, how may the genesis of this pathological experience be explained?

In the first place, a certain basis for the experience is sought in the physical organism of the subject. According to the Epistles, it is said, the apostle was subject to a recurrent malady; this malady is spoken of in 2 Cor. xii. 1-8 in connection with visions and revelations. In Gal. iv. 14, where it is said that the Galatians did not "spit out" when the apostle was with them, an allusion is sometimes discovered to the ancient custom of spitting to avoid contagion. A combination of this passage with the one in 2 Corinthians is thought to establish a diagnosis of epilepsy, the effort being made to show that "spitting out" was particularly prevalent in the case of that disease. The visions then become an additional symptom of the epileptic seizures.[1]

But the diagnosis rests upon totally insufficient data. The visions are not regarded in 2 Corinthians as part of the buffetings of the angel of Satan; on the contrary, the two things are sharply separated in Paul's mind; he rejoices in the visions, but prays the Lord that the buffetings may cease. It is not even said that the visions and the buffetings came close together; there is no real basis for the view that the buffetings consisted in nervous exhaustion following the visions. In Gal. iv. 14, the "spitting out" is probably to be taken figuratively, and the object is "your temptation in my flesh." The meaning then is simply, "You did not reject me or spue me out"; and there is no allusion to the custom of "spitting out" for the purpose of avoiding contagion. It is unnecessary, therefore, to examine the elaborate argument of Krenkel by which he sought to show that epilepsy was particularly the disease against which spitting was practised as a prophylactic measure.

There is therefore absolutely no evidence to show that Paul was an epileptic, unless the very fact of his having visions be thought to furnish such evidence. But such a use of the visions prejudges the great question at issue, which concerns the objective validity of Paul's religious convictions. Furthermore, the fact should always be borne in mind that Paul distinguished the visions very sharply from the experience which he had near Damascus, when he saw the Lord. The visions are spoken of in 2 Corinthians apparently with reluctance, as something which concerned the apostle alone; the Damascus experience was part of the evidence for the resurrection of Christ, and had a fundamental place in the apostle's missionary preaching. All efforts to break down this distinction have failed. The apostle regarded the Damascus experience

[1] See Krenkel, *Beiträge zur Aufhellung der Geschichte und der Briefe des Apostels Paulus*, 1890, pp. 47-125.

as unique—not a mystery like the experiences which are mentioned in 2 Corinthians, but a plain, palpable fact capable of being understood by all.

But if the Damascus experience is to be regarded as an hallucination, it is not sufficient to exhibit a basis for it in the physical weakness of the apostle. Even if Paul was constitutionally predisposed to hallucinations, the experience of this particular hallucination must be shown to be possible. The challenge has often been accepted by modern historians. It is maintained that the elements of Paul's new conviction must have been forming gradually in his mind; the Damascus experience, it is said, merely brought to light what was really already present. In this way, the enormous disparity between effect and cause is thought to be removed; the untold benefits of Paulinism are no longer to be regarded as due to the fortunate chance of an hallucination, induced by the weakness of the apostle and the heat of the desert sun, but rather to a spiritual development which the hallucination merely revealed. Thus the modern view of Paul's conversion, it is thought, may face bravely the scorn of Beyschlag, who exclaimed, when speaking of the naturalistic explanation of Paul's vision, "Oh blessed drop of blood . . . which by pressing at the right moment upon the brain of Paul, produced such a moral wonder." [1] The drop of blood, it is said, or whatever may have been the physical basis of the Damascus experience, did not produce the wonders of the Pauline gospel; it merely brought into the sphere of consciousness a psychological process which had really been going on before.

The existence of such a psychological process, by which the apostle was coming nearer to Christ, is sometimes thought to receive documentary support in one verse of the New Testament. In Acts xxvi. 14, the risen Christ is represented as saying to Paul, "It is hard for thee to kick against the goads." According to this verse, it is said, Paul had been resisting a better conviction, gradually forming in his mind, that the disciples might be right about Jesus and he might be wrong; that, it is said, was the goad which was really driving him. He had indeed been resisting vigorously; he had been stifling his doubts by more and more feverish activity in persecution.

[1] Beyschlag, "Die Bekehrung des Apostels Paulus," in *Theologische Studien und Kritiken*, xxxvii, 1864, p. 241.

But the resistance had not really brought him peace; the goad was really there. And at last, near Damascus, the resistance was overcome; the subconscious conviction which had brought tumult into his soul was at last allowed to come to the surface and rule his conscious life.

At this point, the historian is in grave danger of becoming untrue to his own critical principles. Attention to the Book of Acts, it has been maintained, is not to be allowed to color the interpretation of the Pauline Epistles, which are the primary sources of information. But here the procedure is reversed. In the interests of a verse in Acts, standing, moreover, in a context which on naturalistic principles cannot be regarded as historical, the clear testimony of the Epistles is neglected. For Paul was certainly not conscious of any goad which before his conversion was forcing him into the new faith; he knows nothing of doubts which assailed him during the period of his activity in persecution. On the contrary, the very point of the passage in Galatians, where he alludes to his persecuting activity, is the suddenness of his conversion. Far from gradually coming nearer to Christ he was in the very midst of his zeal for the Law when Christ called him. The purpose of the passage is to show that his gospel came to him without human intermediation. Before the conversion, he says, there was of course no human intermediation, since he was an active persecutor. He could not have spoken in this way if before the conversion he had already become half convinced that those whom he was persecuting were right. Moreover, throughout the Epistles there appears in the apostle not the slightest consciousness of his having acted against better convictions when he persecuted the Church. In 1 Tim. i. 13 he distinctly says that he carried on the persecution in ignorance; and even if Timothy be regarded as post-Pauline, the silence of the other epistles at least points in the same direction. Paul was deeply penitent for having persecuted the Church of God, but apparently he did not lay to his charge the black sin of having carried on the persecution in the face of better convictions. When he laid the Church waste he thought he was doing God service. In the very midst of his mad persecuting activity, he says, apart from any teaching from men—apart, we may certainly infer, from any favorable impressions formed in his mind—the Lord appeared to him and gave him his gospel. Paul stakes everything upon the evidential value of the appearance, which was able suddenly to overcome an altogether hostile attitude. Such is the self-testimony of the apostle. It rests as a serious weight upon all attempts at making the conversion the result of a psychological process.

Certainly the passage in Acts will not help to bear the weight. When the risen Christ says to Paul, "It is hard for thee to kick against the goads," He need not mean at all that the presence of the goad had been known to Paul before that hour. The meaning may be simply that the will of Christ is resistless; all opposition is in vain, the appointed hour of Christ has arrived. Conscious opposition on the part of Paul to a better conviction is certainly not at all implied. No doubt Paul was really miserable when he was a persecutor; all activity contrary to the plan of Christ brings misery. But that he had the slightest inkling of the source of his misery or even of the fact of it need not be supposed. It is even possible that the "hardness" of resistance to the goad is to be found only in the very moment of the conversion. "All resistance," says the risen Christ, "all hesitation, is as hopeless as for the ox to kick against the goad; instant obedience alone is in place."

The weight of the apostle's own testimony is therefore in no sense removed by Acts xxvi. 14. That testimony is unequivocally opposed to all attempts at exhibiting a psychological process culminating in the conversion. These attempts, however, because of the importance which has been attributed to them, must now be examined. In general, they are becoming less and less elaborate; contemporary scholars are usually content to dismiss the psychological problem of the conversion with a few general observations about the secret of personality, or, at the most, a brief word about the possible condition of the apostle's mind. Since the direct interposition of the risen Christ is rejected, it is held that there must have been some psychological preparation for the Damascus experience, but what that preparation was remains hidden, it is said, in the secret places of the soul, which no psychological analysis can ever fully reveal.

If, however, the problem is not thus to be dismissed as insoluble, no unanimity has been achieved among those who attempt a solution. Two principal lines of solution of the problem may perhaps be distinguished—that which begins with the objective evidence as it presented itself to the persecutor, and that which starts with the seventh chapter of Romans and the persecutor's own sense of need. The former line was followed by Holsten, whose monographs still constitute the most elaborate exposition of the psychological process supposed to lie back of the conversion.[1] According to Holsten, the process centered in the consideration of the Cross of Christ. That consideration of course resulted at first in an attitude of hostility on the part of Paul. The Cross was a shameful thing; the proclamation of a crucified Messiah appeared, therefore, to the devout Pharisee as an outrageous blasphemy. But the disciples represented the Cross as in accordance with the will of God, and supported their contention by the evidence for the resurrection; the resurrection was made to overcome the offense of the Cross. But against the evidence for the resurrection, Holsten believes, Paul was helpless, the possibility of resurrection being fully recognized in his Pharisaic training. What then if the resurrection really vindicated the claims of Jesus to be the Messiah? Paul was by no means convinced, Holsten believes, that such was the case. But the possibility was necessarily in his mind, if only for the purposes of refutation. At this point Paul began to advance, according to Holsten, beyond the earlier disciples. On the assumption that the resurrection really did vindicate the claims of Jesus, the Cross would have to be explained. But an explanation lay ready to hand, and Paul applied this explanation with a thoroughness which the earlier disciples had not attained. The earlier disciples removed the offense of the Cross by representing the Cross as part of the plan of God for the Messiah; Paul exhibited the meaning of that plan much more clearly than they. He exhibited the meaning of the Cross by applying to it the category of vicarious suffering, which could be found, for example, in Isaiah liii. At this point the pre-Christian development of Paul was over. The Pauline "gnosis

---

[1] Holsten, *Zum Evangelium des Paulus und des Petrus*, 1868. Against Holsten, see Beyschlag, "Die Bekehrung des Apostels Paulus, mit besonderer Rücksicht auf die Erklärungsversuche von Baur und Holsten," in *Theologische Studien und Kritiken*, xxxvii, 1864, pp. 197-264; "Die Visionshypothese in ihrer neuesten Begründung. Eine Duplik gegen D. Holsten," *ibid.*, xliii, 1870, pp. 7-50, 189-263.

of the Cross" was already formed. Of course, before the conversion it was to Paul entirely a matter of supposition. On the supposition, still regarded as false, that the resurrection had really taken place, the Cross, far from being an offense, would become a glorious fact. All the essential elements of Paul's gospel of the Cross were thus present in Paul's mind before the conversion; the validity of them had been posited by him for the purposes of argument. The only thing that was lacking to make Paul a disciple of Jesus was conviction of the fact of the resurrection. That conviction was supplied by the Damascus experience. The unstable equilibrium then was over; the elements of the Pauline gospel, which were all present before, fell at once into their proper places.

The other way of explaining the conversion starts from the seventh chapter of Romans and the dissatisfaction which Paul is thought to have experienced under the Law. Paul, it is said, was a Pharisee; he made every effort to keep the Law of God. But he was too earnest to be satisfied with a merely external obedience; and real obedience he had not attained. He was therefore tormented by a sense of sin. That sense of sin no doubt led him into a more and more feverish effort to keep the letter of the Law and particularly to show his zeal by persecuting the disciples of Jesus. But all his efforts were vain; his obedience remained insufficient; the curse of the Law still rested upon him. What if the vain effort could be abandoned? What if the disciples of Jesus were right? Of course, he believed, they were not right, but what if they were? What if the Messiah had really died for the sins of believers, in accordance with Isaiah liii? What if salvation were attainable not by merit but by divine grace? These questions, it is supposed, were in the mind of Paul. He answered them still in the negative, but his misery kept them ever before his mind. The Law was thus a schoolmaster to bring him to Christ. He was ready for the vision.

In both of these lines of explanation importance is often attributed to the impression produced upon Paul's mind by the character of the disciples. Whence did they derive their bravery and their joy in the midst of persecution? Whence came the fervor of their love, whence the firmness of their faith? The persecutor, it is said, was impressed against his will.

The fundamental objection to all these theories of psychological development is that they describe only what might have been or what ought to have been, and not what actually was. No doubt Paul ought to have been coming nearer to Christianity; but as a matter of fact he was rather getting further away, and he records the fact in no uncertain terms in his Epistles. There are objections, moreover, to the various theories of development in detail; and the advocates of one theory are often the severest critics of another.

With regard to Holsten's exposition of the "gnosis of the Cross," for example, there is not the slightest evidence that the pre-Christian Jews interpreted Isaiah liii of the vicarious sufferings of the Messiah, or had any notion of the Messiah's vicarious death.[1] It is not true, moreover, as Beyschlag pointed out against Holsten, that Paul was helpless in the face of the evidence for the resurrection.[2] According to Paul's Pharisaic training, the resurrection would come only at the end of the age; a resurrection like the resurrection of Jesus, therefore, was by no means a matter of course, and could be established only by positive evidence of the most direct and unequivocal kind.

With regard to the sense of sin as the goad which forced Paul to accept the Saviour, there is no evidence that before his conversion Paul was under real conviction of sin. It is very doubtful whether Rom. vii. 7-25, with its account of the struggle between the flesh and the higher nature of man, refers to the unregenerate rather than to the regenerate life; and even if the former view is correct, it is doubtful whether the description is taken from the apostle's own experience. At any rate, the struggle, even if it be a struggle in the unregenerate man, is described from the point of view of the regenerate; it is not implied, therefore, that before the entrance of the Spirit of God a man is fully conscious of his own helplessness and of the desperateness of the struggle. The passage therefore, does not afford any certain information about the pre-Christian life of Paul. Undoubtedly before the conversion the conscience of Paul was aroused; he was conscientious in

[1] See Schürer, *Geschichte des jüdischen Volkes*, 4te Aufl., ii, 1907, pp. 648-651 (English Translation, *A History of the Jewish People*, Division II, vol. ii, 1885, pp. 184-187).
[2] Beyschlag, "Die Visionshypothese in ihrer neuesten Begründung," in *Theologische Studien und Kritiken*, xliii, 1870, pp. 19-21.

his devotion to the Law. Probably he was conscious of his failings. But that such consciousness of failure amounted to anything like that genuine conviction of sin which leads a man to accept the Saviour remains very doubtful. Recognized failure to keep the Law perfectly led in the case of Paul merely to greater zeal for the Law, a zeal which was manifested especially in the persecution of a blasphemous sect whose teaching was subversive of the authority of Moses.

Finally, it is highly improbable that Paul was favorably impressed by the bravery of those whom he was persecuting. It may seem strange at first sight that the same man who wrote the thirteenth chapter of 1 Corinthians should have haled helpless men and women to prison without a qualm, or listened without pity to the dying words of Stephen, "Lord, lay not this sin to their charge." But it is very dangerous to argue back from the Christian life of Paul to the life of Paul the Pharisee. Paul himself was conscious of a complete moral transformation as having taken place in him when he saw the Lord near Damascus. What was impossible for him after that transformation may well have been possible before. Moreover, if, despite such considerations, we could argue back from Paul the disciple of Jesus to Paul the Pharisee, there is one characteristic of the apostle which would never have permitted him to persecute those by whom he was favorably impressed—namely, his complete sincerity. The picture of Saul the doubter, torn by conflicting emotions, impressed by the calmness and bravery and magnanimity of those whom he was persecuting, yet stifling such impressions by persecuting zeal, is very romantic, but very un-Pauline.

But in attributing the conversion of Paul altogether to the experience on the road to Damascus, are we not heaping up into one moment what must of very necessity in conscious life be the work of years? Is it conceivable that ideas should have been implanted in the mind of a person not by processes of acquisition but mechanically as though by a hypodermic syringe? Would not such an experience, even if it were possible, be altogether destructive of personality?

The objection serves to correct possible misunderstandings. The view of the conversion which has just been set forth does not mean that when Paul drew near to Damascus on that memorable day he was ignorant of the facts about Jesus. If he had never heard of Jesus, or if having heard of Him he knew absolutely nothing about Him, then perhaps the conversion would have been not only supernatural but inconceivable. But it is not the traditional view of the conversion which is guilty of such exaggerations. They are the product rather of that separation of Paul from the historical Jesus which appears for example in Wrede and in Bousset. According to any reasonable view of Paul's pre-Christian experience, Paul was well acquainted, before the conversion, with many of the facts about Jesus' life and death; what he received on the road to Damascus was a new interpretation of the facts and a new attitude toward them. He had known the facts before, but they had filled him with hatred; now his hatred was changed into love.

Even after exaggerations have been removed, however, the change wrought by the Damascus experience remains revolutionary enough. Is that change conceivable? Could hatred have been changed into love merely by an experience which convinced Paul of the fact of the resurrection? The answer to this question depends altogether upon the nature of the Damascus experience. If that experience was merely an hallucination, the question must be answered in the negative; an hallucination could never have produced the profound changes in the personal life of Paul which have just been contemplated; and the historian would be obliged to fall back, despite the unequivocal testimony of the Epistles, upon some theory of psychological development of which the hallucination would only be the climax. But even those who maintain the supernaturalistic view of the conversion have too often failed to do justice to the content of the experience. One fundamental feature of the experience has too often been forgotten—the appearance on the road to Damascus was the appearance of a person. Sometimes the event has been regarded merely as a supernatural interposition of God intended to produce belief in the fact of the resurrection, as merely a sign. Undoubtedly it was a sign. But it was far more; it was contact between persons. But contact between persons, even under ordinary conditions, is exceedingly mysterious; merely a look or the tone of the voice sometimes produces astonishing results. Who has not experienced the transition from mere hearsay knowledge of a person to actual contact? One meeting is often sufficient to revolutionize the entire impression; indifference or hostility gives place at once to enthusiastic devotion. Those who speak of the transformation wrought in Paul by the appearance of Jesus as magical or mechanical or inconceivable have never reflected upon the mysteries of personal intercourse.

Only, it must have been a real person whom Paul met on the road to Damascus—not a vision, not a mere sign. If it was merely a vision or a sign, all the objections remain in force. But if it was really Jesus, the sight of His face and the words of love which He uttered may have been amply sufficient, provided the heart of Paul was renewed by the power of God's Spirit, to transform hatred into love. To call such an experience magic is to blaspheme all that is highest in human life. God was using no unworthy instrument when, by the personal presence of the Saviour, He transformed the life of Paul.

There is, therefore, no moral or psychological objection in the way of a simple acceptance of Paul's testimony about the conversion. And that testimony is unequivocal. Paul was not converted by any teaching which he received from men; he was not converted as Christians are usually converted, by the preaching of the truth or by that revelation of Christ which is contained in the lives of His followers. Jesus Himself in the case of Paul did in visible presence what He ordinarily does by the means which He has appointed. Upon this immediateness of the conversion, Paul is willing to stake the whole of his life; upon it he bases his apostolic authority.

CHAPTER III

THE TRIUMPH OF GENTILE FREEDOM

CHAPTER III

THE TRIUMPH OF GENTILE FREEDOM

AFTER the conversion, according to the Book of Acts, Paul received the ministrations of Ananias, and was baptized.[1] These details are not excluded by the Epistle to the Galatians. In the Epistle, Paul says that after God had revealed His son in him he did not confer with flesh and blood;[2] but the conference with flesh and blood which he was concerned to deny was a conference with the original apostles at Jerusalem about the principles of the gospel, not a conference with humble disciples at Damascus. An over-interpretation of Galatians would here lead almost to absurdity. Is it to be supposed that after the conversion Paul refused to have anything whatever to do with those who were now his brethren? In particular, is it to be supposed that he who afterwards placed baptism as a matter of course at the beginning of the new life for every Christian should himself not have been baptized? The Epistle to the Galatians does not mention his baptism, but that omission merely illustrates the incompleteness of the account. And if the baptism of Paul, which certainly must have taken place, is omitted from Galatians, other omissions must not be regarded as any more significant. The first two chapters of Galatians are not intended to furnish complete biography. Only those details are mentioned which were important for Paul's argument or had been misrepresented by his Judaizing opponents.

After God had revealed His son in him, Paul says, he went away into Arabia. Apparently this journey to Arabia is to be put very soon after the revelation, though the construction of the word "immediately" in Gal. i. 16 is not perfectly clear. If that word goes merely with the negative part of the sentence, then nothing is said about the time of the journey

[1] Acts ix. 10-19; xxii. 12-16.
[2] Gal. i. 16.

to Arabia; Paul would say merely that in the period just after the revelation of God's Son he did not go up to Jerusalem. There would then be no difficulty in the assertion of Acts which seems to put a stay in Damascus with preaching activity in the synagogues immediately after the baptism. This interpretation is adopted by a number of modern commentators, not only by B. Weiss and Zahn, who might be suspected of a bias in favor of the Book of Acts, but also by Sieffert and Lipsius and Bousset. Perhaps more naturally, however, the word "immediately" in Galatians is to be taken grammatically with the positive part of the sentence or with the whole sentence; the sentence would then mean, "Immediately, instead of conferring with flesh and blood or going up to Jerusalem to those who were apostles before me, I went away into Arabia and again I returned to Damascus." Even so, however, there is no real contradiction with Acts. When Paul tells what happened "immediately" after the revelation he is thinking in terms not of days but of journeys. The very first journey after the conversion—and it took place soon—was not to Jerusalem but to Arabia. When taken in the context the sentence does not exclude a brief preaching activity in Damascus before the journey to Arabia. Grammatically the word "immediately" may go with the positive part of the sentence, but in essential import it goes rather with the negative part. What Paul is really concerned about is to deny that he went up to Jerusalem soon after his conversion.

The Book of Acts does not mention the journey to Arabia and does not make clear where it may be inserted. Sometimes it is placed in the middle of Acts ix. 19, before the words, "And he was with the disciples in Damascus some days." In that case the discussion about the word "immediately" in Gal. i. 16 would be unnecessary; that word could be taken strictly with the positive part of the sentence without contradicting the Book of Acts; the journey to Arabia would have preceded the preaching activity in Damascus. Or the journey may be placed before Acts ix. 22; it would then be the cause of the greater vigor of Paul's preaching. Finally, it may be placed simply within the "many days" of Acts ix. 23. The phrase, "many days," in Acts apparently is used to indicate fairly long periods of time. It must be remembered that the author of Acts is not concerned here about chronology; perhaps he did not trouble himself to investigate the exact period of time that elapsed before the journey to Jerusalem. He was content merely to record the fact that before Paul went to Jerusalem he engaged for a considerable time in preaching in the Damascus synagogues. Certainly he must here be acquitted of any attempt at subserving the interests of harmony in the Church by a falsification of history. It is generally recognized now, against the Tübingen contentions, that if the author of Acts contradicts Galatians, his contradiction is naive rather than deliberate; the contradiction or apparent contradiction at least shows the complete independence of his account. He is not deliberately shortening up the time before Paul's first conference with Peter in the interests of a compromise between a Pauline and a Petrine party in the Church; if he had had the "three years" of Paul before him as he wrote he would have had no objection to using the detail in his history. But investigation of the chronology did not here seem to be important. The detail of the three years was vastly important for Paul's argument in Galatians, where he is showing that for a considerable period after the conversion he did not even meet those from whom he was said to have received his gospel, but it was not at all important in a general history of the progress of the Church.

The extent of the journey to Arabia, both geographically and temporally, is entirely unknown. "Arabia" included not only very remote regions but also a territory almost at the gates of Damascus; and all that may be determined about the length of the Arabian residence is that it was less than three years. Possibly Paul remained only a few weeks in Arabia. In that case the omission of the journey from the general narrative in Acts is very natural. The importance of Arabia in Paul's argument is due simply to the fact that Arabia was not Jerusalem; Paul mentions the journey to Arabia simply in contrast with a journey to Jerusalem which he is excluding in the interests of his argument. The only thing that might seem to require a considerable stay in Arabia is the narrative of Paul's first Jerusalem visit in Acts ix. 26-30; the distrust of Paul displayed by the Jerusalem Christians is more easily explicable if after his conversion he had been living for the most part in a region more remote than Damascus from Jerusalem. A similar consideration might possibly sug-

gest that in Arabia Paul was engaged in meditation rather
than in missionary activity; he had not yet become so well
known as a preacher that the Christians of Jerusalem could
begin to glorify God in him, as they did a little later. Possibly also there is an implied contrast in Gal. i. 16, 17 between conference with the original apostles and direct communion with Christ; possibly Paul means to say, "Instead of
conferring with flesh and blood in Jerusalem, I communed with
the Lord in Arabia." Despite such considerations, the matter
is by no means perfectly clear; it is perfectly possible that
Paul engaged in missionary work in Arabia. But at any rate,
even if that view be correct, he also engaged in meditation.
Paul was never a mere "practical Christian" in the modern
sense; labor in his case was always based upon thought, and
life upon doctrine.

The escape of Paul from Damascus just before his first
visit to Jerusalem is narrated in Acts ix. 23-25 and in 2 Cor.
xi. 32, 33. The mention of the ethnarch of Aretas the Nabatean
king as having authority at or near Damascus causes some
difficulty, and might not have passed unchallenged if it had
been attested by Acts. But as a matter of fact, it is just this
detail which appears, not in Acts, but in an epistle of Paul.

The first visit of Paul to Jerusalem after the conversion
is described in Acts ix. 26-30; xxii. 17-21; Gal. i. 18, 19. In
itself, the account in Acts bears every mark of trustworthiness.
The only detail which might seem surprising is that the Jerusalem Christians would not at first believe that Paul was a
disciple; must not a notable event like the conversion of so
prominent a persecutor have become known at Jerusalem in the
course of three years? But if Paul had spent a large part
of the three years in Arabia, whence news of him could not
be easily obtained, the report of his conversion might have
come to seem like a remote rumor; the very fact of his withdrawal might, as has been suggested, have cast suspicion upon
the reality of his conversion. Emotion, moreover, often lags
behind cold reasoning; the heart is more difficult to convince
than the mind. The Jerusalem Christians had known Paul
only as a cruel and relentless persecutor; it was not so easy for
them to receive him at once as a brother. This one detail is
therefore not at all sufficient to reverse the favorable im-

pression which is made by the Lucan account of the visit as a whole.

The chief objection to the account is usually found in a comparison with what Paul himself says in Galatians. In itself, the account is natural; but does it agree with Paul's own testimony? One apparent divergence may indeed soon be dismissed. In Acts ix. 27 it is said that Paul was introduced to "the apostles," whereas in Gal. i. 19 it is said that Paul saw only James, the brother of the Lord (who was not among the Twelve), and Peter. But possibly the author of Acts is using the term "apostle" in a sense broad enough to include James, so that Paul actually saw two "apostles"—Peter and James— or else the plural is used merely in a generic sense to indicate that Paul was introduced to whatever representative or representatives of the apostolic body may have happened to be present.

Much more weight is commonly attributed to an objection drawn from the general representation of the visit. According to Acts, Paul was associated publicly with the Jerusalem disciples and engaged in an active mission among the Greek-speaking Jews; according to Galatians, it is argued, he was in strict hiding, since he did not become acquainted personally with the churches of Judæa (Gal. i. 22). But the objection, as has already been observed, depends upon an over-interpretation of Gal. i. 22. Whether or no "Judæa" means the country in sharp distinction from the capital, in either case all that is necessarily meant is that Paul did not become acquainted generally with the Judæan churches. The capital may well have formed an exception. If Paul had meant in the preceding verses that he had been in hiding in Jerusalem he would have expressed himself very differently. Certainly the modern representation of the visit is in itself improbable. The picture of Paul entering Jerusalem under cover of darkness or under a disguise and being kept as a mysterious stranger somewhere in a secret chamber of Peter's house is certainly much less natural than the account which the Book of Acts gives of the earnest attempt of Paul to repair the damage which he had done to the Jerusalem Church. It is very doubtful whether concealment of Paul in Jerusalem would have been possible even if Paul had consented to it; he was too well-known in the city. Of course this last argument would be answered if, as Heitmüller and Loisy suppose, Paul had never been in Jerusalem at all, even as a persecutor. But that hypothesis is faced by absolutely decisive objections, as has already been observed.

The whole modern representation of the first visit, therefore, is based solely upon a very doubtful interpretation of one verse, and is in itself highly unnatural. Surely it is much more probable that the real reason why Paul saw only Peter and James among the leaders was that the others were out of the city, engaged in missionary work in Judæa. Their presence in the churches of Judæa would explain the mention of those churches in Gal. i. 22. Paul is indicating the meagerness of his direct contact with the original apostles. The churches of Judæa would become important in his argument if they were the scene of the apostles' labors. Against a very doubtful interpretation of the account in Galatians, which brings it into contradiction with Acts, may therefore be placed an entirely consistent interpretation which, when the account is combined with Acts, produces a thoroughly natural representation of the course of events.

Paul says nothing about what happened during his fifteen-day intercourse with Peter. But it is highly improbable, as even Holsten pointed out, that he spent the time gazing silently at Peter as though Peter were one of the sights of the city.[1] Undoubtedly there was conversation between the two men, and in the conversation the subject of the life and death of Jesus could hardly be avoided. In the Epistle to the Galatians Paul denies, indeed, that he received his gospel from men. But the bare facts about Jesus did not constitute a gospel. The facts were known to some extent to friend and foe alike; Paul knew something about them even before his conversion and then increased his knowledge through intercourse with the disciples at Damascus. The fifteen days spent in company with Peter could hardly have failed to bring a further enrichment of his knowledge.

In 1 Cor. xv. 3-7, Paul gives a summary of what he had

[1] Holsten, *op. cit.*, p. 118, Anm.: "Aber natürlich kann in dem ἱστορῆσαι Κηφᾶν nicht liegen, Paulus sei nach Jerusalem gegangen, um den Petrus fünfzehn tage lang stumm anzuschauen. Die beiden männer werden miteinander über das evangelium Christi geredet haben."

"received"— the death, burial, resurrection, and appearances
of Jesus. The vast majority of modern investigators, of all
snades of opinion, find in these verses a summary of the Jerusalem tradition which Paul received from Peter dur'ng the fifteen
days. Undoubtedly Paul knew some if not all of these facts before he went to Jerusalem; the facts were probably common
property of the disciples in Damascus as well as in Jerusalem.
But it is inconceivable that he should not have tested and supplemented the tradition by what _ eter, whose name stands first
(1 Cor. xv. 5) in the list of the appearances, said in Jerusalem.
Recently, indeed, an attempt has been made by Heitmüller to
represent the tradition as being derived merely from the Christian communities in Damascus or Antioch, and at best only
indirectly from Jerusalem; these communities are thus interposed as an additional link between Paul and the Jerusalem
Church.[1] But the very purpose of the passage in 1 Corinthians is to emphasize the unity of teaching, not between Paul
and certain obscure Christians in Hellenistic communities, but
between Paul and the "apostles." "Whether therefore," Paul
says, "it be I or they, so we preach and so ye believed" (1
Cor. xv. 11). The attempt at separating the factual basis of
the Pauline gospel from the primitive tradition shatters upon
the rock of 1 Corinthians and Galatians. In Galatians, Paul
says he was in direct intercourse with Peter, and in 1 Corinthians he emphasizes the unity of his teaching with that of
Peter and the other apostles.

After leaving Jerusalem Paul went into the regions of
Syria and of Cilicia; the Book of Acts, more specifically, mentions Tarsus (Cilicia) and Antioch (Syria). The period
which Paul spent in Tarsus or in its vicinity is for us altogether obscure. In all probability he engaged in missionary
work and included Gentiles in his mission. Certainly at the
conclusion of the Cilician period Barnabas thought him suitable for the specifically Gentile work at Antioch, and it is
probable that he nad already demonstrated his suitability.
His apostolic consciousness, also, as attested both by the Book
of Acts and by Galatians, suggests that the beginning of his
life-work as apostle to the Gentiles was not too long deferred.

---

[1] Heitmüller, "Zum Problem Paulus und Jesus," in *Zeitschrift für die
neutestamentliche Wissenschaft,* xiii, 1912, pp. 320-337, especially p. 331.

At Antioch, the disciples were first called "Christians" (Acts xi. 26). The objections, especially linguistic, formerly urged against this assertion of Acts have now for the most part been silenced. The assertion is important as showing that the Church was becoming so clearly separate from the synagogue that a separate name had to be coined by the Gentile population. Tremendous importance is attributed to the Christian community at Antioch by Bousset and Heitmüller, who believe that the religion of that community had diverged in fundamental respects from the religion of the primitive Jerusalem Church, and that this extra-Palestinian Christianity, and not the Christianity of Jerusalem, is the basis of the religion of Paul. According to this hypothesis, the independence of Paul which is attested in Galatians is apparently to be regarded as independence merely over against the intimate friends of Jesus; apparently Paul had no objection against taking over the teaching of the Greek-speaking Christians of Antioch. This representation is out of accord with what has just been established about the relations between Paul and the Jerusalem Church. It must be examined more in detail, however, in a subsequent chapter.

After at least a year—probably more—Barnabas and Saul, according to Acts xi. 30; xii. 25, were sent up to Jerusalem to bear the gifts of the Antioch Church, which had been collected in view of the famine prophesied by Agabus. This "famine visit" is the second visit of Paul to Jerusalem which is mentioned in Acts. The second visit which is mentioned in Galatians is the one described in Gal. ii. 1-10, at which Paul came into conference with the pillars of the Jerusalem Church. May the two be identified? Is Gal. ii. 1-10 an account of the visit which is mentioned in Acts xi. 30; xii. 25?[1]

Chronology opposes no absolutely insuperable objection to the identification. The apparent objection is as follows. The famine visit of Acts xi. 30; xii. 25 took place at about the same time as the events narrated in Acts xii, since the narrative of those events is interposed between the mention of the coming of Barnabas and Paul to Jerusalem (Acts xi. 30) and that of their return to Antioch (Acts xii. 25). But the events of

[1] For what follows, compare "Recent Criticism of the Book of Acts," in *Princeton Theological Review*, xvii, 1919, pp. 597-608.

Acts xii include the death of Herod Agrippa I, which certainly occurred in 44 A.D. The famine visit, therefore, apparently occurred at about 44 A.D. But the visit of Gal. ii. 1-10 took place fourteen years (Gal. ii. 1) after the first visit, which in turn took place three years (Gal. i. 18) after the conversion. Therefore the visit of Gal. ii. 1-10 took place seventeen (3+14) years after the conversion. But if that visit be identified with the famine visit and the famine visit took place in 44 A.D., the conversion must have taken place seventeen years before 44 A.D. or in 27 A.D., which of course is impossible since the crucifixion of Jesus did not occur till several years after that time. At first sight, therefore, it looks as though the identification of Gal. ii. 1-10 with the famine visit were impossible.

Closer examination, however, shows that the chronological data all allow a certain amount of leeway. In the first place, it is by no means clear that the famine visit took place at exactly the time of the death of Herod Agrippa I in 44 A.D. The author of Acts has been carrying on two threads of narrative, one dealing with Antioch and the other dealing with Jerusalem. In Acts xi. 19-30 he has carried the Antioch narrative on to a point beyond that reached in the Jerusalem narrative. Now, when the two narratives are brought together by the visit of Barnabas and Paul to Jerusalem, the author pauses in order to bring the Jerusalem narrative up to date; he tells what has been happening at Jerusalem during the period in which the reader's attention has been diverted to Antioch. The events of Acts xii may therefore have taken place some time before the famine visit of Acts xi. 30; xii. 25; the famine visit may have taken place some time after 44 A.D. Information in Josephus with regard to the famine,[1] combined with the order of the narrative in Acts, permits the placing of the famine visit as late as 46 A.D. In the second place, it is by no means certain that the visit of Gal. ii. 1-10 took place seventeen years after the conversion. The ancients sometimes used an inclusive method of reckoning time, in accordance with which "three years" might mean only one full year with parts of two other years; January, 1923, would thus

[1] Josephus, *Antiq.* XX. v. 2. See Schürer, *Geschichte des jüdischen Volkes*, 3te u. 4te Aufl., i, 1901, p. 567 (English Translation, *A History of the Jewish People*, Division I, vol. ii, 1890, pp. 169f.).

be "three years" after December, 1921. According to this method of reckoning, the "fourteen years" of Gal. ii. 1 would become only thirteen; and the "three years" of Gal. i. 18 would become only two years; the visit of Gal. ii. 1-10 would thus be only fifteen (13 + 2) instead of seventeen (14 + 3) years after the conversion. If, then, the visit of Gal. ii. 1-10 be identified with the famine visit, and the famine visit took place in 46 A.D., the conversion took place in 31 A.D. (46 — 15), which is a possible date. Moreover, it is not certain that the "fourteen years" of Gal. ii. 1 is to be reckoned from the first visit; it may be reckoned from the conversion, so that the "three years" of Gal. i. 18 is to be included in it and not added to it. In that case, the conversion took place only fourteen (or, by the inclusive method of reckoning, thirteen) years before the visit of Gal. ii. 1-10; or, if the visit of Gal. ii. 1-10 be identified with the famine visit, fourteen (or thirteen) years before 46 A.D., that is, in 32 A.D. (or 33 A.D.), which is a perfectly possible date.

But of course chronology does not decide in favor of the identification of Gal. ii. 1-10 with Acts xi. 30; xii. 25; at best it only permits that identification. Chronologically it is even slightly more convenient to identify Gal. ii. 1-10 with a visit subsequent to the famine visit. The only subsequent visit which comes seriously in question is the visit at the time of the "Apostolic Council" of Acts xv. 1-29. The advantages of identifying Gal. ii. 1-10 with Acts xi. 30; xii. 25, therefore, must be compared with those of identifying it with Acts xv. 1-29.

If the former identification be adopted, then Paul in Galatians has not mentioned the Apostolic Council of Acts xv. 1-29. Since the Apostolic Council dealt with the same question as that which was under discussion in Galatians, and since it constituted an important step in Paul's relations with the original apostles, it is a little difficult to see how Paul could have omitted it from the Epistle. This objection has often weighed against the identification of Gal. ii. 1-10 with the famine visit. But in recent years the objection has been removed by the hypothesis which places the writing of Galatians actually before the Apostolic Council; obviously Paul could not be expected to mention the Council if the Council had not

yet taken place. This early dating of Galatians has been
advocated by a German Roman Catholic scholar, Weber,[1]
and recently it has won the support of men of widely divergent
points of view, such as Emmet,[2] Kirsopp Lake,[3] Ramsay,[4]
and Plooij.[5] Of course this hypothesis depends absolutely
upon the correctness of the "South Galatian" theory of the
address of the Epistle, which finds "the Churches of Galatia"
of Gal. i. 2 in Pisidian Antioch, Iconium, Lystra and Derbe;
for the churches in "North Galatia," if there were any such,
were not founded till after the Apostolic Council (Acts xvi.
6).[6]

One objection to the early dating of Galatians is derived
from the close relation between that epistle and the Epistle
to the Romans. If Galatians was written before the Apostolic
Council it is the earliest of the extant epistles of Paul and is
separated by a period of some six or eight years from the
epistles of the third missionary journey with which it has
ordinarily been grouped. Thus the order of the Epistles would
be Galatians, 1 and 2 Thessalonians, 1 and 2 Corinthians,
Romans. This order seems to tear asunder the epistles which
naturally belong together. The objection was partially overcome by a bold hypothesis of Lake, who suggested that the
Epistle to the Romans was first composed at an early time
as an encyclical letter, and that later, being modified by the
addition of a Roman address and other suitable details, it
was sent to the Church at Rome.[7] On this hypothesis Galatians and the substance of Romans would be kept together be-

---

[1] *Die Abfassung des Galaterbriefs vor dem Apostelkonzil*, 1900.

[2] "Galatians the Earliest of the Pauline Epistles," in *Expositor*, 7th
Series, vol. ix, 1910, pp. 242-254 (reprinted in *The Eschatological Question
in the Gospels*, 1911, pp. 191-209); *St. Paul's Epistle to the Galatians*, 1912,
pp. xiv-xxii.

[3] *The Earlier Epistles of St. Paul*, 1911, pp. 265-304. In a later book,
Lake has modified his views about the relation between Galatians and Acts.
The historicity of Acts xv. 1-29 is now abandoned. See *Landmarks in the
History of Early Christianity*, 1920, pp. 63-66.

[4] Ramsay, "Suggestions on the History and Letters of St. Paul. I. The
Date of the Galatian Letter," in *Expositor*, VIII, v, 1913, pp. 127-145.

[5] Plooij, *De chronologie van het leven van Paulus*, 1918, pp. 111-140.

[6] Maurice Jones ("The Date of the Epistle to the Galatians," in *Expositor*, VIII, vi, 1913, pp. 193-208) has adduced from the Book of Acts
various arguments against the early date of Galatians, which, though worthy
of attention, are not quite decisive.

[7] Lake, *The Earlier Epistles of St. Paul*, 1911, pp. 361-370.

cause both would be placed early. The hypothesis can appeal to the interesting textual phenomenon in Rom. i. 7, where the words "in Rome" are omitted by a few witnesses to the text. But the evidence is insufficient. And even if Lake's hypothesis were correct, it would not altogether overcome the difficulty; for both Galatians and Romans would be removed from what has usually been regarded as their natural position among the epistles of the third missionary journey. In reply, it could be said that reconstructions of an author's development, unless supported by plain documentary evidence, are seldom absolutely certain; the simplicity of 1 and 2 Thessalonians, as over against the great soteriological epistles, Galatians, 1 and 2 Corinthians, Romans, is no doubt due to the immaturity of the Thessalonian Church rather than to any immaturity in Paul's thinking. There is therefore no absolutely decisive objection against putting the Epistle to the Galatians, with its developed soteriology, before the Thessalonian Epistles.

On the whole, it may be said that the identification of Gal. ii. 1-10 with Acts xi. 30; xii. 25 is perhaps most plausible when it is connected with the early dating of Galatians, before the Apostolic Council. But that identification, whether with or without the early dating of the Epistle, must now be considered on its merits. Is Gal. ii. 1-10 to be identified with the famine visit of Acts xi. 30; xii. 25, or with the Apostolic Council of Acts xv?

The former identification possesses one obvious advantage—by it the second visit in Galatians is the same as the second visit in Acts; whereas if Gal. ii. 1-10 is identified with Acts xv. 1-29 Paul has passed over the famine visit without mention. The identification with the famine visit may therefore conveniently be considered first.

According to this identification, Paul had two conferences with the Jerusalem leaders, one at the time of the famine visit and one some years afterwards at the time of the Apostolic Council. Could the second conference conceivably have followed thus upon the former? If the conference between Paul and the Jerusalem leaders described in Gal. ii. 1-10 took place at the time of the famine visit, then would not the Apostolic Council seem to be a mere meaningless repetition of the former conference? If the matter of Gentile freedom had already been settled (Gal. ii. 1-10) at the famine visit, how could it come up again *de novo* at the Apostolic Council?

This objection is by no means insuperable. The meeting described in Gal. ii. 1-10 may have been merely a private meeting between Paul and the original apostles. Although the presence of Titus, the uncircumcised Gentile, was no doubt a matter of public knowledge, it need not necessarily have given rise to any public discussion, since it was not unprecedented, Cornelius also having been received into the Church without circumcision. But if the famine visit brought merely a private conference between Paul and the original apostles, Gentile freedom was still open to attack, especially if, after the famine visit, there was (as is in any case probable) an influx of strict legalists into the Christian community. There was no public pronouncement of the original apostles to which the advocates of freedom could appeal. There was therefore still urgent need of a public council such as the one described in Acts xv. 1-29, especially since that council dealt not only with the general question of Gentile freedom but also with the problem of mixed communities where Jews and Gentiles were living together. The Apostolic Council, therefore, may well have taken place in the way described in Acts xv. 1-29 even if the conference of Gal. ii. 1-10 had been held some years before.

No absolutely decisive objection, therefore, has yet been found against the identification of Gal. ii. 1-10 with Acts xi. 30; xii. 25. But the *prima facie* evidence has usually been regarded as favoring the alternative identification, since Gal. ii. 1-10 bears much more resemblance to Acts xv. 1-29 than it does to Acts xi, 30; xii. 25. Resemblance to Acts xi. 30; xii. 25 is not, indeed, altogether lacking. In both Galatians ii. 1-10 and Acts xi. 30; xii. 25, Barnabas is represented as going up with Paul to Jerusalem; in both passages there is reference to gifts for the Jerusalem Church; and the revelation referred to in Gal. ii. 2 as the occasion of the journey may be discovered in the revelation of the famine made to Agabus (Acts xi. 28). But the relief of the Jerusalem Church, which is put as the sole purpose of the journey in Acts xi. 30; xii. 25, is quite subordinate in Gal. ii. 1-10; Barnabas is with Paul in Acts xv. 1-29 just as much as he is in Acts xi. 30; xii. 25; and it may be questioned whether in Gal. ii. 2 it is not more natural to think of a revelation coming to Paul rather than one coming through the mouth of Agabus. The strongest argument, however, for identifying Gal. ii. 1-10 with Acts xv. 1-29 is that the main purpose of Paul's visit seems to be the same according to both passages; according to both the matter of circumcision of Gentiles was under discussion, and according to both the result was a triumph for the cause of freedom. This identification must now be considered. Various objections have been raised against it. These objections lead, according to the point of view of the objector, either to an acceptance of the alternative identification (with Acts xi. 30; xii. 25) or else to a rejection of the historicity of the Book of Acts.

The first objection is derived from the fact that if Gal. ii. 1-10 is to be identified with Acts xv. 1-29, Paul has passed over the famine visit without mention. Could he have done so honestly, if that visit had really occurred? In the first two chapters of Galatians Paul is establishing the independence of his apostolic authority; he had not, he says, as the Judaizers maintained, received his authority through mediation of the original apostles. At first, he says, he came into no effective contact with the apostles; it was three years after his conversion before he saw any of them; then he saw only Peter (and James) and that only for fifteen days. Then he went away into the regions of Syria and of Cilicia without ever becoming known by face to the Churches of Judæa; then after fourteen years again he went up to Jerusalem (Gal. ii. 1). Is it not the very point of the passage that after his departure to Syria and Cilicia it was fourteen long years before he again went up to Jerusalem? Would not his entire argument be invalidated if there were an unmentioned visit to Jerusalem between the first visit (Gal. i. 18, 19) and the visit of Gal. ii. 1-10? If such a visit had taken place, would he not have had to mention it in order to place it in the proper light as he had done in the case of the first visit? By omitting to mention the visit in a context where he is carefully tracing the history of his relations with the Jerusalem leaders, would he not be exposing himself to the charge of dishonest suppression of facts? Such considerations have led a great number of investigators to reject the historicity of the famine visit; there never could have been, they insist, a visit between the first visit and the visit of Gal. ii. 1-10; for if there had been, Paul would have been obliged to mention it, not only by his own honesty, but also because of the impossibility of deception. This is one of the points where the narrative in Acts has been most insistently criticized. Here and there, indeed, there have been discordant notes in the chorus of criticism; the insufficiency of the objection has been admitted now and then even by those who are far removed from any concern for the defense of the Book of Acts. Baur himself, despite all his Tübingen severity of criticism, was clear-sighted enough not to lay stress upon this particular objection; [1] and in recent years J. Weiss has been equally discerning.[2] In Galatians Paul is not giving a complete enumeration of his visits to Jerusalem, but merely singling out those details which had formed the basis of the Judaizers' attack, or afforded peculiar support to his own contentions. Apparently the Judaizers had misrepresented the first visit; that is the time, they had said, when Paul came under the authority of the original apostles. In answer to this attack Paul is obliged to deal carefully with that first visit; it came three years after the conversion, he says, and it lasted only fifteen days—surely not long enough to make Paul a disciple of Peter. Then Paul went away into the regions of Syria and Cilicia. Probably, for the first readers, who were familiar with the outlines of Paul's life, this departure for Syria and Cilicia clearly meant the entrance by Paul into his distinctive Gentile work. He was well launched upon his Gentile work, fully engaged in the proclamation of his gospel before he had ever had such contact with the original apostles as could possibly have given him that gospel. At this point as J. Weiss [3] well observes, there is a transition in the argument. The argument based on lack of contact with the original apostles has been finished, and now gives place to an entirely different argument. In the first chapter of Galatians Paul has been showing that at first he had no such contact with the original apostles as could have made him a disciple of theirs; now, in the second chapter he proceeds to show that when he did come into conference with them, they themselves recognized that he was no disciple of theirs but an independent

---

[1] Baur, *Paulus,* 2te Aufl., 1866, pp. 130-132 (English Translation, *Paul,* i, 1873, pp. 118-120). Baur does maintain that Gal. ii. 1 renders improbabl a second visit of Paul to Jerusalem before the conference with the apostle which is narrated in Gal. ii. 1, but points out that in itself the verse capable of a different interpretation.

[2] J. Weiss, *Urchristentum,* 1914, p. 147, Anm. 2.

[3] *Loc. cit.*

apostle. Apparently this conference, like the first visit, had been misrepresented by the Judaizers, and hence needed to be singled out for special treatment. It must be admitted that Paul is interested in the late date at which it occurred—fourteen years after the first visit or fourteen years after the conversion. Probably, therefore, it was the first real conference which Paul held with the original apostles on the subject of his Gentile work. If the famine visit had involved such a conference, probably Paul would have mentioned that visit. But if (as is not improbable on independent grounds) the apostles were away from Jerusalem at the time of the famine visit, and if that visit occurred long after Paul had been well launched upon his distinctive work, and if it had given the Judaizers so little basis for their contentions that they had not thought it worth while to draw it into the discussion, then Paul was not obliged to mention it. Paul is not constructing an argument which would hold against all possible attacks, but rather is meeting the attacks which had actually been launched. In the second chapter, having finished proving that in the decisive early period before he was well engaged in his distinctive work there was not even any extended contact with the original apostles at all, he proceeds to the telling argument that the very men who were appealed to by the Judaizers themselves had admitted that he was entirely independent of them and that they had nothing to add to him. If the famine visit had occurred in the early period, or if, whenever it occurred, it had involved the important event of a conference with the apostles about the Pauline gospel, in either case Paul would probably have been obliged to mention it. But, as it is, the visit, according to Acts xi. 30; xii. 25, did not occur until Paul had already been engaged in the Gentile work, and there is no reason to suppose that it involved any contact with the original apostles. The omission of the famine visit from Galatians, therefore, as a visit distinct from Gal. ii. 1-10, does not absolutely require either the identification of Gal. ii. 1-10 with that famine visit or the denial of the historicity of Acts.

Certain other difficulties emerge, however, when Gal. ii. 1-10 is compared with Acts xv. 1-29 in detail.

In the first place, the leaders of the Jerusalem Church, it is said, are represented in Acts xv. 1-29 as maintaining Pauline principles, whereas in Gal. ii. 1-10 it appears that there was really a fundamental difference between them and Paul. This difficulty constitutes an objection not against the identification of Gal. ii. 1-10 with Acts xv. 1-29 but against the historicity of Acts, for if at any time there was a really fundamental difference of principle between Paul and the original apostles then the whole representation in Acts is radically incorrect. But the objection disappears altogether when Galatians is correctly interpreted. The Epistle to the Galatians does not represent the conference between Paul and the pillars of the Jerusalem Church as resulting in a cold agreement to disagree; on the contrary it represents those leaders as giving to Paul and Barnabas the right hand of fellowship. And Gal. ii. 11-21, rightly interpreted, attests positively a real unity of principle as existing between Paul and Peter.

The one objection that remains against the identification of Gal. ii. 1-10 with Acts xv. 1-29 concerns the "Apostolic Decree" of Acts xv. 28, 29 (compare Acts xv. 19, 20; xxi. 25). According to the Epistle to the Galatians the apostles at the time of the conference "added nothing" to Paul (Gal. ii. 6); according to the Book of Acts, it is argued, they added something very important indeed—namely, the requirements of the Apostolic Decree that the Gentile Christians should "refrain from things offered to idols and from blood and from things strangled and from fornication." Since these requirements are partly at least ceremonial, they seem to constitute an exception to the general principle of Gentile freedom, and therefore an addition to Paul's gospel. If when Paul presented to the original apostles the gospel which he was preaching among the Gentiles, involving the free offer of salvation apart from the Law, the apostles emended that gospel by requiring at least certain parts of the ceremonial Law, were they not "adding" something to Paul?

But are the provisions of the decree really ceremonial? Apparently they are in part ceremonial if the so-called "Neutral text" attested by the Codex Sinaiticus and the Codex Vaticanus be correct. According to this text, which here lies at the basis of all forms of our English Bible, "blood" can hardly refer to anything except meat that has the blood left in it or else blood that might be prepared separately for food; for "things strangled" certainly refers to a closely related provision of the ceremonial Law about food. But at this point an interesting textual question arises. The so-called "Western text" of the Book of Acts, attested by the Codex Bezae and the usual companion witnesses, omits the word translated "things strangled" or "what is strangled" in Acts xv. 20, 29; xxi. 25, and in the first two of these three passages adds the negative form of the Golden Rule. Thus the Western text reads in Acts xv. 28, 29 as follows: "For it has seemed good to the Holy Spirit and to us to lay no further burden upon you except these necessary things—that you refrain from things offered to idols and from blood and from fornication, and that you do not to another whatsoever things you do not wish to be done to you." It is generally agreed that the Golden Rule has here been added by a copyist; but the omission of "things strangled" is thought by many modern scholars to preserve the reading of the autograph. If this short text without "things strangled" be correct, then the provisions of the Decree need not be regarded as ceremonial at all, but may be taken as simply moral. "Things offered to idols" may refer to idolatry in general; "blood" may refer to murder; and "fornication" may be meant in the most general sense. But if the provisions of the Decree were simply moral, then plainly they did not constitute any "addition" to the message of freedom which Paul proclaimed among the Gentiles. Paul himself had of course enjoined upon his converts the necessity of leading a true moral life. If when the original apostles were urged by the Judaizers to impose upon the Gentile converts the requirements of the ceremonial Law, they responded, "No; the only requirements to be imposed upon the Gentiles are that they refrain from deadly sins like idolatry, murder and fornication," that decision constituted merely a most emphatic confirmation of Paul's gospel of freedom.

The textual question cannot here be discussed in detail. In favor of the Western text, with its omission of "things strangled," may be urged not only the general principle of textual criticism that the shorter reading is to be preferred to the longer, but also the special consideration that in this particular passage the shorter reading seems to account for the origin of the two additions; (1) the word translated "things strangled," and (2) the Golden Rule. The short text, supposing it to be the original, was ambiguous; it might be taken either as ceremonial ("blood" meaning the eating of blood) or as moral ("blood" meaning the shedding of blood or murder). Those copyists who took it as ceremonial, it is maintained, fixed the meaning by adding "things strangled" (because animals that were strangled had the blood still in them, so that the eating of them constituted a violation of the ceremonial Law); whereas those who took the Decree as moral fixed the meaning by adding the Golden Rule as the summation of the moral law.[1]

On the other side may be urged the connection which seems to exist between the omission of "things strangled" and the manifest gloss constituted by the Golden Rule. Documentary attestation of a short text, without the Golden Rule and without "things strangled," is exceedingly scanty if not non-existent—Kirsopp Lake can point only to the witness of Irenæus. The omission of "things strangled," therefore, may be only a part of a moralizing of the Decree (carried out also in the addition of the Golden Rule), which would be quite in accord with that habit of scribes by which they tended to ignore in the interests of moral commonplaces what was special and difficult in the text which they were copying. In reply, Lake insists that just at the time and at the place where the short text (without "things strangled") was prevalent, there was a food law for which the long text (with "things strangled") would have afforded welcome support. Why should the text have been modified just where in its original form it supported the prevailing practice of the Church? The conclusion is, Lake believes, that if the Western text prevailed, despite the welcome support which would have been afforded by the other text, it was because the Western text was correct.[2]

Decision as to the textual question will depend to a considerable extent upon the conclusion which is reached with regard to the Western text as a whole. The radical rejection of that text which was advocated by Westcott and Hort has by no means won universal approval; a number of recent scholars are inclined at least to pursue an eclectic course, adopting now the Western reading and now the Neutral reading on the basis of internal evidence in the individual cases. Others believe that the Western text and the Neutral text are both correct, since the Western text is derived from an earlier edition

[1] See Lake, *op. cit.*, pp. 51-53.
[2] *Op. cit.*, pp. 57-59.

of the book, whereas the Neutral text represents a revised edition issued by the author himself.[1] But this hypothesis affords absolutely no assistance in the case f the Apostolic Decree; for the Western reading (if it be interpreted in the purely non-ceremonial way) presents the Decree in a light very different from that in which it appears according to the Neutral reading. It is impossible that the author could have contradicted himself so directly and in so important a matter. Therefore, if one of the two readings is due to the author, the other is due to some one else. Cases like this weigh heavily against the hypothesis of two editions of the book; that hypothesis can be saved only by supposing either that the Western documents do not here reproduce correctly the original Western form of the book, or else that the other documents do not here reproduce the original revised edition. In other words, despite the manuscript evidence, the two editions f the book must here be supposed to have been in harmony. At any rate, then, whether or no the hypothesis of two editions be accepted, a choice must here be made between the Neutral reading and the Western reading; they cannot both be due to the author, since they are contradictory to each other.

On the whole, it must be said that the Western text of the Book of Acts does not commend itself, either as the one genuine form of the book, or as an earlier edition of which the Neutral text is a revision. The Western readings are interesting; at times they may contain genuine historical information; but it seems unlikely that they are due to the author. Here and there indeed the Western documents may preserve a genuine reading which has been lost in all other witnesses to the text—even Westcott and Hort did not altogether exclude such a possibility—but in general the high estimate which Westcott and Hort placed upon the Neutral text is justified. Thus there is a possibility that the short text of the Apostolic Decree, without "things strangled," is genuine, but it is a possibility only.

If then, the Neutral text of the Decree is corect, so that the requirements of the Decree are partly ceremonial, must the

[1] An elaborate attempt has recently been made by Zahn, in addition to former attempts by Blass and Hilgenfeld, to reproduce the original form of the Western text, which Zahn believes to be the earlier edition of the book. See Zahn, *Die Urausgabe der Apostelgeschichte des Lucas,* 1916 (*Forschungen zur Geschichte des neutestamentlichen Kanons,* ix. Teil).

Book of Acts here be held to contradict the Epistle to the
Galatians? If the Decree really was passed at the Apostolic
Council, as Acts xv. 29 represents, would Paul have been
obliged to mention it in Gal. ii. 1-10? Answering these questions
in the affirmative, a great many scholars since the days of
Baur have regarded the account which the Book of Acts gives
of the Apostolic Council as radically wrong; and since the
book has thus failed to approve itself at the point where
it runs parallel to a recognized authority, it must be dis-
trusted elsewhere as well. The Apostolic Council, especially
the Apostolic Decree, has thus become, to use a phrase of B.
W. Bacon, the "crux of apostolic history:" [1]

It is exceedingly unlikely, however, at any rate, that the
Decree has been made up "out of whole cloth"; for it does
not coincide exactly with the usage of the later Church, and
seems to be framed in view of primitive conditions. Even those
who reject the narrative of Acts as it stands, therefore, often
admit that the Decree was really passed by the early Jerusalem
Church; but they maintain that it was passed after Paul's departure from Jerusalem and without his consent. This view
is thought to be supported by Acts xxi. 25, where James, it is
said, is represented, at the time of Paul's last visit to Jerusalem, as calling attention to the Decree as though it were
something new. Acts xxi. 25 is thus thought to preserve a bit
of primitive tradition which is in contradiction to the representation of the fifteenth chapter. Of course, however, the
verse as it stands in the completed book can only be taken by
the unsophisticated reader as referring to what Paul already
knew; and it is a grave question whether the author of Acts
was unskillful enough to allow contradictory representations
to stand unassimilated in his book, as the hypothesis demands.
Acts xxi. 25, therefore, is at any rate not opposed to the view
that the Decree was actually passed with the consent of Paul,
as the fifteenth chapter represents.

But is this representation really in contradiction to the
Epistle to the Galatians? Does Gal. ii. 1-10 really exclude
the Apostolic Decree? In order to answer these questions, it
will be necessary to examine the nature of the Decree.

[1] B. W. Bacon, "Acts versus Galatians: the Crux of Apostolic History,"
in *American Journal of Theology*, xi, 1907, pp. 454-474. See also "Professor Harnack on the Lukan Narrative," *ibid.*, xiii, 1909, pp. 59-76.

The Apostolic Decree, according to Acts xv. 1-29, did not constitute a definition of what was necessary for the salvation of the Gentile Christians, but was an attempt to solve the problem of a limited group of mixed communities where Jews and Gentiles were living together. Such seems to be the implication of the difficult verse, Acts xv. 21, where James, after he has proposed the substance of the Decree, says, "For Moses has from ancient generations in the several cities those who proclaim him, being read in the synagogues every Sabbath." These words seem to mean that since there are Jews in the cities, and since they are devoted to the Law of Moses, the Gentile Christians, in order to avoid offending them, ought to refrain from certain of those features of the Gentile manner of life which the Jews would regard as most repulsive. The Law of Moses had been read in the cities from ancient generations; it was venerable; it deserved at least respect. Such a respectful attitude toward the Jewish way of life would contribute not only to the peace of the Church but also to the winning of the non-Christian Jews.

Was this procedure contrary to the principles of Paul? He himself tells us that it was not. "For though I was free from all men," he says, "I brought myself under bondage to all, that I might gain the more. And to the Jews I became as a Jew, that I might gain Jews; to them that are under the law, as under the law, not being myself under the law, that I might gain them that are under the law; to them that are without law, as without law, not being without law to God, but under law to Christ, that I might gain them that are without law. To the weak I became weak, that I might gain the weak; I am become all things to all men, that I may by all means save some." [1] The Apostolic Decree was simply a particular case of becoming to the Jews as a Jew that Jews might be gained. Indeed it was a rather mild case of that kind; and the conjecture may be ventured that Paul was often very much more accommodating than the Decree would demand. Paul was not the man to insist upon blatant disregard of Jewish feelings where Jews were to be won to Christ.

It must be remembered that Paul, according to his Epistles, did not demand that Jewish Christians should give up keeping the Law, but only required them not to force the keep-

[1] 1 Cor. ix. 19-22, American Revised Version.

ing of the Law upon the Gentiles. No doubt the observance of the Law on the part of Jewish Christians was to be very different in spirit from their pre-Christian legalism; they were no longer to regard the Law as a means of salvation. But after salvation had been obtained, they might well believe that it was God's will for them to continue to live as Jews; and Paul, according to his Epistles, had no objection to that belief. But how were the Jewish Christians to carry out their observance of the Law? Various requirements of the Law were held to imply that Israelites should keep separate from Gentiles. How then could the Jewish Christians live in close brotherly intercourse with the Gentile members of the Christian community without transgressing the Law of Moses? There is no reason to believe that Paul from the beginning had a hard and fast solution of this problem. Undoubtedly, the tendency of his practice led toward the complete abandonment of the ceremonial Law in the interests of Christian unity between Jews and Gentiles. He was very severe upon those Jewish Christians who, though convinced in their hearts of the necessity of giving precedence to the new principle of unity, yet separated themselves from the Gentiles through fear of men (Gal. ii. 11-21). But there is no reason to think that he condemned on principle those who truly believed that Jewish Christians should still keep the Law. With regard to these matters he was apparently content to wait for the clearer guidance of the Spirit of God, which would finally work out the unity of the Church. Meanwhile the Apostolic Decree was an attempt to solve the problem of mixed communities; and that attempt was in harmony with the principles which Paul enunciated in 1 Cor. ix. 19-22.

Moreover, the Apostolic Decree was in accord with Paul's principle of regard for the weaker brother (1 Cor. viii; Rom. xiv). In Corinth, certain brethren were offended by the eating of meat which had been offered to idols. Paul himself was able to eat such food; for he recognized that the idols were nothing. But for some of the members of the Christian community the partaking of such food would mean the deadly sin of idolatry; and out of regard for them Paul is ready to forego his freedom. The case was very similar in the mixed communities contemplated in the Apostolic Decree. The similarity, of course, appears on the surface in the first prohibition of the Decree, which concerns things offered to idols. But the two other prohibitions about food are not really very different. The use of blood was intimately associated with heathen cults, and the eating of meat with the blood still in it ("things strangled") would also, because of deep-seated religious ideas, seem to a devout Jew to involve idolatry. It is very doubtful, therefore, whether those prohibitions of the Decree which we are accustomed to designate as "ceremonial" were felt to be ceremonial by those for whose benefit the Decree was adopted. They were probably not felt to be ceremonial any more than the prohibition of things offered to idols was felt to be ceremonial by the weaker brethren at Corinth. Rather they were felt to involve the deadly sin of idolatry

Finally, the Apostolic Decree was of limited range of application; it was addressed, not to Gentile Christians generally, but only to those in Antioch, Syria, and Cilicia (Acts xv. 23). The Book of Acts, it is true, does declare, after the mention of Derbe and Lystra in connection with the beginning of the second missionary journey, that Paul and Silas "as they went on their way through the cities . . . delivered them the decrees to keep which had been ordained of the apostles and elders that were at Jerusalem" (Acts xvi. 4). According to this passage the observance of the Decree does seem to have been extended into Lycaonia, and thus beyond the limits set forth in the Decree itself. But if Paul chose to make use of the document beyond the range originally contemplated, that does not alter the fact that originally the Jerusalem Church undertook to deal only with Antioch and Syria and Cilicia. In Acts xxi. 25, indeed, the reference of James to the Decree does not mention the geographical limitation. But James was thinking no doubt particularly of those regions where there were the largest bodies of Jews, and he does not say that the Jerusalem Church, even if the Decree represented its own desires for all Gentiles, had actually sent the Decree to all. The general reference in Acts xxi. 25 may therefore fairly be interpreted in the light of the more particular information given in Acts xv. 23. It is thus unnecessary to follow Wendt, who, after a careful examination of all the objections which have been urged against the historicity of the Decree, concludes that the Decree was actually passed by the Jerusalem Church in the presence of Paul as the Book of Acts represents, but supposes that the author of Acts has erred in giving the decision a wider range of application than was really contemplated.[1] A correct interpretation of the passages in question will remove even this last vestige of objection to the Lucan account.

But if the Decree was addressed only to Antioch and Syria and Cilicia, it was not imposed upon specifically Pauline churches. The Gentile work at Antioch had not been started by Paul, and it is a question how far he regarded the churches of Syria and Cilicia in general as belonging to his peculiar province. Undoubtedly he had labored long in those regions, but others had shared his labors and in some places had even preceded him. These other missionaries had come from Jerusalem. Paul may well therefore have recognized the authority of the Jerusalem leaders over the churches of Syria and Cilicia in a way which would not have been in place at Ephesus or Corinth, especially since the Jewish Christian element in the Syrian and Cilician churches was probably very strong.

The adoption of the Apostolic Decree by the Jerusalem Church was thus not derogatory in general to the apostolic dignity of Paul, or contrary to his principles. But is the Decree excluded, in particular, by the words of Paul in Galatians? Paul says that the pillars of the Jerusalem Church "added nothing" [2] to him (Gal. ii. 6). The meaning of these words must be examined with some care.

Undoubtedly the word here translated "added"—it may perhaps be better translated "imparted nothing to me in addition"—is to be understood in conjunction with Gal. ii. 2, where the same Greek word is used, but without the preposition which means "in addition." The sense of the two verses— they are separated by the important digression about Titus— is thus as follows: "When I laid my gospel before the leaders, they laid nothing before me in addition." That is, they declared, after listening to Paul's gospel, that they had nothing to add to it; Christ had given it to Paul directly; it was sufficient and complete. The question, therefore, in connection with the Apostolic Decree is not whether the Decree was or was not something important' that the Jerusalem leaders im-

---

[1] Wendt, *Die Apostelgeschichte*, 1913, in Meyer, *Kritisch-exegetischer Kommentar über das Neue Testament*, 9te Aufl., p. 237.

[2] οὐδὲν προσανέθεντο.

parted to Paul, but only whether it constituted an addition to his gospel. If it constituted an addition to his gospel, then it is excluded by Paul's words in Galatians, and is unhistorical. But as it has been interpreted above, it certainly did not constitute an addition to Paul's gospel. Paul's gospel consisted in the offer of salvation to the Gentiles through faith alone apart from the works of the law. The Jerusalem leaders recognized that gospel; they had absolutely nothing to add to it; Paul had revealed the way of salvation to the Gentiles exactly as it had been revealed to him by God. But the recognition of the Pauline gospel of salvation by faith alone did not solve all the practical problems of the Christian life; in particular it did not solve the problem of the mixed churches. It would have been unnatural if the conference had not proceeded to a consideration of such problems, and Paul's words do not at all exclude such consideration.

Certainly some sort of public pronouncement on the part of the Jerusalem leaders was imperatively demanded. The Judaizers had made trouble in Antioch, Syria, and Cilicia— that much of the account in Acts is generally admitted to be historical and is certainly necessary to account for the very fact that Paul went to Jerusalem, the revelation which came to him being given by God in relation to a very definite situation. Against his inclination Paul went to Jerusalem in order to stop the propaganda of the Judaizers by obtaining a pronouncement from the very authorities to which they appealed. Is it to be supposed that he returned to Antioch without the pronouncement which he had sought? If he had done so his journey would have been in vain; the Judaizers would have continued to make trouble exactly as before. Some kind of public pronouncement was therefore evidently sought by Paul himself from the Jerusalem leaders. No doubt the very seeking of such a pronouncement was open to misunderstanding; it might seem to involve subordination of Paul to the authorities to whom apparently he was appealing as to a higher instance. Paul was keenly aware of such dangers, and waited for definite guidance of God before he decided to make the journey. But if he had come back from Jerusalem without any such pronouncement of the authorities as would demonstrate the falsity of the Judaizers' appeal to them, then the disadvantages of the conference would have been incurred in vain. In all probability, therefore, the conference of Gal. ii. 1-10, if it took place at the time reached by the narrative at the beginning of the fifteenth chapter of Acts, resulted in a pronouncement from the Jerusalem Church. And the Apostolic Decree was just such a pronouncement as might have been expected. It was public; it was an emphatic vindication of Gentile freedom and an express rebuke of the Judaizers; and it dealt with some at least of the practical difficulties which would result from the presence of Jews and Gentiles in the churches of Syria and Cilicia.

The identification of Gal. ii. 1-10 with Acts xv. 1-29, therefore, does not raise insuperable difficulties against the acceptance as historical of the narrative in Acts. But it must be remembered that the alternative identification—with Acts xi. 30; xii. 25—is also possible. The comparison between Acts and Galatians, therefore, has certainly not resulted disastrously for the Book of Acts; there are three ways in which Acts can be shown to be in harmony with Paul. These three possibilities may now conveniently be summed up in the light of the examination of them in the preceding pages.

(1) Galatians ii. 1-10 may be regarded as an account of the famine visit of Acts xi. 30; xii. 25; and on the basis of this identification the Epistle may be dated before the Apostolic Council of Acts xv. 1-29. The course of events would then be somewhat as follows: First there was a private conference between Paul and the original apostles (Gal. ii. 1-10) at the time of the famine visit (Acts xi. 30; xii. 25). Then followed the first missionary journey of Paul and Barnabas to Southern Galatia (Acts xiii, xiv). That journey brought a great influx of Gentiles into the Church and aroused the active opposition of the Judaizers. The trouble seems to have been accentuated by the coming to Antioch of certain men from James (Gal. ii. 11-13). It is not clear whether they themselves were to blame, or whether, if they were, they had any commission from James. At any rate, Peter was induced to give up the table companionship with Gentile Christians which formerly he had practiced at Antioch, and Barnabas also was carried away. Paul rebuked Peter publicly. But the Judaizers continued to disturb the peace of the Church, and even demanded, as a thing absolutely necessary to salvation, that the Gentile Christians should be circumcised and should

keep the Law of Moses. The Judaizing activity extended **also** into Galatia, and Paul wrote the Epistle to the Galatians in the midst of the conflict. At Antioch it was finally determined to bring the matter to the attention of the Jerusalem leaders in order to show that the Judaizers had no right to appeal to those leaders, and in order to silence the Judaizers by a public pronouncement of the Jerusalem Church. A revelation induced Paul to agree to this plan. The result was the Apostolic Council of Acts xv. 1-29.

Undoubtedly this account of the matter overcomes certain difficulties. It has won considerable support, and can no longer be regarded as a mere apologetic expedient.

(2) The Western text of the Apostolic Decree may be regarded as correct. The Decree may then be taken as forbidding only the three deadly sins of idolatry, murder, and fornication, so that it cannot by any possibility be taken as a limitation of Gentile freedom or an addition to Paul's gospel of justification by faith alone. This solution has been adopted by Von Harnack and others; and by Kirsopp Lake,[1] certainly without any "apologetic" motive, it has actually been combined with (1).

(3) Finally, Gal. ii. 1-10 being identified with Acts xv. 1-29, and the Neutral text of the Apostolic Decree being adopted, harmony between Acts and Galatians may be established by that interpretation of both passages which has been proposed above. According to this interpretation, the Decree was not regarded as necessary to salvation or intended as an addition to Paul's gospel, but was an attempt to solve the special and temporary problem of the mixed communities in Syria and Cilicia.

This last solution being adopted provisionally (though (1) certainly has much in its favor), the outcome of the Apostolic Council must be considered in connection with the events that followed. Apparently Paul in Galatians is telling only what happened in a private conference between himself and the Jerusalem leaders, the account of the public action of the Church being found in Acts. James and Peter and John recognized the independence of Paul's apostleship; Paul had been intrusted with the apostleship to the Gentiles as Peter

---

[1] In *The Earlier Epistles of St. Paul*, 1911. It will be remembered that Lake has now radically modified his views. See above, p. 81, footnote 3.

with that to the circumcision. After listening to Paul's account of the wonderful works of God by which his ministry had been blessed, and after coming into direct contact with the grace which had been given to him, the pillars of the Jerusalem Church gave to him and Barnabas the right hand of fellowship that they should go to the Gentiles while the Jerusalem leaders should go to the circumcision. This division of labor has often been egregiously misinterpreted, especially by the Tübingen school and all those in subsequent years who have not been able to throw off the shackles of Tübingenism. The question has often been asked whether the division was meant geographically or ethnographically. Was Paul to preach everywhere outside of Palestine both to Jews and Gentiles, while the original apostles were to labor in Palestine only; or was Paul to preach to Gentiles wherever found, while the original apostles were to labor for Jews wherever found? In other words, to whose province were assigned the Jews of the Dispersion—to the province of Paul and Barnabas, or to the province of the original apostles? It has sometimes been maintained that Paul understood the division geographically, but that the Jerusalem leaders understood it ethnographically; so that Peter transgressed Paul's geographical interpretation when he went to labor in Antioch. But the very raising of the whole question is in itself a fundamental error. The division was not meant in an exclusive or negative sense at all; it was not intended to prevent Peter from laboring among Gentiles or Paul from laboring among Jews. The same gospel was being preached by both Paul and Peter; they gave each other the right hand of fellowship. What was meant was simply a general recognition of the dispensation of God which had so far prevailed. By that dispensation Paul and Barnabas had been sent particularly to the Gentiles and the Jerusalem apostles to the Jews. If either group was hindered in its work, the interests of the Church would suffer. Both groups, therefore, were absolutely necessary in order that both Jews and Gentiles should be won.

In one particular, indeed, the Jerusalem leaders requested expressly that the division of labor should not be taken too strictly; they hoped that Paul would not be so much engrossed in his Gentile work as to forget the poor of the Jerusalem Church (Gal. ii. 10). It should be observed very carefully that this request about the poor forms an exception, not at all to the full recognition of Paul's gospel, but only to the division of labor as between Jews and Gentiles. It does not go with the remote words of verse 6 ("for to me those who were of repute added nothing"), but with the immediately adjacent words in verse 9. Paul does not say, therefore, "To me those of repute added (or imposed) nothing except that I should remember the Jerusalem poor." If he had said that, then perhaps it would be difficult to explain the omission of the Apostolic Decree; for the Decree as much as the request for aid of the Jerusalem poor was something that the Jerusalem leaders laid upon him. But the fact is that neither the Decree nor the request about the poor has anything whatever to do with Paul's gospel or the attitude of the Jerusalem leaders toward it. What is really meant by the request for aid is simply this: "You are the apostle to the Gentiles; it is a great work; we wish you Godspeed in it. But even in so great a work as that, do not forget your needy Jewish brethren in Jerusalem."

After the conference at Jerusalem Paul and Barnabas returned to Antioch. According to the Book of Acts the letter of the Jerusalem Church was joyfully received; it meant a confirmation of Gentile freedom and relief from the attacks of the Judaizers. But new disturbances began, and Peter was concerned in them. He had gone to Antioch. There is not the slightest reason to think that his arrival occasioned anything but joy. The notion that Paul was jealously guarding his rights in a Gentile church and resented the coming of Peter as an intrusion has not the slightest basis either in Acts or in the Pauline Epistles. But at Antioch Jews and Gentiles were living together in the Church, and their juxtaposition presented a serious problem. The Gentile Christians, it will be remembered, had been released from the obligation of being circumcised and of undertaking to keep the Mosaic Law. The Jewish Christians, on the other hand, had not been required to give up their ancestral mode of life. But how could the Jewish Christians continue to live under the Law if they held companionship with Gentiles in a way which would render the strict observance of the Law impossible? Should the precedence be given to the observance of the Law on the part of the Jewish Christians or to the new principle of Christian unity? This question had not been settled by the Apostolic Council, for even if the Gentile Christians observed the provisions of the Apostolic Decree, table companionship with them would still have seemed to involve a transgression of the Law. Peter, however, took a step beyond what had already been settled; he relaxed the strictness of his Jewish manner of life by eating with the Gentiles. He was convinced of the revolutionary change wrought by the coming of Christ, and gave practical expression to his conviction by holding full companionship with all his brethren. After a time, however, and perhaps during an absence of Paul from the city, certain men came from James, and their coming occasioned difficulty. It is not said that these men were commissioned by James, and some readers have thought that "from James" means merely "from Jerusalem," James being named merely as representative of the church over which he presided. But even if the newcomers stood in some closer relationship to James, or even had been sent by him, it is an unwarranted assumption that James was responsible for the trouble that they caused, or had sent them to Antioch with the purpose of limiting the freedom of Peter's conduct. They may have abused whatever commission they had received. Moreover, it must be remembered that they are not expressly blamed by Paul. If they clung conscientiously to the keeping of the Law, as they had been accustomed to do at Jerusalem, Paul would perhaps not necessarily condemn them; for he did not on principle or in all circumstances require Jewish Christians to give up the keeping of the Law. But Peter had really transcended that point of view; and when, therefore, he now, from fear of these newcomers, withdrew from the Gentiles, he was concealing his true convictions. It was the inconsistency of his conduct that Paul felt called upon to rebuke. That inconsistency could not fail to have a bad effect upon the Gentile Christians. Peter had received them into true fellowship. But now apparently he regarded such liberal conduct as a thing to be ashamed of and to be concealed. The Gentile Christians could not help drawing the conclusion that they were at best only on the outskirts of the Christian community; the chief of the original apostles of Jesus was apparently ashamed of his association with them. Despite the liberty granted by the Apostolic Council, therefore, the Gentile Christians were again tempted to remove the disabilities which rested upon them, by accepting circumcision and so becoming full members of the Church. Evidently the keeping of the Law on the part of Jewish Christians was a half-way position. But when it was pursued conscientiously, as a duty still resting upon men of Jewish descent, it might possibly be dealt with gently by Paul. When, however, it was undertaken for fear of men, in the face of better understanding, it became "hypocrisy" and was rebuked sharply. If the transcending of the Law, in the interests of Christian unity, had once been grasped as a necessary consequence of the redemption wrought by Christ, then to repudiate it was to bring discredit upon Christ Himself, and make His death of none avail.

The influence of Peter's withdrawal from the Gentile Christians soon began to make itself felt; other Jewish Christians followed Peter's example, and even Barnabas was carried away. A serious crisis had arisen. But God had not deserted His Church. The Church was saved through the instrumentality of Paul.

To Paul had been revealed the full implications of the gospel; to him the freedom of the Gentiles was a matter of principle, and when principle was at stake he never kept silent. Regardless of all petty calculations about the influence that might be lost or the friendships that might be sacrificed, he spoke out boldly for Christ; he rebuked Peter openly before the assembled Church. It should always be observed, however, that it was not the principles of Peter, but his conduct, which Paul was rebuking. The incident is therefore misused when it is made to establish a fundamental disagreement between Paul and Peter. On the contrary, in the very act of condemning the practice of Peter, Paul approves his principles; he is rebuking Peter just for the concealment of his correct principles for fear of men. He and Peter, he says, were perfectly agreed about the inadequacy of the Law, and the all-sufficiency of faith in Christ; why then should Peter act in contradiction to these great convictions? The passage, Gal. ii. 11-21, therefore, far from establishing a fundamental disagreement between Peter and Paul really furnishes the strongest possible evidence for their fundamental unity.

But how did Peter take the rebuke which was administered to him? There should be no real doubt about the answer to

this question. Details, indeed, are uncertain; it may perhaps
be doubtful when Peter acquiesced or how he expressed his
acquiescence. But that he acquiesced at some time and in some
manner is indicated by the whole subsequent history of the
Church. A contrary conclusion has, indeed, sometimes been
drawn from the silence of Paul. If Peter was convinced by
Paul at Antioch, would not Paul have been sure to mention
so gratifying a result? Would he not have appealed, against
the contentions of the Judaizers in Galatia, to so signal a
recognition of his apostolic authority? This argument ignores
the true character of the passage. During the writing of Gal.
ii. 11-21 Paul has altogether ceased to think of Peter. What
he had said to Peter at Antioch happened to be exactly the same
thing that he desired to say, at the time of the writing of the
letter, to the Galatians. In reporting, not with pedantic verbal
accuracy but in substance, what he had said to Peter at Antioch, he has entered upon the very heart of his gospel, which
had been despised by the Judaizers in Galatia. Long before the
end of the glorious passage, Gal. ii. 11-21, he has forgotten
all about Peter and Barnabas and Antioch, and is thinking
only about the grace of Christ and the way in which it was
being made of none effect by those who would desert it for a
religion of works. To expect him to descend from the heights
in order to narrate the outcome of the incident at Antioch
is to do woeful injustice to the character of the apostle's
mind and the manner of his literary activity. Gal. ii. 11-21
forms a transition between the first main division of the Epistle,
in which Paul is answering the personal attack of the Judaizers, and the second main division, in which he is defending
the contents of his gospel. Before the end of the passage
Paul has plunged into the principal thing that he wanted to
say to the Galatians, who were making void the cross of
Christ. The presentation in Gal. ii. 11-21 of what Bengel [1]
called the "marrow of Christianity" leads inevitably, therefore, not to a pedantic narration of what Peter did, but to the
exclamation of Gal. iii. 1, "O foolish Galatians, who did be-
witch you, before whose eyes Jesus Christ was openly set forth
crucified?"

Thus the silence of Paul about the outcome of the incident
at Antioch does not at all establish the outcome as unfavor-

[1] On Gal. ii. 19.

able. But there are positive indications on the other side. Of course, if Gal. ii. 1-10 were identified with the famine visit, the whole question would be settled. In that case, the incident of Gal. ii. 11-21 would have been followed by the Apostolic Council, at which the harmony of Peter and Paul found full expression. But even if the identification of Gal. ii. 1-10 with the Apostolic Council be adopted, there are still plain indications that the outcome of the Antioch incident was favorable.

In the first place, Paul mentions Peter in 1 Cor. ix. 5 with respect, as an apostle to whose example appeal may be made; in 1 Cor. iii. 22 he classes Peter with himself and with Apollos as a possession of all Christians; [1] and in 1 Cor. xv. 1-11 he includes as part of his fundamental missionary preaching the appearance of the risen Christ to Peter, and appeals to the unity which existed between his own preaching and that of the other apostles (verses 5, 11).[2]

In the second place, Paul concerned himself earnestly, according to 1 and 2 Corinthians and Romans, with the collection for the Jerusalem poor. If the incident at Antioch had meant a repudiation of the "right hand of fellowship" which Peter in common with James and John had given to Paul at Jerusalem (Gal. ii. 9), it is difficult to see how Paul could have continued to engage in a form of brotherly service which was the most touching expression of that fellowship. If there was a permanent breach between Peter and Paul, the contribution for the poor saints at Jerusalem could hardly have been collected.

In the third place, the agitation of the Judaizers seems to have died down during the third missionary journey. It appears, indeed, at Corinth, according to the Corinthian Epistles, but seems there to have lacked that insistence upon the keeping of the Law which had made it so dangerous in Galatia. In the epistles of the captivity—Colossians and Philemon, Ephesians, Philippians—it appears, if at all, only in the obscure reference in Phil. iii. 2ff., which may relate to non-Christian Judaism rather than to Jewish Christianity. This subsidence of the Judaizing activity is difficult to understand if the benefits of the Jerusalem conference had been annulled by a serious breach at Antioch.

Finally, the whole subsequent history of the Church is

---

[1] Knowling, *The Witness of the Epistles,* 1892, p. 14, note 1.
[2] Knowling, *loc. cit.*

explicable only if there was fundamental unity between Peter and Paul. Ever since the formation of the Old Catholic Church at the close of the second century the Church was founded upon the twin pillars of Peter and Paul. How was this unity produced if in the apostolic age there was fundamental disunion? The existence of this problem was fully recognized by F. C. Baur, and the recognition of it constitutes one element of greatness in Baur's work. But the elaborate solution which Baur proposed has had to be abandoned. Baur supposed that the harmony between Pauline and Petrine Christianity was produced by a gradual compromise effected during the second century. Subsequent investigation has pushed the harmony very much further back. The unity between Peter and Paul appears, for example, plainly expressed in the letter of Clement of Rome (about 95 A. D.), who appeals to the two great apostles as though both were of recognized authority; it appears also in the first Epistle of Peter, which even if not genuine is important as attributing to Peter, as though the attribution were a matter of course, a conception of the gospel thoroughly in harmony with that of Paul; it appears in the early traditional account of John Mark, by which Mark is made to be a follower of Peter (compare 1 Peter v. 13) and to have received from Peter the substance of his Gospel, so that when his cordial relations with Paul are remembered (Col. iv. 10; Philem. 24) he constitutes an important link between Peter and Paul. What is more important, however, than all details, is the undoubted fact that before the end of the first century epistles of Paul and genuine tradition about Jesus, which latter must at first have been connected with the Jerusalem Church, appear side by side as possessing high authority in the Church. Finally, the testimony of the Book of Acts is now admitted to be at any rate very much earlier than Baur supposed; and that testimony, so far as the harmony between Paul and Peter is concerned, is unequivocal. Thus the explanation which Baur proposed for the final healing of the supposed breach between Peter and Paul is unsatisfactory. But no other explanation has been discovered to take its place. The very existence of the Church would have been impossible if there had been a permanent breach between the leader in the Gentile mission and the leader among the original disciples of Jesus.

The Book of Acts does not mention the difficulty which

arose at Antioch with regard to table companionship between
Jews and Gentiles. But it does mention another disagreement
between Paul and Barnabas. Barnabas desired to take John
Mark along on the second missionary journey, while Paul was
unwilling to take with him again the one who had turned bac'k
on the former journey and had not gone to those South
Galatian churches which it was now proposed to revisit. It
was maintained by the Tübingen school of criticism that the
lesser quarrel has here been inserted by the author of Acts
with the express purpose of covering up the more serious disagreement which was the real reason for the separation of
Barnabas and Paul. But the insertion of a quarrel is rather
an unnatural way to cover up the fact that there was another
quarrel; it would have been better to keep altogether silent
about the disagreement. Moreover, the good faith of the
author is now generally accepted. There is another possible
way of explaining the omission of the incident of Gal. ii. 11-21
from the Book of Acts. It may be surmised that the incident
was so unimportant in its consequences, Peter and Barnabas
were so quickly convinced by Paul, that a historian who was
concerned, not with personal details about the relations between
Paul and the other leaders, but with the external progress
of the gospel, did not find it necessary to mention the incident
at all.

After the separation of Barnabas from Paul at the beginning of the second missionary journey, it is not recorded that
the two men were ever associated again in missionary work.
But in 1 Cor. ix. 6 Barnabas is spoken of with respect—"Or
I only and Barnabas, have we not a right to forbear working."
Evidently Paul was interested in the work of Barnabas, and
was not ashamed to appeal to his example. In Col. iv. 10,
moreover, "Mark, the cousin of Barnabas" is mentioned, and
is commended to the attention of the Colossian Christians.
Mark here forms a link between Paul and Barnabas as he
does between Paul and Peter. Evidently the estrangement at
Antioch was not permanent even in the case of Mark, against
whom there was the special objection that he had withdrawn
from the work at Perga. According to 2 Tim. iv. 11, Mark
became exactly what he had not been at Perga, "useful" to
Paul "for ministering." And if the testimony of 2 Timothy
be rejected, the same cordial relationship between Paul and

Mark appears also in Col. iv. 10, 11; Philem. 24. The scanty indications all point very decidedly away from any permanent estrangement as resulting from the incidents at Antioch.

During the second and third missionary journeys, the agitation of the Judaizers, as has already been observed, seems to have subsided. In Corinth, indeed, according to 1 and 2 Corinthians, Paul appears in deadly conflict with certain men who sought to undermine his apostolic authority. Baur made much of this conflict; indeed, he based his reconstruction of apostolic history upon the Corinthian Epistles almost as much as upon Galatians. The starting-point of his investigation was found in the party watchwords mentioned in 1 Cor. i. 12, "I am of Paul; and I of Apollos; and I of Cephas; and I of Christ." The "Christ-party" of the verse, identified with the opponents attacked in 2 Cor. x-xiii, Baur believed to have been an extreme Judaizing party. This extreme Judaizing party, Baur maintained, appealed with some show of reason to the original apostles in Jerusalem. Thus the Corinthian Epistles like the Epistle to the Galatians were made to establish what was to Baur the fundamental fact of apostolic history, a serious conflict of principle between Paul and the original apostles.[1]

Subsequent investigation, however, has cast at least serious doubt upon the Tübingen exegesis, even where it has not discredited it altogether. The whole matter of the Christ-party of 1 Cor. i. 12 is felt to be exceedingly obscure, so obscure that J. Weiss, for example, in his recent commentary on 1 Corinthians, has felt constrained to cut the Gordian knot by regarding the words, "And I of Christ', as an interpolation.[2] Where this heroic measure has not been resorted to, various interpretations have been proposed. Sometimes, for example, the Christ-party has been thought to have consisted of those who rejected the other watchwords, but in such a proud and quarrelsome way that the watchword, "I am of Christ," which should have belonged to all, became only the shibboleth of another party. Sometimes, again, the Christ-party has been regarded as a gnosticizing party which boasted of direct communica-

[1] Baur, "Die Christuspartei in der korinthischen Gemeinde," in *Tübinger Zeitschrift für Theologie*, 1831, 4 Heft, pp. 61-206.
[2] J. Weiss, *Der erste Korintherbrief*, 1910, in Meyer, *op. cit.*, 9te Aufl., p. xxxviii.

tions with the risen Christ. At any rate, it is very difficult
to find in the words "I am of Christ" any clear designation of
Judaizers who appealed against Paul to James or to their
own connections with Jesus in Palestine. On the contrary,
the reader of the first four chapters of 1 Corinthians may
well be doubtful whether there were any distinct parties at all.
It looks rather as though what Paul was rebuking were merely
a spirit of division, which manifested itself now in one watchword and now in another. The Corinthian Christians seem
to have been "sermon-tasters"; they were proud of their "wisdom," and laid undue stress upon the varying form of the
gospel message to the neglect of the content. It is noteworthy
that in 1 Cor. i-iv Paul does not enter upon any anti-Judaistic
polemic, but addressed himself to those who in a spirit of
pride and quarrelsomeness sought after wisdom. "If you would
be truly wise and truly 'spiritual,'" he says, "then cease your
contentions." Paul was perhaps combating not any definite
parties, but only the party spirit.

It must be admitted that there were in the Corinthian
Church persons who emphasized against Paul the advantages
of Palestinian origin and of direct connection with Jesus.
But there is no reason to bring these opponents of Paul into
any close relation to the original apostles and to James. The
letters of recommendation (2 Cor. iii. 1) may have come elsewhere than from the apostles; indeed the mention of letters
from the Corinthians as well as to them would seem to make
the passage refer to a general habit of credential-bearing
rather than to any special credentials from Jerusalem. The
opponents desired to push themselves into other men's spheres
of labor; and in order to do so they were in the habit of arm-
ing themselves with commendatory epistles. The reference is
quite general and to us quite obscure; it is only by exceedingly
bold specialization that it can be made to attest the existence
of letters of commendation from the Jerusalem leaders. Moreover, even if the opponents did have some sort of endorsement
from Jerusalem, they may have abused the confidence which
had been reposed in them. The Tübingen exegesis of 2 Cor.
xi. 5; xii. 11, by which "the chiefest apostles" were identified
with the pillars of the Jerusalem Church should be rejected; and
the phrase (which is rather to be translated "those who are
apostles overmuch") should be taken as designating simply the

Corinthian agitators themselves. Thus, the "apostles over-much" of 2 Cor. xi. 5 become the same as the "false apostles" of verse 13, the latter verse being used in order to interpret the former. In 1 Cor. i. 12, Peter is mentioned as being appealed to by one of the "parties" in the Corinthian Church. It has sometimes been maintained, on the basis of this verse, that Peter had actually been present in Corinth as had Apollos and Paul, who appear in two of the other party watchwords. But the matter is at least very doubtful. As chief of the original disciples of Jesus Peter might well have evoked the special admiration of certain members of the Corinthian Church without having ever been personally present. There does not seem to be the slightest evidence for supposing that the admirers of Peter mentioned in 1 Cor. i. 12 were extreme Judaizers; and there is no decisive reason for identifying them with the opponents who appear in 2 Cor. x-xiii. Certainly there is no reason for making Peter responsible for the factiousness of those who used his name. It must be remembered that Paul rebukes the "Paul party"—if it be a party—as much as any of the others, and distinctly commends Apollos, who was appealed to by the "Apollos party." Evidently the faults of the "parties" were not due at all to those whose names the parties used. In 1 Cor. iii. 21, 22, Paul says, "All things are yours, whether Paul or Apollos or Cephas." Here Peter is put as part of the common possession of all Christians. There could not possibly be a clearer recognition of the complete fellowship which Paul regards as existing between himself and Peter. Finally, in 1 Cor. xv. 11, Paul calls attention expressly to the fundamental unity between himself and the other apostles: "Whether then it be I or they, so we preach, and so ye believed." [1] The Corinthian Epistles certainly lend no support to the Tübingen contention; they certainly provide no evidence of a breach between Paul and the original disciples of Jesus.

At the time of his last visit to Jerusalem, Paul came again into contact with James, the brother of the Lord, and with the Jerusalem Church. The arrival at Jerusalem is narrated in one of the we-sections of the Book of Acts, and it is there said, "The brethren received us gladly" (Acts xxi. 17). The use of the first person plural disappears after the following

[1] See Knowling, as cited above, p. 104, footnotes 1 and 2.

verse, where the meeting of Paul with James is described, but it is very difficult to separate Acts xxi. 20, for example, from the we-section. Of course there could be no use of the "we" when the narrator did not participate in what was being described. In Acts xxi. 20, it is said that James and the presbyters "glorified God" on account of what had been done among the Gentiles through the ministry of Paul. Whatever view may be taken of the composition of Acts, therefore, the warm reception of Paul on the part of the Jerusalem leaders seems to be attested by an eyewitness. Such a reception would be very difficult to explain if the relations between Paul and Jerusalem had been what they are represented as being by the Tübingen scholars.

According to Acts xxi. 20-26, James brought to Paul's attention the scruples of the Jewish Christians, who were "zealous for the law." These Jewish Christians had been told that Paul was teaching the Jews of the Dispersion not to circumcise their children or to walk "in the customs." With regard to the Gentile Christians, James has nothing to say except to call attention to the Apostolic Decree which the Jerusalem Church itself had adopted. But in order to allay the suspicions of the Jewish Christians, James suggests that Paul should participate in a Jewish vow. According to Acts xxi. 26, Paul complied with the request.

Such compliance was regarded by the Tübingen scholars as absolutely incompatible with Paul's character, and therefore as unhistorical. But recent criticism has been becoming, to say the least, less certain about the matter. The incident is narrated in a concrete way which creates a most favorable impression; indeed, the passage seems even to belong to the supposed we-section source. Moreover, a sober study of the Pauline Epistles has shown that the attitude of Paul toward Judaism and toward the Law was by no means what Baur and Zeller, through a one-sided interpretation of the polemic of Galatians, had supposed. In particular, the sharing of Paul in a Jewish vow is only an exemplification of the principle which Paul lays down in 1 Cor. ix. 19-22 of becoming all things to all men. Where could the principle possibly have applied if it did not apply to the situation in Jerusalem at the time of Paul's last visit? Where, if not there, could

Paul have felt bound to become to the Jews as a Jew in order
that he might gain Jews (1 Cor. ix. 20)? There seems to
have been no attempt at that time to force the Law upon
Gentiles, and no tendency to regard it even for Jews as
necessary to salvation. Compliance with Jewish custom would
therefore not be open to the misunderstanding which might
have made it inadvisable during the midst of the Judaistic
controversy. The devotion of the Jewish Christians to the
Law seems never to have been condemned by Paul on principle.
Should he then run counter to Jewish feeling by pursuing a
crassly Gentile manner of life in the very midst of Judaism,
when the national life, in the troublous years before the Jewish war, was running high? The answer to this question is
at any rate not so simple as was formerly supposed. Participation by Paul in a Jewish vow in Jerusalem is not beyond
the limits of that devotion to the Jewish people which the
Epistles undoubtedly attest. And it is not really derogatory
to the character of Paul. Where the truth of the gospel
was concerned, Paul was absolutely unswerving and absolutely without regard for personal considerations; but when
the "weaker brethren" of his own nation could be won without
sacrifice of principle, he was fully capable of becoming to the
Jews as a Jew.

While Paul was in prison in Jerusalem and in Cæsarea,
what was the attitude of James and of the Jerusalem Church?
The Book of Acts does not say, and far-reaching conclusions
have sometimes been drawn from its silence. The Jerusalem
leaders, it is said, were at least lukewarm in their defense of
Paul; they themselves were zealous for the Law, and they
had only been half-convinced of the loyalty of Paul; it is no
wonder, then, that they were not anxious to bring Jewish
disfavor upon themselves by championing the cause of Paul.

This representation can find no support whatever in the
sources. Certainly it is not supported by the silence of Acts.
The disciples of Jesus were certainly not in positions of political
influence at Jerusalem; indeed only a few years later even
James, despite his strict Jewish manner of life, fell victim to
the fury of his enemies. If at such a time and under such
circumstances the Jerusalem disciples accomplished nothing
for Paul, the fact does not attest any coldness in their sym-

pathy, or any repentance for the joy with which, on the unequivocal testimony of a we-section, they had greeted him on
his arrival.

The Book of Acts does not mention the collection which
according to 1 and 2 Corinthians and Romans Paul carried
up to Jerusalem for the poor of the Jerusalem Church, except
perhaps in the bare allusion in Acts xxiv. 17. But no great
significance is to be attached to the omission. It must be
remembered that the Book of Acts is not concerned primarily
with the inner development of the churches, but rather with
the external progress of the gospel out from Jerusalem to the
Gentile world. How meager, for example, as compared with
the Corinthian Epistles, is the account which Acts gives of
affairs at Corinth! To infer, therefore, from the silence of
Acts about the collection that the collection was not graciously
received is to make use of the argument from silence in a most
adventurous and unwarranted manner. The inference is definitely opposed, moreover, by the testimony of a we-section in
Acts xxi. 17, where Paul is said to have been warmly received
on his arrival in Jerusalem. That verse refers perhaps to
the reception of Paul merely in a little group at the house of
Mnason. But the warmth of his reception there was at least
of good presage for the reception which took place the next
day in the assembly of the elders. Rom. xv. 31 is sometimes
thought to indicate anxious solicitude on the part of Paul
lest the collection should not be acceptable to the Jerusalem
Church. But the words will not bear the weight which is
hung upon them. When Paul asks his readers to pray that
he may be rescued from them that are disobedient in Judæa
(that is, the non-Christian Jews), and that the offering
which he is carrying to Jerusalem may be acceptable to the
saints, he certainly does not indicate any fear lest the offering
may not be acceptable. The offering had been much on his
heart; it was being carried to Jerusalem at the imminent risk
of life; these perils were being encountered out of love
for the Jerusalem brethren. Surely it is natural for the bearer
of such an offering to wish that it may be acceptable. That
wish is natural in the case of any gift, no matter how certain
the giver may be that the recipient will be grateful. It was
still more natural in the case of the Pauline collection. Moreover, even if Paul was solicitous about the reception of the

gift, his solicitude may well have concerned merely those members of the Jerusalem Church mentioned in Acts xxi. 20-22, who were suspicious of Gentile Christianity. There is no reason, therefore, for connecting the solicitude of Paul with the original apostles or with James.

It will not be necessary for the present purpose to attempt any review of the missionary journeys of Paul. The outline of Paul's life is here being considered merely for its bearing upon the relations which Paul sustained (1) to the original disciples of Jesus, (2) to Judaism, and (3) to paganism. The first of these relationships has been chiefly in view. Enough has, however, perhaps been said to establish the following propositions:

(1)   The relation between Paul and the original disciples of Jesus was cordial; there is no reason to interpret the "right hand of fellowship" which the leaders of the Jerusalem Church gave to Paul in any other than its full meaning, and no reason to suppose that the good relationship was broken off at any later time.

(2)   The early training of Paul was thoroughly Jewish, and was fundamentally Palestinian, not Hellenistic; and Paul never relinquished his attachment to his own people.

(3)   Paul's attitude toward paganism, after the conversion as well as before it, was an attitude of abhorrence. If common ground was ever sought with his pagan hearers, it was only as a starting-point for the denunciation of idolatry and the proclamation of a revealed gospel.

CHAPTER IV
PAUL AND JESUS

CHAPTER IV

PAUL AND JESUS [1]

THE review of Paul's life has prepared the way for the principal subject of investigation. What was the origin of the religion of Paul?

The most obvious answer to that question is that the religion of Paul was based upon Jesus. That is the answer which has always been given in the Church. The Church has always accepted the apostle Paul, not at all as a religious philosopher, but simply and solely as a witness to Jesus. If he was not a true disciple of Jesus, then the authority which he has always possessed and the influence which he has wielded have been based upon a misconception.

But exactly the same answer was given by Paul himself. Paul regarded himself as a servant of Christ, and based his whole life upon what Christ had done and what Christ was continuing to do. "It is no longer I that live," he says, "but Christ liveth in me." Unquestionably this Christ, upon whom Paul based his life, was identified by Paul with Jesus of Nazareth, a person who had lived in Palestine a few years before. A mighty change in the mode of existence of Jesus had indeed, Paul believed, been wrought by the resurrection; a life of humiliation had given place to a life of glory. But it was the same person who lived throughout. There is in the Pauline Epistles not a trace of any distinction between "Jesus" and "Christ," as though the former were the name of the historic personage who lived in Galilee and the latter the name of the risen Lord. On the contrary, the name Jesus is applied freely to the risen Lord, and the name Lord—the loftiest of all titles—is applied to the Jesus who suffered and died. It was "the Lord of glory," according to Paul, who was crucified

[1] In the present chapter there are some coincidences of thought and expression with the paper by the same author entitled "Jesus and Paul" in *Biblical and Theological Studies* by the Members of the Faculty of Princeton Theological Seminary, 1912,   547-578.

(1 Cor. ii. 8). The same phenomenon appears everywhere in the Epistles: the Lord of glory lived the life of a servant on earth; and Jesus, the man who had recently lived in Palestine, was to be worshiped by all in heaven and on earth (Phil. ii. 10, 11).

There is, therefore, in the Pauline Epistles not the slightest trace of any gnosticizing separation between Jesus the historic person, and Christ the divine Lord. There is, moreover, as W. Morgan rightly observes,[1] not the slightest trace of any "adoptionist Christology," by which a man Jesus could be conceived of either as growing up gradually into divinity or as received into divinity by a catastrophic event like the resurrection. On the contrary, Paul says expressly that the Jesus who lived in Palestine existed, before His appearance upon earth, in the form of God; and the entrance of that person upon human life is represented as a voluntary act of love. His higher nature, therefore, existed from the beginning; indeed He was, according to Paul, the instrument in the creation of the world.

Finally, there is no trace in Paul of any doctrine of "kenosis," by which the higher nature of Christ might have been regarded as so relinquished while He was on earth that the words and deeds of the historic person would become matter of indifference. Such a representation is refuted not only by what has just been said about the application of the term "Lord" to the historic Jesus, but also by the references of Paul to actual words and deeds of Jesus. These references are few; their scantiness may require explanation. But they are sufficient to show that Paul regarded the words of the historic Jesus as possessing absolute authority and His example as normative for the Christian life.

Thus the testimony of Paul is plain. He regarded Christ as Lord and Master, and he identified that Christ fully with the Jesus who had lived but a few years before. This testimony must be faced and invalidated by those who would find the origin of Paul's religion elsewhere than in Jesus of Nazareth.

Such is the testimony of Paul. But what was the testimony of his contemporaries? In the environment of Paul were to be found some men who had been intimate friends of

[1] W. Morgan, *The Religion and Theology of Paul*, 1917.

Jesus; presumably they were acquainted with Jesus' character and teaching. What was their attitude toward Paul? Did they regard him as an innovator with respect to Jesus, or did they admit him to the company of Jesus' true disciples? Since they knew both Jesus and Paul, their testimony as to the relationship between the two is obviously worth having. At this point appears the importance of Baur's work. It is the merit of Baur that however faulty his solution he placed at least in the forefront of interest the problem of the relationship between Paul and the intimate friends of Jesus. That relationship, Baur believed, was fundamentally a relationship of conflict; Paul and Peter, according to Baur, established at best only a *modus vivendi*, an agreement to disagree; really they were separated by a deep-seated difference of principle. But at this point a further problem arises. If Paul and Peter were really in disharmony, how did they ever come to be regarded as in harmony? If there was a deep-seated difference of principle between Paul and Peter, how did it come about that the Catholic Church was founded not upon Paul taken alone, or upon Peter taken alone, but upon Paul and Peter taken together?

Here, again, Baur displayed his true intellectual greatness by detecting and facing the problem. He saw clearly what has seldom been seen with equal clearness since his day, that the historian must explain the transition not only from the historical Jesus to apostolic Christianity, but from apostolic Christianity to the Old Catholic Church. And for this latter problem he proposed a solution which was not wanting in grandeur. But his solution, despite its grandeur, has succumbed. Baur's reconstruction of the second century, with the supposed gradual compromise between Pauline and Petrine Christianity, resulting finally in the Christianity of the Old Catholic Church, was one of the first elements in his system which had to be abandoned; it was destroyed, in the first place, by the criticism of A. Ritschl, and, in the second place, by the painstaking labors of Lightfoot, Zahn, Von Harnack and others, by which, through a study of second-century documents and their literary relationships, it was shown that the New Testament books cannot be scattered at will anywhere throughout the second century in the interests of a theory of development. Ritschl showed that the importance

of specifically Jewish Christianity had been enormously exaggerated by Baur; and the study of patristics tended to place
the New Testament books much earlier than the late dating
which the theory of Baur required.

Thus Baur did not succeed in overcoming the fundamental
objection raised against him by the very existence of a Church
that appealed both to Peter and to Paul. If Peter and Paul
were really in fundamental disharmony, how did the Church
come to bring them together so confidently and at such an
early time? This question has never been answered. The
very existence of the Church is a refutation of Baur; the
Church never could have existed unless the apostles had been
in fundamental agreement.

But Baur may also be refuted directly, in a purely exegetical way, by an examination of the sources to which he
himself appealed. Baur established his hypothesis of a conflict between Paul and Peter on the basis of the Pauline
Epistles. Subsidiary evidence, thought to be found in other
books of the New Testament, was soon shown to be illusory.
Thus Baur and the early Tübingen scholars detected an anti-
Pauline polemic in the Book of Revelation, which they attributed to John the son of Zebedee. This use of the Apocalpse
was soon abandoned even by Baur's own disciples. The theory
of Baur, therefore, stands or falls with his interpretation of
the Pauline Epistles, especially 1 and 2 Corinthians and Galatians.

The Corinthian Epistles, as has been observed in the last
chapter, afford no real support to the hypothesis of an inter-
apostolic conflict. There is not the slightest reason to connect the troublemakers at Corinth with the original apostles
or with James; and the whole subject of the "Christ-party"
in 1 Cor. i. 12 is now felt to be very obscure. The evidence
of an apostolic conflict narrows down, therefore, to the second
chapter of Galatians.

Undoubtedly there are expressions in that chapter which
if taken alone might indicate ill-will between Paul and the
Jerusalem leaders. In Gal. ii. 2, 6, for example, James and
Peter and John are called "those who seemed," [1] and in the
latter verse the phrase is explained by the fuller designation,
"those who seemed to be something." In Gal. ii. 9, the same

[1] οἱ δοκοῦντες.

persons are designated as "those who seemed to be pillars."
In themselves these words are capable of an interpretation
which would be derogatory to the persons so designated. The
meaning might conceivably be that the Jerusalem leaders only
"seemed" or "were thought" to be something, or only thought
themselves to be something (compare Gal. vi. 3), whereas they
really were nothing. But this interpretation is, of course,
quite impossible, since Paul certainly recognized Peter and
John as genuine apostles and James the brother of the Lord
as a man of real authority in the Church. The most that may
be maintained, therefore, is that the choice of the peculiar
phrases indicates a certain irritation of Paul against the
Jerusalem leaders; instead of calling them pillars (which certainly he recognized them as being) he shows his irritation,
it is said, by calling them "those who were thought to be
pillars."

The presence of indignant feeling in the passage must
clearly be admitted; but the question is whether the indigna-
tion is directed against the Jerusalem leaders themselves or
only against the Judaizers who falsely appealed to them. The
latter view is correct. It must be remembered that what Paul
in Gal. ii. 1-10 desires most of all to prevent is the impression
that he is appealing to the Jerusalem apostles as to a higher
instance. He is not basing the authority of his preaching
upon any authorization that the apostles gave him; he is not
saying that he has a right to be heard because those who were
the pillars of the Church endorsed his message. Such a representation of the conference would have cast despite upon all
the work which he had done before, and would have made it
necessary for him in the future to prove constantly against
all Judaizers and other opponents his agreement with the
Jerusalem authorities. The profound consciousness which he
had of his apostolic authority did not permit any such course
of action; and such restrictions would have hindered his work
wherever he went. It was absolutely essential in the economy
of God that the leader of the Gentile work should have independent authority and should not be obliged to appeal again
and again to authorities who were far away, at Jerusalem.
Hence what Paul desires to make clear above all in Gal. ii.
1-10 is that though he appealed to the Jerusalem authorities
it was not necessary for his own sake for him to appeal to

them. They were great, but their greatness had absolutely nothing to do with his authority; for they added nothing to him. It was therefore not the real greatness of the original apostles which caused him to appeal to them (for he needed no authorization from any man no matter how great), but only the greatness which was attributed to them by the Judaizers. They really were great, but it was only the false use which had been made of their greatness by the Judaizers which caused him to lay his gospel before them. The Judaizers were to be refuted from the lips of the very authorities to whom they appealed.

It should be observed that the terms which are now under discussion are incapable of real translation into English. The equivalent English words might seem to imply that the reputed greatness of the Jerusalem leaders was not also a real greatness. There is no such implication in the Greek. The shortest of the phrases, which may be paraphrased "those of repute," was used in Greek sometimes in a way thoroughly honorable to the persons designated. Possibly the repetition of the phrases, which seems somewhat strange, was due to the employment of the same phrases by the Judaizing opponents. The peculiarities of the passage may perhaps be due partly to the fact that Paul is here using catchwords of his adversaries.

At any rate, if the reader refuses to interpret these expressions in a way derogatory to the original apostles, such refusal is not due merely to a pious desire to preserve harmony in the apostolic college; it is due rather to the way in which Paul himself everywhere speaks of the apostles, and to the "right hand of fellowship" which according to this very passage they extended to him. It is good exegetical method to interpret things that are obscure by things that are plain; but what is plainest of all in this passage is that the very authorities to whom the Judaizers appealed against Paul recognized the hand of God in his work and bade him Godspeed.

If Gal. ii. 1-10 affords no support to the theory of Baur, the latter part of the same chapter (Gal. ii. 11-21) is not really any more favorable. This passage does indeed attest a rebuke which Paul administered to Peter at Antioch. Peter is even accused of "hypocrisy." The Greek word [1] is indeed not

[1] ὑπόκρισις.

quite so harsh as the English word derived from it; it means
the "playing of a part" and so here the concealment of true
convictions. Nevertheless, the incident remains regrettable
enough; evidently real moral blame was attached by Paul to
Peter's conduct. But what is really significant is that in the
very act of condemning Peter's practice Paul commends his
principles; he appeals to a great fund of Christian conviction
which he and Peter had in common (Gal. ii. 14-21). It will
not do to say that in this passage Paul is giving no report of
what he said to Peter, but is expounding his own views to the
Galatians. For in Gal. ii. 14 he begins to tell what he said
to Peter "before them all"; and there is not the slightest indication of a break before the end of the chapter. Certainly the
break cannot come after verse 14; for the thought of that
verse is quite incomplete in itself and becomes intelligible only
when explained by what follows. The passage is best explained, therefore, if it be taken as embodying the substance
of what Paul said to Peter at Antioch, though doubtless there
is no attempt at verbal reproduction of the language. At
any rate, however much of Gal. ii. 14-21 be a report of what
was said at Antioch, and however much be what Paul now
wishes to say to the Galatians, one thing is clear—when Paul
begins in verse 14 to report what he said to Peter, he means
to call attention to something in which he and Peter were
agreed; he means to say: "You and I, though we had all the
advantages of the Law, relinquished such advantages, in order
to be justified by faith in Christ. How then can we force the
Gentiles to seek salvation by a way which even in our own
case was futile?" Whatever else Paul said to Peter, this much
he certainly said. The context makes the matter perfectly
clear. It must always be remembered that Paul blames Peter
not for false opinions, but for "hypocrisy"—that is, for concealment of true opinions. In verse 14, moreover, he says
expressly that Peter was living after a Gentile manner. The
verb is in the present tense—"if thou being a Jew livest as do
the Gentiles and not as do the Jews." Paul means to say that
a principle essentially similar to that of the Gentile Christians,
according to which in their case the keeping of the Mosaic Law
was relinquished, was the fixed basis of Peter's life. Peter's
present withdrawal from the Gentiles was a mere temporary
aberration. Before the coming of the men from James, he had

seen clearly that the great new principle of faith in Christ took precedence of the Law, even for Jewish Christians; and after the departure of the men he would presumably revert to his old freedom. Indeed even now, even while he was withdrawing himself from his Gentile brethren, the real principle of his life had not been changed; he was still "living as do the Gentiles." But he was concealing his real life for fear of men. The very nature of the charge which Paul brought against Peter, therefore, attests a fundamental unity of principle between the two apostles. Paul condemned Peter for "hypocrisy"; not for false principles, but for concealment of true principles. In principle, therefore, Paul and Peter were agreed.

Accordingly, even the very passage which at first sight lends most color to the hypothesis of Baur, really, when it is correctly interpreted, provides the most striking refutation of that hypothesis. The very chapter which attests the appeal of Paul's bitter opponents to the original apostles, and records a sharp rebuke which Paul administered to Peter, really furnishes the best evidence of apostolic unity. It is the second chapter of Galatians which mentions the right hand of fellowship extended to Paul by James and Peter and John, and it is the second chapter of Galatians which represents the divergence between Paul and Peter as divergence of practice, not of principle. Even if the Epistle to the Galatians stood alone, it would establish the fundamental unity of the apostles. But as a matter of fact, the Epistle to the Galatians does not stand alone; it must be interpreted in the light of other sources. The one-sided interpretation of Galatians, with neglect of other epistles of Paul and of the Book of Acts, has been one of the most fruitful causes of error in the study of the apostolic age. For example, Gal. ii should never be read except in the light of 1 Cor. xv. 1-11. The two passages emphasize two different aspects of Paul's relation to those who had been apostles before him; and only when both the two aspects are considered is the full truth attained. Gal. ii emphasizes the independence of Paul's gospel; Paul had not received it through the instrumentality of men. 1 Cor. xv. 1-11 emphasizes the harmony of Paul's gospel with that of the original apostles, whom Christ had commissioned as directly and as truly as He had commissioned Paul. Both passages are contained in sources admitted by all to be sources of primary importance; yet either passage might be misunderstood if it were taken alone.

Thus the danger of interpreting Gal. ii entirely without reference to anything else is signally manifested by a comparison with 1 Cor. xv. 1-11. The First Epistle to the Corinthians must be allowed to cast light upon Galatians. But if so, may not the same privilege be granted to the Book of Acts? As a matter of fact, the privilege is being granted to the Book of Acts by a larger and larger number of modern scholars. Baur demanded that the Pauline Epistles should be interpreted by themselves, entirely without reference to Acts. But as J. Weiss [1] pertinently remarks, such interpretation is quite impossible; the Epistles taken by themselves are unintelligible; they can be interpreted only when placed in the biographical outline provided by the historian. Of course, that outline might be discredited by a comparison with the Epistles; the divergences might really be contradictions. Comparison of Acts with the Epistles is therefore a matter of fundamental importance. But that comparison, as it has been undertaken at some length in the two preceding chapters of the present discussion, has resulted favorably to the Book of Acts. The divergences between Acts and Pauline Epistles are no more to be regarded as contradictions than are the divergences between various passages in the Epistles themselves; and at many points the historical work casts a flood of light upon the words of Paul.

Thus the imposing construction of Baur was erected by neglecting all sources except Galatians and Corinthians, and then by misinterpreting these. When all the available sources are used, and estimated at their true value, the hypothesis of a fundamental conflict between Paul and the original apostles disappears. There was indeed a bitter conflict in the apostolic age, but, as Ritschl observed against Baur, it was a conflict not between Paul and the original apostles, but between all the apostles, including both Paul and Peter, on the one side, and an extreme Judaizing party on the other. The extreme Judaizing party, not having the support of the original disciples of Jesus, soon ceased to be influential. The various sects of schismatic Jewish Christians which appear in the second century—"Ebionites" and the like—if they had any

[1] See above, p. 40, footnote 1.

roots at all in the apostolic age (which is more than doubtful), could trace their spiritual descent not from the original apostles, but from the Judaizers. It is no wonder then that they were left behind in the march of the Church. They were left behind not because Peter was left behind—for Peter appears as at least one of the foundations upon which the Old Catholic Church was built—but because Peter had left them behind, or rather because Peter had never given them his support at all. They were left behind because from the beginning their spiritual ancestors in the apostolic age had not really belonged with apostolic Christianity, but had been "false brethren privily brought in."

One fact, indeed, still requires explanation. If Paul and the original apostles were in such perfect agreement, how is it that the Judaizers in the apostolic age could appeal to the original apostles against Paul? The existence of that appeal cannot altogether be denied. The exact nature of the appeal is not indeed altogether clear. It is by no means clear that the Judaizers appealed to the original apostles in support of the content of the Judaizing message; it is by no means clear that they made Peter or James teach the necessity of the Mosaic Law for salvation. What is clear is only that they appealed to the original apostles in their personal attack against Paul; they contrasted Paul, who had become a disciple only after the crucifixion, with those who had been intimate with Jesus. They used Peter to discredit the apostolic authority of Paul, but it is not so clear that they used Peter to discredit the content of Paul's message.

If, however, they did appeal to Peter in this latter way, if they did appeal to Peter in support of their legalistic contentions, such an appeal does not overthrow the conclusions which have just been reached about the harmony of Peter and Paul; it does not really make Peter an advocate of legalism. For even if Peter was not an advocate of legalism the appeal of the Judaizers to him can be explained. It can be explained not by the principles of Peter, but by his practice. The early disciples in Jerusalem continued to observe the Jewish fasts and feasts; they continued in diligent attendance upon the Temple services. Outwardly, they were simply devout Jews; and the manner of their life might therefore have given some color to the Judaizing contentions.

Inwardly, it is true, the early disciples were not simply devout Jews; they were really trusting for their salvation no longer to their observance of the Law but to Jesus their Saviour. The whole spirit of their lives, moreover, was quite different from that which prevailed in legalistic Judaism; anxious thought for the morrow, gloomy contemplation of the triumphs of the oppressor, had given place to exultant joy. The early disciples, indeed, like the Jews, were still waiting for the establishment of the kingdom of God. But their waiting was no longer full of sorrow. The Messiah was taken from them for a time; but He had already appeared and had brought salvation.

Thus the early Jerusalem Church was really quite distinct from contemporary Judaism; the real principle of its life was fresh and new. But to a superficial observer, on account of the continuance of old customs, the new principle might not appear; to a superficial observer, the observance of Jewish customs on the part of the early disciples might seem to be legalism. And certainly the Judaizers were superficial. Apparently they had come into the Church in the period of quiet that followed the persecution of Stephen; they had come in from the sect of the Pharisees, and they continued to be Pharisees at heart. As Pharisees they welcomed the coming of the Messiah, but they did not understand the teaching of this Messiah. They looked for a continuance of the prerogatives of Israel. Jesus was the Messiah, but was He not the Jewish Messiah, would He not bring about the triumph of the chosen people? Would not all the peoples of the earth come to do obeisance to Israel by submitting to Israel's Law? To such observers, the Jewish practice of the original apostles would furnish welcome support; these observers would not care to look beneath the surface; they would say simply to the Gentile Christians of Galatia: "The original disciples of Jesus obey the Mosaic Law; must not you do likewise?"

At a later time such an appeal could not have been made; at a later time even the practice of the original apostles ceased to conform to Jewish custom. The tradition according to which the apostle Peter finally went to Rome is emerging triumphant [1] from the fires of criticism; and if Peter went to Rome, it is inconceivable that he separated himself from Gen-

[1] See, for example, Lietzmann, *Petrus and Paulus in Rom*, 1915.

tile Christians. Even in the early days, in Antioch, he had begun to abandon his Jewish manner of life; surely he must have abandoned it more fully when he went to the capital of the Gentile world. The tradition as to the Ephesian residence of the apostle John also points to the abandonment of the Law on the part of the original apostles, and to their definite entrance upon the Gentile mission. That tradition has been rejected only by attending to late and dubious evidence to the neglect of what is plain. But it is not necessary to appeal to details. All that has been said above about the position of Peter in the mind of the Church shows that even the practice of the original apostles finally adapted itself to the needs of the expanding Gentile work.

But in the early period, in Jerusalem, before it had become evident that the Jewish people as such was to reject the gospel message, the apostles continued to observe the Law. And by doing so, they gave the Judaizers some color of support. Thus if the Judaizers did appeal to the original apostles in support of their legalistic claims, the appeal does not establish any real unity of principle between them and the original apostles, or any divergence of principle between the original apostles and Paul. But as a matter of fact it is by no means perfectly clear that the appeal was made; it is by no means clear that the Judaizers appealed to the original apostles for the content of their legalistic message rather than merely for their attack upon the independent apostleship of Paul. It is possible that they said no more than this: "Paul was not one of the original disciples of Jesus; his authority is merely a derived authority; he is, therefore, no more worthy to be heard than we; and we can tell you something new—the followers of the Messiah must unite themselves with the chosen people and obey the Law of God."

At any rate, even if the Judaizers did appeal to the original apostles for the content of their message, the appeal was a false appeal; the original apostles repudiated the Judaizers, and recognized Paul as a true apostle, with authorization as direct as their own.

Thus Baur was wrong. But suppose Baur were right about the point which has just been discussed; suppose even the most impossible admissions be made; suppose it be granted that the original apostles differed fundamentally from Paul.

Even then the testimony of the original apostles to the true connection between Paul and Jesus is not invalidated. For even if the original apostles differed fundamentally from Paul, the difference concerned only the place of the Mosaic Law in the Christian economy, and did not concern the Pauline conception of the person of Christ. So much at least must be insisted upon against Baur. The really astounding fact, which emerges from all discussion of the apostolic age, is that the Pauline conception of the person of Christ, whatever may be said of the Pauline doctrine of Gentile freedom, was never criticized by the original apostles. Indeed, so far as can be seen, it was never criticized even by the Judaizers themselves. Apparently it never occurred to Paul that his conception of the heavenly Christ required defense. About other things there was controversy; the doctrine of Christian freedom, for example, had to be defended against all sorts of objections and by the use of all sorts of evidence. But about the person of Christ there was not one word of debate. "Not by man but by Jesus Christ," Paul says at the beginning of Galatians. Evidently the Judaizers said, "Not by Jesus Christ but by man." But apparently it never occurred to Paul that any one might say, "By Jesus Christ and therefore by man." The Judaizers, apparently, as well as Paul, recognized the alternative between Jesus Christ and man; like Paul they separated Jesus Christ from ordinary humanity and placed Him on the side of God. The same phenomenon appears everywhere in the Pauline Epistles—the tremendous doctrine of the person of Christ is never defended, but always assumed. Indeed, in the earlier epistles the doctrine is never even set forth in any systematic way; it is simply presupposed. In Colossians, indeed, it is more definitely set forth, and apparently in opposition to errorists who failed to recognize its full implications. Even in Colossæ, however, the doctrine does not seem to have been denied; the errorists apparently did not deny the supreme place of Jesus in the scale of being, but merely erred in attaching undue importance to other beings. What is really significant in Colossians is the character of the errorists. Evidently they were not conservative disciples, who appealed against the heavenly Christ of Paul to the facts about the historic Jesus. On the contrary, they were gnostics, engaged in unhistorical speculations, and as far removed as possible from anything that primitive Palestinian Christianity might conceivably have been. So when Paul first has to defend his doctrine of the exclusive and supreme importance of Christ, he defends it not against conservative disciples, who could appeal either with or without reason to the original apostles, but against gnostic speculation. With regard to the person of Christ Paul appears everywhere in perfect harmony with all Palestinian Christians.

The fact is of such importance that it must be examined in the light of all possible objections. Is there any trace in the Pauline Epistles of a primitive view of Jesus different from the lofty Christology of Paul?

One such trace has occasionally been found in 2 Cor. v. 16. In that verse, after Paul has spoken of the complete break that comes in a man's life when he accepts the benefits of Christ's death, he says: "Wherefore we henceforth know no man after the flesh: even though we have known Christ after the flesh, yet now we know him so no more." Some interpreters have discovered in the words, "even though we have known Christ after the flesh," a reference to a fleshly conception of Christ which laid stress upon His Davidic descent, His connection with the Jewish people, and in general His ordinary human relationships, to the neglect of His higher, divine nature. That fleshly conception of Christ might then be regarded as the primitive conception, which Paul himself shared until a mature stage of his Christian life. But this latter suggestion is excluded not only by the whole tenor of the Epistles (in which Paul never displays the slightest consciousness of any such revolution in his idea of Christ), but also especially by the present passage. The passage deals with the complete and immediate break which comes in a man's way of thinking when the death of Christ becomes representative of him—that is, at the beginning of his Christian life. It is therefore entirely out of accord with the context to suppose that Paul is contrasting an immature stage of his own Christian life with the present mature stage. But he is also not alluding to any lower, fleshly conception of Christ as being held by others. The interpretation which finds in the passage a human Messiah in contrast to the divine Christ of Paul, errs fundamentally in making the words "according to the flesh" modify "Christ," whereas as a matter of fact they clearly modify the verb "know." Paul says not, "Even if we have known a Christ according to the flesh, we know such a Christ no longer," but, "Even if we have known Christ with a fleshly kind of knowledge, we know Him in such a way no longer." He is not speaking of two different conceptions of Christ, but of two different ways of knowing Christ. There is in the passage, therefore, not the slightest reference to any primitive conception of the person of Christ different from Paul's conception.

In 2 Cor. xi. 4 Paul speaks of "another Jesus" whom his opponents in Corinth were proclaiming or might proclaim. Was this "other Jesus" the historical Jesus, in distinction from the heavenly Christ of Paul? Does this verse refer to a primitive, Palestinian conception of Jesus different from the conception held by Paul?

The verse is certainly very difficult; it constitutes a famous *crux interpretum*. But just for that reason, it should not be made the foundation for far-reaching theories. There is not the slightest hint elsewhere in 2 Corinthians that the opponents presented a view of the person of Christ different from that of Paul; indeed what is characteristic of the polemic in this Epistle is that doctrinal questions are absent. There is not even any evidence that the opponents, though apparently they laid stress upon Jewish descent, Palestinian connections, and the like, and so may perhaps loosely be called "Judaizers," insisted upon the keeping of the Mosaic Law. Apparently Paul does not feel required to defend the content of his gospel at all. Certainly he does not feel required to defend his doctrine of the person of Christ. But if the opponents had really proclaimed a human Jesus different from the divine Christ of Paul, it is inconceivable that Paul should not have defended his view. If there is one thing that is fundamental in the religion of Paul, it is his conception of Christ as divine Redeemer. Any denial of that conception would certainly have called forth anathemas at least as severe as those which were hurled against the legalists in Galatia. Yet in 2 Cor. x-xiii, though these chapters contain perhaps the bitterest polemic to be found anywhere in the Pauline Epistles, there is no trace of any defense of the Pauline conception of the person of Christ. The natural suggestion is that such defense is absent because

it was not called forth by anything that the opponents said.
It is adventurous exegetical procedure to hang a heavy weight
upon the very obscure verse, 2 Cor. xi. 4.

As a matter of fact, however, the obscurities of that verse
are not hopeless, and rightly interpreted the verse contains
no hint of a primitive conception of Jesus different from
that which was proclaimed by Paul. The translation of the
American Revised Version may first be presented as a basis
of discussion, though it is probably incorrect in important
particulars. In that version the three verses 2 Cor. xi. 4-6[1]
read as follows: "For if he that cometh preacheth another
Jesus, whom we did not preach, or if ye receive a different
spirit, which ye did not receive, or a different gospel, which
ye did not accept, ye do well to bear with him. 5 For I
reckon that I am not a whit behind the very chiefest apostles.
6 But though I be rude in speech, yet am I not in knowledge; nay, in every way have we made this manifest unto
you in all things." By a modification of this translation at the
end of verse 4, the whole passage might mean: "Bear with
me in my boasting. I am 'boasting' or defending myself
only in order that you may not be deceived by the opponent
who comes to you. For if he comes arrogantly proclaiming
another Jesus, another Spirit, and another gospel, ye bear
with him only too well. Bear with *me* then when I defend
myself. For I am not a bit behind these 'preëminent' apostles,[2]
since despite what they say I have really made the whole truth
known to you."

Even according to this interpretation there is no real
reference to a Jesus of the opponents different from Paul's
Jesus. The "other Jesus" of the opponents existed, rather,
merely in their own inordinate claims. They had no other
Jesus, no other Spirit, and no other gospel to offer. They
asserted, indeed, that the teaching of Paul was insufficient;
they asserted that they had fuller information about Jesus,

---

[1] 4. εἰ μὲν γὰρ ὁ ἐρχόμενος ἄλλον Ἰησοῦν κηρύσσει ὃν οὐκ ἐκηρύξαμ·ν, ἢ πνεῦμα ἕτερον
λαμβάνετε ὃ οὐκ ἐλάβετε, ἢ εὐαγγέλιον ἕτερον ὃ οὐκ ἐδέξασθε, καλῶς ἀνέχεσθε. 5. λογί-
ζομαι γὰρ μηδὲν ὑστερηκέναι τῶν ὑπερλίαν ἀποστόλων. 6. εἰ δὲ καὶ ἰδιώτης τῷ λόγῳ,
ἀλλ'οὐ τῇ γνώσει, ἀλλ'ἐν παντὶ φανερώσαντες ἐν πᾶσιν εἰς ὑμᾶς.

[2] The translation preferred in the American Revision, "very chiefest
apostles," seems to be based upon the mistaken view that the ὑπερλίαν
ἀπόστολοι are the original apostles at Jerusalem. This view is rejected
in the above paraphrase, which diverges from the American Revision in
other ways also.

about the Spirit, and about the gospel. They said, "Paul has not made the full truth known to you." Yet they had really nothing new to offer. Paul had really given to the Corinthians the whole Jesus, the whole Spirit, and the whole gospel.

As a matter of fact, however, this interpretation is unsatisfactory. It is obliged to supply a link to connect verse 4 with verse 5—namely, the thought, "Bear with me." That thought is here entirely unexpressed; verse 1, where it is expressed, is too far back to be in view. Thus if the pronoun "him" is supplied with the verb at the end of verse 4, there is no clear connection with verse 5; the "for" of verse 5 is very obscure. If, however, the pronoun "me," not "him," is supplied with the verb at the end of verse 4, all is plain. Since the pronoun does not appear at all in the Greek, the translator is free to supply it as the context demands; and the context apparently demands the pronoun "me." The meaning of the passage is then as follows: "Bear with me in my 'boasting.' My boasting is undertaken to prevent you from being deceived. For if the one who comes to you seeks to commend himself by claiming fuller knowledge of Jesus, the Spirit, or the gospel, then you do well to bear with me in my boasting, you do well to listen to my defense. For I am not afraid of the comparison with the opponent. It is not true that I have concealed from you anything about Jesus, about the Spirit, or about the gospel; on the contrary I have made everything known to you."

The exegetical question is somewhat complicated by a question of the text in verse 4. Manuscript evidence is rather evenly divided between the present tense of the verb at the end of the verse and the imperfect tense.[1] Unquestionably the imperfect tense is the more difficult reading; it is favored therefore by the well-known principle of textual criticism that the more difficult reading is to be preferred to the easier. If the imperfect be read, it may perhaps be explained as the imperfect tense in the apodosis of a condition contrary to fact; there would then be a transition from one form of condition to another. Paul would then say: "If he who comes is preaching another Jesus, another Spirit, and another gospel —if such were the case you would do well to bear with my defense of my own preaching." If indeed the pronoun "him"

---

[1] Between ἀνέχεσθε and ἀνείχεσθε (or ἠνείχεσθε).

be supplied at the end of verse 4, as is usually done, the imperfect might be taken simply as referring to past time, and the meaning would be: "If he who comes is preaching another Jesus, another Spirit, and another gospel—when that took place ye were bearing with the newcomer only too well." But even so the imperfect is extremely harsh, and on the whole it is more probable that it has crept in by a copyist's error—perhaps in conformity to the same imperfect in verse 1, where the imperfect is used to express a wish.

What has caused the vast majority of commentators to supply "him" rather than "me" at the end of verse 4 is apparently the parallel with 2 Cor. xi. 19, 20, where Paul certainly expresses the thought, "Bear with me, for you bear with my arrogant opponents only too well." The parallel does indeed constitute the strongest argument in favor of the ordinary view of verse 4 which supplies the pronoun "him," and regards the adverb "well" as sarcastic—"only too well." But the argument is not decisive. The connection with verse 5 really fixes the pronoun which is to be supplied at the end of the preceding verse. Paul is defending himself against the charge, implied in verse 6, that he had not made the full truth known. The opponents had claimed to have further information about Jesus, the Spirit, and the gospel. "But," says Paul, "if that is their claim, ye do well to listen to my defense. For I have made Jesus and the Spirit and the gospel just as fully known to you as they have." The thought is perfectly clear if only the pronoun "me" be supplied at the end of verse 4.

If, however, exegetical tradition be followed, and the pronoun "him" be supplied, the essential implications of the passage are not really different. In no case is anything said about a conception of Jesus really differing from that of Paul. One interpretation, indeed, definitely excludes such an implication. The passage may mean, "If the one who comes to you preaches another Jesus—in that case you would do well to bear with him. But as a matter of fact there is only one Jesus. Therefore you will do well to be content with me. For I have made Jesus fully known to you." According to this interpretation, which has much to be said in its favor, Paul refutes the opponents and their arrogant claims of bringing something superior to Paul's message, by a reference to the obvious fact that there is only one Jesus. "If they had

another Jesus," Paul says, "then they might claim to bring
you something that I did not bring. But since, unfortunately
for them, there is of course only one Jesus, and since I made
that Jesus fully known to you, they cannot maintain any supe-
riority." This interpretation is probably to be preferred among
all those which supply the pronoun "him" rather than "me"
at the end of verse 4.

At any rate, whichever interpretation be adopted, Paul
would surely have expressed himself very differently if the
opponents had presented an account of Jesus radically contradictory to his own. In that case he could hardly have
appealed merely to the completeness of his presentation. Instead, he would have had to establish the truth of his presentation. As it is, the "other Jesus" of the Judaizers existed only
in their own inordinate claims. They really had no other
Jesus to offer; Paul had made the whole Jesus known. The
passage contains no hint, therefore, of a primitive conception of
Jesus differing from the lofty conception proclaimed by Paul.

Thus the Pauline Epistles contain not the slightest trace
of any conflict with regard to the person of Christ. About
other things there was debate, but about this point Paul
appears to have been in harmony with all Palestinian Christians. Even the Judaizers seem to have had no objection to
the heavenly Christ of Paul. But if the Judaizers, who were
Paul's bitter opponents, had no objection to Paul's view of
Christ, it could only have been because the original apostles
on this point gave them not even that slight color of support
which may have been found with regard to the way of salvation in the apostles' observance of the Law. The fact is of
enormous importance. The heavenly Christ of Paul was also
the Christ of those who had walked and talked with Jesus of
Nazareth.

Let it not be said that this conclusion involves an undue
employment of the argument from silence; let it not be said
that although the original apostles did not share Paul's conception of the heavenly Christ, Paul did not find it necessary to enter into the debate in his Epistles. For on this
matter Paul could not possibly have kept silent. He was not
in the habit of keeping silent when the essential things of
his gospel were called in question—the anathemas which he
pronounced against the Judaizers in Galatia and the sharp

rebuke which he administered to the chief of the apostles at Antioch are sufficient proof of his fearlessness. But what can possibly be regarded as essential to his gospel if it was not his doctrine of Christ as divine Redeemer? That doctrine was the very warp and woof of his being; without it he was less than nothing. Yet the historian is asked to believe that Paul submitted tamely, without a word of protest, to the presentation of a purely human Jesus. The thing is unthinkable. Paul would not have submitted to the preaching of such a Jesus if the preachers had all been angels from heaven.

What is really most significant in the Pauline Epistles therefore, is the complete absence of any defense of the Pauline doctrine of Christ, the complete absence, indeed, of any systematic presentation of that doctrine. The Pauline view of Christ is everywhere presupposed, but nowhere defended. The phenomenon is very strange if the modern naturalistic account of Jesus be correct. According to that account, the historical Jesus, a great and good man, came after His death to be regarded as a divine Redeemer; one conception of Jesus gave place to a very different conception. Yet the surprising thing is that the mighty transition has left not the slightest trace in the primary sources of information. The chief witness to the transcendent conception of Jesus as divine Redeemer is quite unconscious of introducing anything new; indeed he expressly calls attention to the harmony of his proclamation with that of the intimate friends of Jesus. There is only one possible conclusion—the heavenly Christ of Paul was also the Christ of those who had lived with Jesus of Nazareth. They had seen Jesus subject to all the petty limitations of human life; they had seen Him hungry and thirsty and weary; they had toiled with Him over the hills of Galilee; yet they gave the right hand of fellowship to one who regarded Him as the divine Redeemer seated on the throne of all being, and they were quite unconscious of any conflict between their view and his.

Thus Paul was not regarded as an innovator with respect to Jesus by Jesus' intimate friends. He was not regarded as an innovator even with regard to those elements in his message —such as freedom from the Law—about which no definite guidance was to be found in the teaching or example of Jesus.

Still less was he regarded as an innovator in his account of Jesus' person. With regard to that matter even the Judaizers did not venture to disagree.

But if Paul regarded himself, and was regarded by the original apostles, as a true disciple of Jesus, how did he obtain the necessary knowledge of Jesus' life? Was his knowledge limited to intuition or remote hearsay; or had he opportunities for authentic information?

That question has really been answered by the outline of Paul's life in Chapters II and III. It has been shown that even before his conversion, in Palestine, Paul must have become acquainted with the facts about Jesus' life and death. The facts were common property; even indifference could not have made a man completely ignorant of them. But far from being indifferent, Paul was deeply interested in Jesus, since he was an active persecutor of Jesus' disciples. After the conversion, Paul was undoubtedly baptized, and undoubtedly came into some contact with Christians in Damascus. The presumption is strongly in favor of the presence there of some who had known Jesus in the days of His flesh; the independence of which Paul is speaking in Galatians is independence over against the Jerusalem apostles, not over against humble disciples in Damascus, and it does not relate to information about details. Three years after the conversion Paul visited Peter at Jerusalem. and also met James the brother of Jesus. It is quite inconceivable that the three men avoided the subject of Jesus' words and deeds. The fifteen days spent with Peter at Jerusalem brought Paul into contact with the most intimate possible source of information about Jesus.

According to the Book of Acts, Paul came into contact with Barnabas at the time of his first Jerusalem visit. Whatever may be thought of this detail, the later association of Barnabas with Paul, at Antioch and on the first missionary journey, is generally or universally recognized as historical. It is confirmed by the association of the two men at the time of the conference with the Jerusalem pillars (Gal. ii. 1). Thus Paul spent several years in the most intimate association with Barnabas. Who then was Barnabas? According to Acts iv. 36, 37, he was a man of Cyprus by descent, but he was also a member of the primitive Jerusalem Church. The kind of information contained in this passage represents just that element in the early chapters of Acts which is being generally accepted by recent criticism. With regard to the community of goods in the early Jerusalem Church, it is sometimes supposed that the author of Acts has erred in generalizing and exalting to the position of a principle what was really done in many cases by generous individuals. But in order that there might be unhistorical generalization, there must have been something to generalize. Details, therefore, like the generous act of Barnabas in selling a field and devoting the proceeds to the needs of the brethren, are thought to constitute the solid tradition with which the author of Acts is operating. Objections in plenty may be raised against this treatment of the narrative as a whole, but certainly the concreteness of the little detached note about Barnabas makes a specially favorable impression. It will probably be admitted to-day by the majority of scholars that Barnabas really had a place in the primitive Jerusalem Church. But if so, his close connection with Paul is of the utmost importance. How could Paul possibly have been for years intimately associated with Barnabas in the proclamation of the gospel without becoming acquainted with the facts about Jesus? Is it to be supposed that Barnabas, who had lived at Jerusalem, proclaimed Jesus as Saviour without telling in detail what sort of person Jesus had been, and what He had said and done? Or is it to be supposed that Paul closed his ears to what his brother missionary said?

At the beginning of the first missionary journey, Barnabas and Paul were accompanied by John Mark, and Mark appears again in the company of Paul, as one of Paul's trusted helpers, in Col. iv. 10 and Philem. 24. This John Mark certainly came from the Jerusalem Church; for the house of his mother is mentioned as a meeting-place for the Jerusalem disciples in the incomparably vivid account in Acts xii. 1-17 of the escape of Peter from prison. Whatever may be thought of the Book of Acts as a whole, the twelfth chapter is recognized as embodying primitive tradition. Even Wellhausen was somewhat impressed with the lifelike detail of this narrative; the chapter, Wellhausen admitted, contains elements of high historical value.[1] Certainly, then, the mother of John Mark and presumably Mark himself were members of the primitive Jerusa-

[1] Wellhausen, *Kritische Analyse der Apostelgeschichte*, 1914, pp. 22f.

lem Church. Tradition, moreover, as preserved by Papias of
Hierapolis, connects Mark with Peter and represents the Second Gospel (attributed to Mark) as based upon Peter's preaching.[1] The connection of Mark with Peter is confirmed by 1
Peter v. 13. In general, recent criticism is favorably dis-
posed toward the Papian tradition about the Second Gospel;
that tradition is often admitted to have some basis in fact.
Of course the words of Papias about Mark's connection with
Peter naturally refer, at least in part, to a time later than
the formative period of Paul's life. But no doubt the later relationship was at least prepared for in the early days when Mark
and Peter were together in Jerusalem.[2] John Mark, therefore,
constitutes an important link, not only between Paul and the
Jerusalem Church, but also between Paul and one of the most
intimate friends of Jesus. Paul would have been able to learn
the facts about Jesus' life from Mark if he had not learned
them elsewhere.

The conference between Paul and the Jerusalem leaders,
described in Gal. ii. 1-10, whether or no it was identical with
the Apostolic Council of Acts xv. 1-29, would naturally bring
an enrichment in Paul's knowledge of Jesus' earthly ministry.
It is hardly to be supposed that at the conference any more
than at the first visit of Paul to Jerusalem the subject of
the words and deeds of Jesus was carefully avoided. Such
avoidance would have been possible only if the Jerusalem
Church itself had been indifferent to its own reminiscences of
Jesus' earthly ministry. But that the Jerusalem Church was
not indifferent to its own reminiscences is proved by the preser-
vation (evidently at Jerusalem) of the tradition contained in
the Gospels. The existence of the Gospels shows that the
memory of Jesus' words and deeds was carefully treasured up
in the Jerusalem Church from the earliest times. Paul could
hardly have come into contact with such a church without obtaining information about Jesus. He could not have failed to
obtain information even if he had been anxious to avoid it.

---

[1] In Eusebius, *Hist. Eccl.* iii, 39, 15.
[2] B. W. Bacon (*Jesus and Paul*, 1921, pp. 15f.) believes that the connection between Peter and Mark is probably to be placed only in the
early years, principally before the first association of Mark with Paul.
This view, which is insufficiently grounded, involves a rejection of the
common view, attested, for example, by 1 Peter v. 13, according to which
Mark was also with Peter at a later time.

But as a matter of fact he was not anxious to avoid it; his apostolic independence, as will be observed below, does not really presuppose any such absurd attitude on his part.

On the third missionary journey Paul was accompanied by Silas (the "Silvanus" of the Pauline Epistles). According to the Book of Acts, Silas, like Barnabas and Mark, came originally from the Jerusalem Church, though his connection with Jerusalem is not traced so far back. He is said to have been one of the two men who accompanied the Apostolic Decree from Jerusalem to Antioch (Acts xv. 27). This assertion of course will not escape unchallenged. It shares no doubt to some extent the criticism which has been directed against the Decree itself. But the tendency in recent years is to find a larger and larger historical basis for the concrete assertions of the author of Acts. So the mention of Judas and Silas as coming from Jerusalem creates a favorable impression. It cannot be ruled out merely because it stands only in Acts, or merely because it is connected with the Decree. Even the Decree, it will be remembered, is now often admitted to be a Decree of the Jerusalem Church or to represent the substance of such a decree, even by those scholars who suppose that Acts is wrong in representing Paul as being present when the Decree was passed. The tradition which lies back of Acts xv, therefore, cannot lightly be rejected. There is certainly some evidence, therefore, for connecting Silas with the Jerusalem Church. Of course, if the narrative in Acts be accepted as it stands, as it is being accepted more and more generally to-day, then the connection of Silas with the Jerusalem Church is firmly established. That connection is not without its importance. It shows that even when engaged in his specifically Gentile work, Paul had not shut himself off from the sources of information about Jesus.

The mention of Andronicus and Junias in Rom. xvi. 7 is not without interest. According to the most natural interpretation of the verse, Andronicus and Junias are declared to have been in Christ before Paul was in Christ. They were, therefore, primitive disciples. Certain other details are more obscure. Does Paul mean that Andronicus and Junias were themselves "apostles," the word "apostle" being used here in a broad sense? In that case, the verse may be translated, "Salute Andronicus and Junias, my kinsmen and fellow-prisoners, who are noteworthy among the apostles who were before me in Christ." Or is it merely said that Andronicus and Junias were regarded highly by the apostles, had a good reputation among them? In that case, the relative pronoun is no doubt to be taken with the words "Andronicus and Junias" rather than with the word "apostles"; and two details are mentioned: (1) that Andronicus and Junias had a good reputation among the apostles, and (2) that they were converted earlier than Paul. Also the meaning of the word translated "kinsmen" is doubtful. The word may mean merely "members of the same race," that is, "Jews"; or it may mean "members of the same family," that is, "relatives." Still another interpretation is favored by Böhlig, who thinks that the word designates Andronicus and Junias as members of the Jewish colony at Tarsus, the boyhood home of Paul.[1] But however the interesting exegetical problems may be solved, it seems evident that Andronicus and Junias had become Christians earlier than Paul, and that they were therefore representatives of primitive Christianity. The presence of such men in the Church at Rome—or in the Church at Ephesus, if the common separation of Rom. xvi. from the rest of Romans (on insufficient grounds) be adopted—is interesting. It exemplifies the kind of personal connection that was undoubtedly maintained between primitive Christianity and the Gentile churches. Even far away in the Gentile world Paul was not altogether removed from contact with those who had been Christians before him. Wherever and however Andronicus and Junias had become disciples, whether in Jerusalem or elsewhere, whether by the instrumentality of Jesus Himself or by the instrumentality of His apostles, in any case they had become disciples in the very earliest days of the Church's life. It is hardly to be supposed that they were ignorant of the facts about Jesus, and in all probability there were other such persons, even in Pauline churches.

But it is not necessary to lay stress upon Andronicus and Junias, when Peter and James and Barnabas and Mark all came into close contact with Paul. Paul had abundant opportunity for acquainting himself with the words and deeds of Jesus.

Three important facts have thus far been established; (1) Paul regarded himself as a disciple of Jesus of Nazareth,

[1] Böhlig, *Die Geisteskultur von Tarsos,* 1913, pp. 140-142.

(2) he was so regarded by the intimate friends of Jesus, (3) he had abundant sources of information about Jesus' life. The natural conclusion is that Paul was a true disciple of the real Jesus.

This conclusion is thought to be overthrown by two considerations. In the first place, it is said, Paul himself attests his own indifference to historical information about Jesus; and in the second place, such indifference is confirmed by the paucity of references in the Epistles to Jesus' words and deeds. These two considerations lead into the heart of the problem, and must be examined with some care.

The indifference of Paul toward historical information about Jesus is thought to be attested chiefly by 2 Cor. v. 16 and by the Epistle to the Galatians. In 2 Cor. v. 16 Paul says, "Even if we have known Christ according to the flesh, yet now we know Him so no more." What can these words mean, it is asked, except that ordinary information about Jesus, dealing with the details of His earthly life, the kind of information that one man can obtain of another by sight and hearing, has become valueless for the Christian? The Christian, Paul says, is interested not at all in what eyewitnesses may say or in what he himself may remember about the earthly life of Jesus; he is interested only in the direct contact which he has at present with the risen Lord.

This interpretation ignores the fact that the assertion in 2 Cor. v. 16 about the knowledge of Christ is only an application of the general assertion at the beginning of the verse about the knowledge of persons in general. "So that," says Paul, "we from now on know no one after the flesh." Paul says, therefore, not only that he does not know Christ after the flesh, but also that he does not know any man after the flesh, and the two assertions must obviously be interpreted in the same way. Therefore the interpretation which has been proposed for the knowledge of Christ, if it is to commend itself, must also be applied to the knowledge of every man.

But when it is so applied it results in absurdity. It would make Paul indifferent not only to ordinary information about Jesus, but also to ordinary information about men in general. But as a matter of fact Paul was not indifferent to ordinary information about men in general. On the contrary, he was exceedingly careful about getting information just as accurate as could possibly be secured. Was Paul a visionary, with his head always in the clouds, indifferent to the concrete problems of individual men, indifferent to what men had to tell him about their various earthly relationships, indifferent to their bodily needs? The First Epistle to the Corinthians is a magnificent refutation of such a caricature. That Epistle represents Paul as a pastor of souls, unsurpassed in his insight into the practical problems of his converts, unsurpassed in the tact with which he applied great principles to special circumstances. But the same characteristics appear everywhere in Paul. Everywhere Paul is the true friend, the true patriot, and the true man; everywhere he exhibits that careful attention to detail, that careful recognition of special relationships, which is lacking in genuinely mystical piety. Some pastors are accustomed to say the same thing no matter what questions are laid before them; they can only enunciate general principles without applying them to special problems; they are incapable of special friendships and incapable of analyzing actual situations. It is not so in the case of Paul. In the Pauline Epistles special problems are solved in the light of eternal principles; but the special problems as well as the eternal principles are subjected to the most careful examination. Paul was not indifferent to ordinary knowledge of his fellow-men.

Thus when Paul says that he knows no man after the flesh he does not mean that he ignored the ordinary knowledge which comes through sight and hearing. But if that kind of knowledge is not excluded from the relations between Paul and men in general, it is also not excluded from the relations between Paul and Christ; for the latter part of the verse is evidently placed in parallel with the former part. It is evidently the same kind of knowledge which is excluded in both cases. Paul does not mean, therefore, that he was indifferent to ordinary sources of information about Christ.

What he does mean is that he regarded those ordinary sources of information not as an end in themselves, but as a means to an end. The natural man according to Paul does not understand the true significance of the words and deeds of his fellow-men; he does not use them to attest spiritual facts. The man who is in Christ, on the contrary, even when he uses ordinary means of information, is acquiring knowledge of spiritual relationships, relationships which exist in the new world. So it is also with the knowledge of Christ. The natural man may acquire a certain knowledge of Christ; he may learn what Christ said and did and what were the worldly circumstances of His life. But such knowledge is a knowledge according to the flesh; it does not attain to the true significance even of those facts which are learned. The man who is in Christ, on the other hand, may operate partly with the same materials; but even when he is operating with the same materials, even when he is obtaining by sight or by hearsay knowledge of the words and deeds of Jesus, these facts now are invested with a higher significance. The natural man detects only the outward appearance of the words and deeds of Jesus; the man who is in Christ makes them attest facts that have significance in the new world. No doubt the higher knowledge of Christ of which Paul is speaking is not limited to this spiritual use of ordinary sources of information; no doubt there is also a direct intercourse between the believer and the risen Lord. But the spiritual use of the ordinary sources of information is certainly not excluded. Paul does not mean that he was indifferent to what Jesus said and did.

Thus 2 Cor. v. 16, rightly interpreted, does not attest any indifference on the part of Paul toward the information about Jesus which came to him through contact with Jesus' disciples. Such indifference, however, is also thought to be attested by the Epistle to the Galatians. In Gal. i, ii, Paul emphasizes his complete independence over against the original disciples. He received his gospel, he says, not by the instrumentality of men, but by direct revelation from the risen Christ. Even after the revelation he felt no need of instruction from those who had been apostles before him. It was three years before he saw any of them, and then he was with Peter only fifteen days. Even when he did finally have a conference with the original apostles, he received nothing from them; they recognized that God had already entrusted him with his gospel and that they had nothing to add. What can this passage mean, it is asked, except that Paul was indifferent to tradition, and derived his knowledge of Christ entirely from revelation?

In answer, it is sufficient to point to 1 Cor. xv. 1-11. Was Paul indifferent to tradition? In 1 Cor. xv. 3 he himself attests the contrary; he places tradition—something that he had received—at the very foundation of his missionary preaching. "For I delivered unto you among the first things," he says, "that which I also received." The word "received" here certainly designates information obtained by ordinary word of mouth, not direct revelation from the risen Christ; and the content of what was "received" fixes the source of the information pretty definitely in the fifteen days which Paul spent with Peter at Jerusalem. It is almost universally admitted that 1 Cor. xv. 3ff. contains the tradition of the Jerusalem Church with regard to the death and resurrection of Jesus.

The comparison with 1 Cor. xv. 1-11 thus exhibits the danger of interpreting the Epistle to the Galatians in one-sided fashion. If Galatians stood by itself, the reader might suppose that at least the resurrection of Christ, the central fact of Paul's gospel, was founded, in Paul's preaching, upon Paul's own testimony alone. In Galatians Paul says that his gospel was not derived from men. But his gospel was grounded upon the resurrection of Christ. Surely, it might be said, therefore, he based at least the resurrection not at all upon the testimony of others but upon the revelation which came to him from Christ. Is it possible to conceive of the author of Galatians as appealing for the foundation of his gospel to the testimony of Peter and the twelve and other brethren in the primitive Church—to the testimony of exactly those men whose mediatorship he is excluding in Galatians? Yet as a matter of fact, that is exactly what Paul did. That he did so is attested not by the Book of Acts or by any source upon which doubt might be cast, but by one of the accepted epistles. The Epistle to the Galatians must always be interpreted in the light of 1 Cor. xv. 1-11.

What then does Paul mean in Galatians when he says that he received his gospel directly from Christ? The answer is perfectly plain. He does not mean that when he drew near to Damascus on that memorable day he knew none of the facts about Jesus; he does not mean that after that day his knowledge of the facts was not enriched by intercourse with Jesus' friends. What Jesus really gave him near Damascus was not so much the facts as a new interpretation of the facts. He had known some of the facts before, but they had filled him with hatred. The Galilean prophet had cast despite upon the Law; He had broken down the prerogatives of Israel; it was blasphemous, moreover, to proclaim a crucified malefactor as the Lord's Anointed. Paul had known the facts before; he had known them only too well. Now, however, he obtained a new interpretation of the facts; he obtained that new interpretation not by human intermediation, not by reflection upon the testimony of the disciples, not by the example of the holy martyrs, but by revelation from Jesus Himself. Jesus Himself appeared to him. He might have appeared in anger, to destroy him for his unspeakable sin. Instead, He appeared in love, to call him into fellowship and into glorious service, to commission him as apostle of the One whose Church he had laid waste. That is what Paul means when he says that he received his gospel directly from the risen Christ.

The truth is, it never occurred to Paul to regard the bare facts about Jesus as constituting a "gospel"; it never even occurred to Paul to reflect upon all the sources of information about the facts. To us the sources of information about Jesus are limited: therefore they are searched out and numbered and weighed. But to Paul the sources of information were so numerous that they could not be catalogued. It never occurred to him to regard with supreme gratitude the particular source from which he derived any particular bit of information about Jesus any more than we regard with special gratitude the newspaper from which we derive our knowledge of current events. If one newspaper had not printed the news, others would have done so; the sources of information are so numerous that we do not reflect upon them. So it was in the case of Paul's information about Jesus. Bare detailed information about the words and deeds of Jesus did not in Paul's mind constitute a "gospel"; they constituted only the materials upon which the gospel was based. When he says, therefore, that he did not receive his gospel from men he does not mean that he received no information from Peter or Barnabas or Mark or James or the five hundred brethren who had seen the risen Lord. What he does mean is that he himself was convinced of the decisive fact—the fact of the resurrection—not by the testimony of these men, but by the divine interposition on the road to Damascus, and that none of these men told him how he himself was to be saved or what he was to say to the Gentiles about the way of salvation. Materials for the proof of his gospel might come to him from ordinary sources of information, but his gospel itself was given to him directly by Christ.

Thus Paul does not directly attest any indifference on his part toward tradition about the life of Jesus. But is not such indifference revealed by the extreme paucity of references in the Pauline Epistles to what Jesus said and did?

In answer to this question it must be admitted that direct citations in the Pauline Epistles of words of Jesus, and direct references to the details of Jesus' life, are surprisingly few. In 1 Cor. vii. 10, Paul appeals to a command of the Lord about divorce, and carefully distinguishes such commands from what he himself is saying to the Corinthians (verses 12, 25). In 1 Cor. ix. 14, he calls attention to an ordinance of the Lord to the effect that they that proclaim the gospel should live of the gospel. In these passages it cannot be doubted that the commands of "the Lord" are commands that Jesus gave during His earthly ministry; they are certainly not commands given to Paul by the risen Christ. For the words which Paul himself wrote to his churches, by virtue of his apostolic authority, themselves constituted commands of the Lord in the broad sense, in that the authority of the Lord was behind them (1 Cor. xiv. 37); here, therefore, when such apostolic commands are distinguished from commands of the Lord, the commands of the Lord must be taken in a narrower sense. They can only be commands given by Jesus during His earthly ministry.[1]

These passages show that Paul was in the habit of distinguishing what Jesus said on earth to His disciples from what the risen Lord said to him directly by revelation. They show, moreover, that Paul was in possession of a fund of information about the words of Jesus. It may be a question why he did not draw upon the fund more frequently; but at any rate, the fund was there.

In 1 Thess. iv. 15, the assurance that those who are alive at the Parousia shall not precede those that have died is grounded in a word of the Lord ("For this we say to you in a word of the Lord").[2] Here again the "word of the Lord" is probably to be regarded as a word which Jesus spoke while He was on earth, rather than as a revelation made by the risen

[1] Compare Knowling, *The Witness of the Epistles.* 1892, pp. 319f.
[2] τοῦτο γὰρ ὑμῖν λέγομεν ἐν λόγῳ κυρίου.

Lord directly to Paul. If this interpretation be correct, then this passage contains another incidental reference to a fund of information about the words of Jesus.

Most important of all, however, is the report of the institution of the Lord's Supper in 1 Cor. xi. 23ff. The report is introduced by the words, "For I received from the Lord that which also I delivered unto you." What does Paul mean by the expression "received from the Lord"? Does he mean that the information was given him directly by the risen Christ, or that he received it by ordinary word of mouth from the eyewitnesses? The former interpretation has been favored in the first place by some who occupy a strictly supernaturalistic point of view, to whom therefore it does not seem strange that the risen Christ should give to His apostle even detailed information about past events; it has also been favored by some who start from naturalistic presuppositions, and, regarding Paul as a mystic and a visionary, seek to separate him as far as possible from historical tradition about Jesus. But from either of these two points of view the interpretation is unsatisfactory. Why should the risen Christ give to His apostle detailed information which could be obtained perfectly well by ordinary inquiry from the eyewitnesses? Such revelation would be unlike the other miracles of the Bible. God does not rend the heaven to reveal what can be learned just as well by ordinary word of mouth. But this interpretation is equally unsatisfactory from the naturalistic point of view. Did Paul really suppose the risen Christ to have given him all this detailed information about the night of the betrayal and the rest? How could such a visionary experience be explained? The only possible answer, on naturalistic presuppositions, would be that the vision merely made use of materials which were already in Paul's mind; Paul already had information from the eyewitnesses about the Supper, but after he had forgotten whence he had received the information it welled up again from his subconscious life in the form of a vision. This explanation involves a psychological absurdity. The area of Paul's consciousness was not so limited as it is represented in modern reconstructions as being. If Paul received information from the eyewitnesses about what Jesus said and did on the night of the betrayal, we can be sure that he remembered the information and remembered where he had got it. It was not necessary for him to receive it all over again in a vision.

There are therefore serious *a priori* objections against finding in the words "received from the Lord" in 1 Cor. xi. 23 a reference to direct revelation. But this interpretation is not really favored by the words as they stand. The word "from," in the clause "I received from the Lord," is not the only word used for "from" after the word "received"; this word seems to indicate not the immediate but the ultimate source of what is received.[1] Furthermore, the word "received" [2] in 1 Cor. xv. 3 certainly refers to ordinary information obtained from eyewitnesses; it is natural therefore to find a similar usage of the word in 1 Cor. xi. 23. It is natural to interpret one passage after the analogy of the other. In 1 Cor. xv. 3ff. Paul is certainly appealing to ordinary tradition; probably, therefore, he is also doing so in 1 Cor. xi. 23ff. The report of the institution of the Lord's Supper is thus to be added to those passages which contain definite citations of the words of Jesus.

This report also belongs with those passages in the Epistles which attest knowledge of the details of Jesus' life. It is sometimes said that Paul is interested only in two facts about Jesus, the death and the resurrection. Yet in 1 Cor. xi. 23 he refers even to such a detail as the betrayal, and fixes the time of its occurrence—"the night in which He was betrayed." Other details about the life of Jesus may be gleaned from the Epistles. Jesus, according to Paul, was a Jew, He was descended from David, He was subject to the Mosaic Law, He had brothers, of whom one is named, He carried on a ministry for the Jews (Rom. xv. 8). With regard to the crucifixion and resurrection, moreover, Paul was interested not merely in the bare facts themselves; he was also interested in the details connected with them. Thus in 1 Cor. xv. 4 he mentions the burial of Jesus as having formed a part of his fundamental missionary preaching; and he also gives in the same connection an extended list of appearances of the risen Christ. It is possible that when Paul writes to the Galatians that Jesus Christ crucified had been pictured or placarded before their eyes (Gal. iii. 1), he is referring, not merely to the

---

[1] ἀπό is here used, not παρά.

[2] παρέλαβον.

forcibleness with which the one fact of Christ's death was proclaimed in Galatia, but also to the vividness with which the story was told in detail. So vivid was the story of the crucifixion as Paul told it in Galatia that it was as though the Galatians had before their eyes a great picture of Jesus on the cross.

Moreover, the references of Paul to Jesus' life concern not merely details; some of them also attest warm appreciation of Jesus' character. The character of Jesus is indeed, according to Paul, exhibited primarily by the great central act of love by which He came to earth to die for the salvation of men. In Phil. ii. 5ff., the unselfishness of Christ, which is held up for imitation by the Philippian Christians, is found no doubt primarily in the incarnation and in the Cross; in Gal. ii. 20, the love of Christ, upon which the faith and the gratitude of believers are based, is found in the one great fact of Christ's death ("who loved me and gave himself for me"). But there are also passages in the Epistles which show that Paul was impressed with the character of Jesus not only as it was manifested by the incarnation and by the atoning death, but also as it appeared in the daily life of Jesus throughout His earthly ministry. The plainest of such passages, perhaps; are 2 Cor. x. 1 and Rom. xv. 2, 3. When Paul speaks of the meekness and gentleness of Christ, he refers evidently to the impression which Jesus made upon His contemporaries; and when he says that Christ "pleased not himself" but bore reproaches patiently, he is evidently thinking not only of the gracious acts of incarnation and atonement but also of the conduct of Jesus from day to day. In 2 Cor. viii. 9 ("though He was rich yet for your sakes He became poor"), although the reference may be primarily to the poverty of any human life as compared with the glories of the preëxistent Christ, yet the peculiar choice of words is probably due to the details of Jesus' life of hardship; Paul would hardly have spoken in this way if Jesus while He was on earth had lived in the magnificence of an earthly kingdom. Even in Phil. ii. 7, though the "form of a servant" refers primarily to human existence as distinguished from the glories of heaven, yet there seems to be also an impression of the special humility and poverty of Jesus' earthly life; and the Cross is put as the climax of an obedience which appeared also in Jesus' life as a whole (verse 8). Back of these passages there lies warm appreciation of Jesus' character as it appeared in the days of His flesh. Imitation of Christ (1 Thess. i. 6; 1 Cor. xi. 1) had its due place in the life and teaching of Paul, and that imitation was founded not only upon one act, but upon many acts, of the Lord. When Paul speaks of his own life of constant self-sacrifice, in which he seeks not his own comfort but the salvation of others, as being led in imitation of Christ (1 Cor. x. 32-xi. 1), he has before his mind the lineaments of just that Jesus who is known to us in the Gospels—that Jesus who had not where to lay His head, who went about doing good, and who preached the gospel to the poor.

Thus the paucity of references in the Pauline Epistles to the teaching and example of Jesus has sometimes been exaggerated. The Epistles attest considerable knowledge of the details of Jesus' life, and warm appreciation of His character.

Undoubtedly, moreover, Paul knew far more about Jesus than he has seen fit, in the Epistles, to tell. It must always be remembered that the Epistles do not contain the missionary preaching of Paul; they are addressed to Christians, in whose case much of the primary instruction had already been given. Some things are omitted from the Epistles, therefore, not because they were unimportant, but on the contrary just because they were fundamental; instruction about them had to be given at the very beginning and except for special reasons did not need to be repeated. Except for certain misunderstandings which had arisen at Corinth, for example, Paul would never have set forth in his Epistles the testimony by which the fact of the resurrection of Jesus was established; yet that testimony, he says, was fundamental in his missionary preaching. If it were not for the errorists at Corinth we should never have had the all-important passage about the appearances of the risen Christ. It is appalling to reflect what far-reaching conclusions would in that case have been drawn by modern scholars from the silence of Paul. So it is also with the account of the institution of the Lord's Supper in 1 Cor. xi. 23ff. That account is inserted in the Epistles only because of certain abuses which had happened to arise at Corinth. Elsewhere Paul says absolutely nothing about the institution of the Supper; indeed, in the Epistles other than 1 Corinthians he says nothing about the Supper at all. Yet the Lord's Supper was undoubtedly

celebrated everywhere in the Pauline churches, and no doubt
was grounded everywhere in an account of its institution.
Thus the resurrection appearances and the institution of the
Lord's Supper, despite the fact that they were absolutely fundamental in Paul's teaching, appear each only once in the
Epistles.   May there not then have been other things just as
prominent in Paul's teaching which are not mentioned at all?
These two things are mentioned only because of the misunderstandings that had arisen with regard to them.   Certain
other things just as important may be omitted from the Epistles only because in their case no misunderstandings had happened to arise.   It must always be remembered that the Epistles
of Paul are addressed to special needs of the churches.   It
cannot be argued, therefore, that what is not mentioned in the
Epistles was not known to the apostle at all.

Thus the incidental character of Paul's references to the
life and teaching of Jesus shows clearly that Paul knew
far more than he has seen fit in the Epistles to tell.   The
references make the impression of being detached bits taken
from a larger whole.   When, for example, Paul says that the
institution of the Lord's Supper took place on the night in
which Jesus was betrayed, he presupposes on the part of his
readers an account of the betrayal, and hence an account of the
traitor and of his position among the apostles.   So it is in
other cases where Paul refers to the life and teaching of
Jesus.   The references can be explained only as presupposing a
larger fund of information about the words and deeds of Jesus.
Unquestionably Paul included in his fundamental teaching an
account of what Jesus said and did.

Indeed, if he had not done so, he would have involved
himself in absurdity.   As J. Weiss has pointed out with admirable acuteness, a missionary preaching which demanded faith
in Jesus without telling what sort of person Jesus was would
have been preposterous.[1]   The hearers of Paul were asked to
stake their salvation upon the redeeming work of Jesus.   But
who was this Jesus?   The question could scarcely be avoided.
Other redeemers, in the pagan religion of the time, were protected from such questions; they were protected by the mists
of antiquity; investigations about them were obviously out of

[1] J. Weiss, *Das älteste Evangelium*, 1903, pp. 33-39.

place. But Paul had given up the advantages of such vague-
ness. The redeemer whom he proclaimed was one of his own
contemporaries, a Jew who had lived but a few years before
and had died the death of a criminal. Investigation of this
Jesus was perfectly possible; His brothers, even, were still
alive. Who was He then? Did He suffer justly on the cross?
Or was He the Righteous One? Such questions could hardly
be avoided. And as a matter of fact they were not avoided.
The incidental references in the Epistles, scanty though they
are, are sufficient to show that an account of the words and
deeds of Jesus formed an important part of the teaching of
Paul.

The presumption is, therefore, that Paul was a true disciple
of Jesus. He regarded himself as a disciple; he was so regarded by his contemporaries; he made use of Jesus' teaching
and example. But is this presumption justified? Was it
the real Jesus whom Paul followed? The question can be
answered only by a comparison of what is known about Paul
with what is known about Jesus.

But at the very beginning of the comparison, a fundamental
difficulty arises. How may Jesus be known? Paul is known,
through his own letters. But how about Jesus? The sources
of information about Jesus are the four Gospels. But are the
Gospels trustworthy?

If they are trustworthy, then it will probably be admitted
that Paul was a true disciple of Jesus. For the Gospels,
taken as a whole, present a Jesus like in essentials to that
divine Lord who was sum and substance of the life of Paul.
The Jesus of the Gospels is no mere prophet, no mere inspired
teacher of righteousness, no mere revealer or interpreter of
God. He is, on the contrary, a supernatural person; a heavenly Redeemer come to earth for the salvation of men. So much
is usually being admitted to-day. Whatever may have been
the real facts about Jesus, the Gospels present a supernatural
Jesus. This representation is contained not merely in one of
the Gospels; it is contained in all of them. The day is past
when the divine Christ of John could be confronted with a
human Christ of Mark. On the contrary, Mark and John, it
is now maintained, differ only in degree; Mark as well as John,
even though it should be supposed that he does so less clearly

and less consistently, presents a Jesus similar in important respects to the divine Redeemer of the Epistles of Paul.[1]

Thus if Paul be compared with the Jesus of the Gospels, there is full agreement between the two. The Jesus of all the Gospels is a supernatural person; the Jesus of all the Gospels is a Redeemer. "The Son of Man," according to the shortest and if modern criticism be accepted the earliest of the Gospels, "came not to be ministered unto, but to minister, and to give his life a ransom for many" (Mk. x. 45). But it is not necessary to depend upon details. The very choice of material in the Gospels points to the same conclusion; the Gospels like the Epistles of Paul are more interested in the death of Jesus than in the details of His life. And for the same reason. The Gospels, like the Epistles of Paul, are interested in the death of Jesus because it was a ransom from sin.

But this similarity of the Jesus of the Gospels to the Christ of the Pauline Epistles has led sometimes, not to the recognition of Paul as a disciple of Jesus, but to the hypothesis that the Gospels are dependent upon Paul. If the Gospels are introducing into their picture of Jesus elements derived not from the real Jesus but from the mythical Christ of the Epistles, then of course they will display similarity to the Epistles; but such similarity will scarcely be very significant. In comparing the Epistles with the Gospels, the historian will then be comparing not Paul with Jesus, but Paul with Paul.

If, therefore, Paul is to be compared with Jesus, it is said, those elements which are derived from Paul must first be separated from the Gospels. Even after this separation has been accomplished, however, there remains in the Gospel picture of Jesus a certain amount of similarity to the Pauline Christ; it is generally admitted that the process by which Jesus was raised to the position of a heavenly being was begun before the appearance of Paul and was continued in some quarters in more or less independence of him. Thus if Paul is to be compared with the real Jesus, as distinguished from the Christ of Christian faith, the historian, it is said, must first separate from the Gospel picture not merely those details which were derived distinctly from Paul, but also the whole of the super-

[1] See, for example, J. Weiss, *Das Urchristentum*, 1914-1917, pp. 540, 547, 548.

natural element.[1] Mere literary criticism will not accomplish the task; for even the earliest sources which can be distinguished in the Gospels seem to lift Jesus above the level of ordinary humanity and present Him not merely as an example for faith but also as the object of faith.[2] Even in the earliest sources, therefore, the historian must distinguish genuine tradition from dogmatic accretions; he must separate the natural from the supernatural, the believable from the unbelievable; he must seek to remove from the genuine figure of the Galilean prophet the tawdry ornamentation which has been hung about him by naïve and unintelligent admirers.

Thus the Jesus who is to be compared with Paul, according to the modern naturalistic theory, is not the Jesus of the Gospels; he is a Jesus who can be rediscovered only through a critical process within the Gospels. And that critical process is very difficult. It is certainly no easy matter to separate natural and supernatural in the Gospel picture of Jesus, for the two are inextricably intertwined. In pulling up the tares, the historian is in danger of pulling up the wheat as well; in the removal of the supernatural elements from the story of Jesus, the whole of the story is in danger of being destroyed. Certain radical spirits are not afraid of the consequence; since the Jesus of the Gospels, they say, is a supernatural person, He is not a real person; no such person as this Jesus ever lived on earth. Such radicalism, of course, is absurd. The Jesus of the Gospels is certainly not the product of invention or of myth; He is rooted too deep in historical conditions; He towers too high above those who by any possibility could have produced Him. But the radical denials of the historicity of Jesus are not without interest. They have at least called attention to the arbitrariness with which the separation of historical from unhistorical has been carried on in the production of the "liberal Jesus."

But suppose the separation has been completed; suppose the historical Jesus has been discovered beneath the gaudy colors which had almost hopelessly defaced His portrait. Even then

---

[1] For what follows, see, in addition to the paper mentioned at the be ginning of the chapter, "History and Faith," in *Princeton Theological Review*, xiii, 1915, pp. 337-351.

[2] See Denney, *Jesus and the Gospel*, 1909.

the troubles of the historian are not at an end. For this historical Jesus, this human Jesus of modern liberalism, is a monstrosity; there is a contradiction at the very center of His being. The contradiction is produced by His Messianic consciousness. The human Jesus of modern liberalism, the pure and humble teacher of righteousness, the one who kept His own person out of His message and merely asked men to have faith in God like His faith—this Jesus of modern liberalism thought that He was to come with the clouds of heaven and be the instrument in judging the earth! If Jesus was pure and unselfish and of healthy mind, how could He have applied to Himself the tremendous conception of the transcendent Messiah? By some the problem is avoided. Some, like Wrede, deny that Jesus ever presented Himself as the Messiah; others, like Bousset, are at least moving in the same direction. But such radicalism cannot be carried out. The Messianic element in the consciousness of Jesus is rooted too deep in the sources ever to be removed by any critical process. It is established also by the subsequent development. If Jesus never thought Himself to be the Messiah and never presented Himself as such, how did His disciples come to regard Him as the Messiah after His death? Why did they not simply say, "Despite His death, the Kingdom of God is coming?" Why did they say rather, "Despite His death, He is the Messiah?" [1] They could only have done so if Jesus had already presented Himself to them as Messiah when He had been with them on earth.

In recent criticism, such radicalism as that which has just been discussed is usually avoided. The presence of the Messianic element in the consciousness of Jesus cannot altogether be denied. Sometimes, indeed, that element is even made the determining factor in all of Jesus' teaching. So it is with the hypothesis of "consistent eschatology" of A. Schweitzer and others.[2] According to that hypothesis Jesus expected the Kingdom of God to come in a catastrophic way in the very year in which he was carrying on His ministry in Galilee, and all His teaching was intended to be a preparation for the great catastrophe. Even the ethic of Jesus, therefore, is thought to have been constructed in view of the approaching

---

[1] J. Weiss, "Das Problem der Entstehung des Christentums," in *Archiv für Religionswissenschaft*, xvi, 1913, p. 456.
[2] A. Schweitzer, *Geschichte der Leben-Jesu-Forschung*, 1913, pp. 390-443.

end of the world, and is thus regarded as unsuitable for a permanent world order. This hypothesis not only accepts the Messianic consciousness of Jesus, but in one direction at least it even exaggerates the implications of that consciousness.

Usually, however, this extreme also is avoided, and the historian pursues, rather, a policy of palliation. Jesus did come to regard Himself as the Messiah, it is said, but He did so only late in His ministry and almost against His will. When He found that the people were devoted to sin, and that He alone was fighting God's battle, He came to regard Himself as God's chosen instrument in the establishment of the Kingdom. Thus He had a tremendous consciousness of a mission. But the only category in which He could express that consciousness of a mission was the category of Messiahship. In one form, indeed, that category was unsuitable; Jesus would have nothing to do with the political aspirations associated with the expected king of David's line. But the expectation of the Messiah existed also in another form; the Messiah was sometimes regarded, not as a king of David's line, but as the heavenly Son of Man alluded to in Daniel and more fully described in the Similitudes of Enoch. This transcendent form of Messiahship, therefore, was the form which Jesus used. But the form, it is maintained, is a matter of indifference to us, and it was not really essential to Jesus; what was really essential was Jesus' consciousness of nearness to God.

Such palliative measures will not really solve the problem. The problem is a moral and psychological problem. How could a pure and holy prophet of righteousness, one whose humility and sanity have made an indelible impression upon all subsequent generations—how could such a one lapse so far from the sobriety and sanity of His teaching as to regard Himself as the heavenly Son of Man who was to be the instrument in judging the world? The difficulty is felt by all thoughtful students who proceed upon naturalistic principles. There is to such students, as Heitmüller says, something almost uncanny about Jesus.[1] And the difficulty is not removed by putting the genesis of the Messianic consciousness late in Jesus' life. Whether late or early, Jesus did regard Himself as the Messiah, did regard Himself as the one who was to come with the clouds of heaven. There lies the problem. How

[1] Heitmüller, *Jesus*, 1913, p. 71.

could Jesus, with His humility and sobriety and strength, ever have lapsed so far from the path of sanity as to assume the central place in the Kingdom of God?

Here, again, radical minds have drawn the logical conclusions. The Messianic consciousness, they say, is an example of megalomania; Jesus, they say, was insane. Such is said to be the diagnosis of certain alienists. And the diagnosis need cause no alarm. Very likely it is correct. But the Jesus who is being investigated by the alienists is not the Jesus of the New Testament. The liberal Jesus, if he ever existed, may have been insane. But that is not the Jesus whom the Christian loves. The alienists are investigating a man who thought he was divine and was not divine; about one who thought He was divine and was divine they have obviously nothing to say.

Two difficulties, therefore, face the reconstruction of the liberal Jesus. In the first place, it is difficult to separate the natural from the supernatural in the Gospel picture of Jesus; and in the second place, after the separation has been accomplished, the human Jesus who is left is found to be a monstrosity, with a contradiction at the very center of His being. Such a Jesus, it may fairly be maintained, could never have existed on earth.

But suppose He did exist, suppose the psychological impossibilities of His character be ignored. Even then the difficulties of the historian are not overcome. Another question remains. How did this human Jesus ever come to give place to the superhuman Jesus of the New Testament? The transition evidently occurred at a very early time. It is complete in the Epistles of Paul. And within Paul's experience it was certainly no late development; on the contrary it was evidently complete at the very beginning of his Christian life; the Jesus in whom he trusted at the time of his conversion was certainly the heavenly Christ of the Epistles. But the conversion occurred only a very few years, at the most, after the crucifixion of Jesus. Moreover, there is in the Pauline Epistles not the slightest trace of a conflict between the heavenly Christ of Paul and any "other Jesus" of the primitive Jerusalem Church; apparently the Christ of Paul was also the Christ of those who had walked and talked with Jesus of Nazareth. Such is the evidence of the Epistles. It is confirmed by the Gospels. Like Paul, the Gospels present no mere teacher of righteousness, but a heavenly Redeemer. Yet the Gospels make the impression of being independent of Paul. Everywhere the Jesus that they present is most strikingly similar to the Christ of Paul; but nowhere—not even where Jesus is made to teach the redemptive significance of His death (Mk. x. 45)—is there the slightest evidence of literary dependence upon the Epistles. Thus the liberal Jesus, if he ever existed, has disappeared from the pages of history; all the sources agree in presenting a heavenly Christ. How shall such agreement be explained?

It might conceivably be explained by the appearances of the risen Christ. If, at the very beginning of the Church's life, Jesus appeared to His disciples, after His death, alive and in heavenly glory, it is conceivable that that experience might have originated the lofty New Testament conception of Jesus' person. But what in turn caused that experience itself? On naturalistic principles the appearances of the risen Christ can be explained only by an impression which the disciples already had of the majesty of Jesus' person. If they had listened to lofty claims of Jesus like those which are recorded in the Gospels, if they had witnessed miracles like the walking on the water or the feeding of the five thousand, then, conceivably, though not probably, they might have come to believe that so great a person could not be holden of death, and this belief might have been sufficient, without further miracle, to induce the pathological experiences in which they thought they saw Him alive after His passion. But if the miraculous be removed from the life of Jesus, a double portion of the miraculous must be heaped up upon the appearances. The smaller be the Jesus whom the disciples had known in Galilee, the more unaccountable becomes the experience which caused them to believe in His resurrection. By one path or another, therefore, the historian of Christian origins is pushed off from the safe ground of the phenomenal world toward the abyss of supernaturalism. To account for the faith of the early Church, the supernatural must be found either in the life of Jesus on earth, or else in the appearances of the risen Christ. But if the supernatural is found in one place, there is no objection to finding it in both places. And in both places it is found by the whole New Testament.

Three difficulties, therefore, beset the reconstruction of

the "liberal Jesus." In the first place, it is difficult to disengage His picture from the miraculous elements which have defaced it in the Gospels; in the second place, when the supposed historical Jesus has been reconstructed, there is a moral contradiction at the center of His being, caused by His lofty claims; in the third place, it is hard to see how, in the thinking of the early disciples, the purely human Jesus gave place without the slightest struggle to the heavenly Christ of the Pauline Epistles and of the whole New Testament.

But suppose all the difficulties have been removed. Suppose a human Jesus has been reconstructed. What is the result of comparing that human Jesus with Paul? At first sight there seems to be nothing but contradiction. But closer examination discloses points of agreement. The agreement between Jesus and Paul extends even to those elements in the Gospel account of Jesus which are accepted by modern naturalistic criticism.

In the first place, Jesus and Paul present the same view of the Kingdom of God. The term "kingdom of God" is not very frequent in the Epistles; but it is used as though familiar to the readers, and when it does occur, it has the same meaning as in the teaching of Jesus. The similarity appears, in the first place, in a negative feature—both in Jesus and in Paul, the idea of the Kingdom is divorced from all political and materialistic associations. That fact may seem to us to be a matter of course. But in the Judaism of the first century it was far from being a matter of course. On the contrary, it meant nothing less than a revolution in thought and in life. How did Paul, the patriot and the Pharisee, come to separate the thought of the Kingdom from political associations? How did he come to do so even if he had come to think that the Messiah had already appeared? How did he come to do so unless he was influenced in some way by the teaching of Jesus? But the similarity is not merely negative. In positive aspects also, the Kingdom of God in Paul is similar to that which appears in the teaching of Jesus. Both in Jesus and in Paul, the implications of entrance are ethical. "Or know ye not," says Paul, "that the unrighteous shall not inherit the kingdom of God" (1 Cor. vi. 9). Then follows, after these words, as in Gal. v. 19-21, a long list of sins which exclude a man from participation in the Kingdom. Paul is here continuing faithfully the teaching of Him who said, "Repent ye; for the kingdom of heaven is at hand." Finally both in Jesus and in Paul the Kingdom appears partly as present and partly as future. In the above passages from Galatians and 1 Corinthians, for example, and in 1 Cor. xv. 50, it is future; whereas in such passages as Rom. xiv. 17 ("for the kingdom of God is not eating and drinking but righteousness and peace and joy in the Holy Spirit"), the present aspect is rather in view. The same two aspects of the Kingdom appear also in the teaching of Jesus; all attempts at making Jesus' conception thoroughly eschatological have failed. Both in Jesus and in Paul, therefore, the Kingdom of God is both transcendent and ethical. Both in Jesus and in Paul, finally, the coming of the Kingdom means joy as well as judgment. When Paul says that the Kingdom of God is "righteousness and peace and joy in the Holy Ghost," he is like Jesus not merely in word but in the whole spirit of the message; Jesus also proclaimed the coming of the Kingdom as a "gospel."

In the second place, Paul is like Jesus in his doctrine of the fatherhood of God. That doctrine, it will probably be admitted, was characteristic of Jesus; indeed the tendency in certain quarters is to regard it as the very sum and substance of all that Jesus said. Certainly no parallel to Jesus' presentation of God as Father has been found in extra-Christian literature. The term "father" is indeed applied to God here and there in the Old Testament. But in the Old Testament it is usually in relation to the people of Israel that God is thought of as Father rather than in relation to the individual. Even in the Old Testament, it is true, the conception of the fatherhood of God is not without importance. The consciousness of belonging to God's chosen people and thus being under God's fatherly care was immensely valuable for the life of the individual Israelite; it was no mere product of an unsatisfying state religion like the religions of Greece or Rome. There was preparation in Old Testament revelation, here as elsewhere, for the coming of the Messiah. In Jewish literature outside of the Old Testament, moreover, and in rabbinical sources, the conception of God as Father is not altogether absent.[1] But it appears comparatively seldom, and it lacks altogether the true content of Jesus' teaching. Despite all

[1] Bousset, *Die Religion des Judentums*, 2te Aufl., 1906, pp. 432-434.

previous uses of the word "father" as applied to God, Jesus was ushering in a new era when He taught His disciples to say, "Our Father which art in heaven."

This conception of the fatherhood of God appears in Paul in just the same way as in Jesus. In Paul as well as in Jesus it is not something to be turned to occasionally; on the contrary it is one of the constituent elements of the religious life. It is no wonder that the words, "God our Father," appear regularly at the beginnings of the Epistles. The fatherhood of God in Paul is not something to be argued about or defended; it is altogether a matter of course. But it has not lost, through repetition, one whit of its freshness. The name "Father" applied to God in Paul is more than a bare title; it is the welling up of the depths of the soul. "Abba, Father" on the lips of Paul's converts was exactly the same, not only in form but also in deepest import, as the word which Jesus first taught His disciples when they said to Him, "Lord, teach us to pray."

But the fatherhood of God in Paul is like the teaching of Jesus in even more definite ways than in the fervor of the religious life which it evokes. It is also like Jesus' teaching in being the possession, not of the world, but of the household of faith. If, indeed, the fatherhood of God in Jesus' teaching were like the fatherhood of God in modern liberalism—a relationship which God sustains toward men as men—then it would be as far removed as possible from the teaching of Paul. But as a matter of fact, both Paul and Jesus reserved the term Father for the relation in which God stands to the disciples of Jesus. One passage, indeed (Matt. v. 45; Luke vi. 35), has been quoted as making God the Father of all men. But only by a strange misinterpretation. It is strange how in the day of our boasted grammatico-historical exegesis, so egregious an error can be allowed to live. The prejudices of the reader have triumphed here over all exegetical principles; a vague modernism has been attributed to the sternest, as well as most merciful, Prophet who ever walked upon earth. When Jesus says, "Love your enemies, and pray for them that persecute you; that ye may be sons of your Father who is in heaven: for he maketh his sun to rise on the evil and the good, and sendeth rain on the just and the unjust," He certainly does not mean that God is the Father of all men both evil and good.

God cares for all, but He is not said to be the Father of all. On the contrary, it may almost be said that the very point of the passage is that God cares for all although He is not the Father of all. That it is which makes Him the example for those who are to do good not merely to friends or brothers but also to enemies.

This interpretation does not mean that God does not stand toward all men in a relation analogous to that of a father to his children; it does not mean that He does not love all or care for all. But it does mean that however close may be the relationship which God sustains to all men, the lofty term Father is reserved for a relationship which is far more intimate still. Jesus extends to all men those common blessings which the modern preacher sums up in the term "fatherhood of God"; but He extends to His own disciples not only those blessings but infinitely more. It is not the men of the world—not the "publicans," not the "Gentiles"—who can say, according to the teaching of Jesus, "Our Father which art in Heaven." Rather it is the little group of Jesus' disciples—which little group, however, all without exception are freely invited to join.

So it is exactly also in the teaching of Paul. God stands, according to Paul, in a vital relation to all men. He is the author of the being of all; He cares for all; He has planted His law in the hearts of all. He stands thus in a relation toward all which is analogous to that of father to child. The Book of Acts is quite in accord with the Epistles when it makes Paul say of all men, "For we are also His offspring." But in Paul just as in Jesus the lofty term "Father" is reserved for a more intimate relationship. Paul accepts all the truth of natural religion; all the truth that reappears in the vague liberalism of modern times. But he adds to it the truth of the gospel. Those are truly sons of God, he says, who have been received by adoption into God's household, and in whose hearts God's Spirit cries, "Abba, Father."

There was nothing narrow about such a gospel; for the door of the household of faith was opened wide to all. Jesus had died in order to open that door, and the apostle went up and down the world, enduring peril upon peril in order to bring men in. There was need for such service, because of sin. Neither in Jesus nor in Paul is sin covered up, nor the necessity of a great transformation concealed. Jesus came not to reveal to men that they were already children of God, but to make them God's children by His redeeming work.

In the third place, Paul is like Jesus in presenting a doctrine of grace. Of course he is like the Jesus of the Gospels; for the Jesus of the Gospels declared that the Son of Man came to give His life a ransom for many. But He is even like the Jesus of modern reconstruction. Even the liberal Jesus taught a doctrine of grace. He taught, it for example, in the parables of the laborers in the vineyard and of the servant coming in from the field. In those two parables Jesus expressed His opposition to a religion of works, a religion which can open an account with God and seek to obtain salvation by merit.[1] Salvation, according to Jesus, is a matter of God's free grace; it is something which God gives to whom He will. The same great doctrine really runs all through the teaching of Jesus; it is the root of His opposition to the scribes and Pharisees; it determines the confidence with which He taught His disciples to draw near to God. But it is the same doctrine, exactly, which appears in Paul. The Paul who combated the legalists in Galatia, like the Jesus who combated the scribes and Pharisees, was contending for a God of grace.

Let it not be objected that Jesus maintained also the expectation of a judgment. For in this particular also He was followed by Paul. Paul also, despite his doctrine of grace, expected that the Christians would stand before the judgment-seat. And it may be remembered in passing that both in Jesus and in Paul the judgment-seat is a judgment-seat of Christ.

In the fourth place, the ethical teaching of Paul is strikingly similar to that of Jesus. It is necessary only to point to the conception of love as the fulfilling of the law, and to the substitution for external rules of the great principles of justice and of mercy. These things may seem to us to be matters of course. But they were not matters of course in the Jewish environment of Paul. Similarity in this field between Jesus and Paul can hardly be a matter of chance. Many resemblances have been pointed out in detail between the ethical

[1] Compare W. Morgan, *The Religion and Theology of Paul,* 1917, p. 155: "The essential import of Paul's doctrine [of justification by faith] is all contained in the two parables of the Pharisee and the publican and the servant coming in from the field."

teaching of Jesus and that of Paul. But the most important
is the one which is most obvious, and which just for that reason has sometimes escaped notice. Paul and Jesus, in their
ethical teaching, are similar because of the details of what
they say; but they are still more similar because of what they
do not say. And they are similar in what they do not say
despite the opposition of their countrymen. Many parallels for
words of Jesus may have been found in rabbinical sources. But
so much more, alas, is also found there. That oppressive plus
of triviality and formalism places an impassable gulf between
Jesus and the Jewish teachers. But Paul belongs with Jesus,
on the same side of the gulf. In his ethic there is no formalism, no triviality, no casuistry—there is naught but "love,
joy, peace, longsuffering, kindness, goodness, faithfulness,
meekness, self-control." What has become of all the rest?
Was it removed by the genius of Paul? It is strange that
two such men of genius should have arisen independently and
at the same time. Or was the terrible plus of Pharisaic formalism and triviality burned away from Paul when the light
shone around him on the way to Damascus and he fell at the
feet of the great Teacher?

Points of contact between Jesus and Paul have just been
pointed out in detail, and the list of resemblances could be
greatly increased. The likeness of Paul to Jesus extends even
to those features which appear in the Jesus of modern liberalism. What is more impressive, however, than all similarity in
detail is the similarity in the two persons taken each as a
whole. The Gospels are more than a collection of sayings
and anecdotes; the Pauline Epistles are more than a collection
of reasoned discussions. In the Gospels, a person is revealed,
and another person in the Epistles. And the two persons
belong together. It is impossible to establish that fact fully
by detailed argument any more than it is possible to explain
exactly why any two persons are friends to-day. But the
fact is plain to any sympathetic reader. The writer of the
Pauline Epistles would have been at home in the company
of Jesus of Nazareth.

What then was the true relation between Paul and Jesus?
It has been shown that Paul regarded himself as a disciple of
Jesus, that he was so regarded by those who had been Jesus'
friends, that he had abundant opportunity for acquainting

himself with Jesus' words and deeds, that he does refer to them occasionally, that he could have done so oftener if he had desired, that the imitation of Jesus found a place in his life, and that his likeness to Jesus extends even to those elements in Jesus' life and teaching which are accepted by modern naturalistic criticism as authentic. At this point the problem is left by the great mass of recent investigators. Wrede is thought to be refuted already; the investigator triumphantly writes his Q. E. D., and passes on to something else.

But in reality the problem has not even been touched. It has been shown that the influence of Jesus upon Paul was somewhat greater than Wrede supposed. But that does not make Paul a disciple of Jesus. The true relationships of a man are determined not by things that lie on the periphery of his life, but by what is central [1]—central both in his own estimation and in his influence upon subsequent generations. And what was central in Paul was certainly not the imitation of Jesus. At that point, Wrede was entirely correct; he has never really been silenced by the chorus of protest with which his startling little book was received. It is futile, therefore, to point to the influence of Jesus upon Paul in detail. Such a method may be useful in correcting exaggerations, but it does not touch the real question. The plain fact remains that if imitation of Jesus had been central in the life of Paul, as it is central, for example, in modern liberalism, then the Epistles would be full of the words and deeds of Jesus. It is insufficient to point to the occasional character of the Epistles. No doubt the Epistles are addressed to special needs; no doubt Paul knew far more about Jesus than in the Epistles he has found occasion to tell. But there are passages in the Epistles where the current of Paul's religious life runs full and free, where even after the lapse of centuries, even through the dull medium of the printed page, it sweeps the heart of the sympathetic reader on with it in a mighty flood. And those passages are not concerned with the details of Jesus' earthly life. They are, rather, the great theological passages of the Epistles— the second chapter of Galatians, the fifth chapter of 2 Corinthians, and the eighth chapter of Romans. In these chapters, religion and theology are blended in a union which no critical

[1] Wrede, *Paulus,* 1904, p. 93 (English Translation, *Paul,* 1907, p. 161).

analysis can ever possibly dissolve; these passages reveal the very center of Paul's life.

The details of Jesus' earthly ministry no doubt had an important place in the thinking of Paul. But they were important, not as an end in themselves, but as a means to an end. They revealed the character of Jesus; they showed why He was worthy to be trusted. But they did not show what He had done for Paul. The story of Jesus revealed what Jesus had done for others: He had healed the sick; He had given sight to the blind; He had raised the dead. But for Paul He had done something far greater than all these things—for Paul He had died.

The religion of Paul, in other words, is a religion of redemption. Jesus, according to Paul, came to earth not to say something, but to do something; He was primarily not a teacher, but a Redeemer. He came, not to teach men how to live, but to give them a new life through His atoning death. He was, indeed, also a teacher, and Paul attended to His teaching. But His teaching was all in vain unless it led to the final acceptance of His redemptive work. Not the details of Jesus' life, therefore, but the redemptive acts of death and resurrection are at the center of the religion of Paul. The teaching and example of Jesus, according to Paul, are valuable only as a means to an end, valuable in order that through a revelation of Jesus' character saving faith may be induced, and valuable thereafter in order that the saving work may be brought to its fruition in holy living. But all that Jesus said and did was for the purpose of the Cross. "He loved me," says Paul, "and gave Himself for me." There is the heart and core of the religion of Paul.

Jesus, according to Paul, therefore, was not a teacher, but a Redeemer. But was Paul right? Was Jesus really a Redeemer, or was He only a teacher? If He was only a teacher, then Paul was no true follower of His. For in that case, Paul has missed the true import of Jesus' life. Compared with that one central error, small importance is to be attributed to the influence which Jesus may have exerted upon Paul here and there. Wrede, therefore, was exactly right in his formulation of the question. Paul regarded Jesus as a Redeemer. If Jesus was not a Redeemer, then Paul was no true follower of Jesus, but the founder of a new religion. The liberal theologians have tried to avoid the issue. They have pointed out exaggerations; they have traced the influence of Jesus upon Paul in detail; they have distinguished religion from theology, and abandoning the theology of Paul they have sought to derive his religion from Jesus of Nazareth. It is all very learned and very eloquent. But it is also entirely futile. Despite the numerous monographs on "Jesus and Paul," Wrede was entirely correct. He was correct, that is, not in his conclusions, but in his statement of the question. He was correct in his central contention—Paul was no true disciple of the "liberal Jesus." If Jesus was what the liberal theologians represent Him as being—a teacher of righteousness, a religious genius, a guide on the way to God—then not Jesus but Paul was the true founder of historic Christianity. For historic Christianity, like the religion of Paul, is a religion of redemption.

Certainly the separation of religion from theology in Paul must be abandoned. Was it a mere theory when Paul said of Jesus Christ, "He loved me and gave Himself for me"? Was it merely theological speculation when he said, "One died for all, therefore all died; and he died for all, that they that live should no longer live unto themselves, but unto him who for their sakes died and rose again"? Was it mere theology when he said, "Far be it from me to glory save in the cross of our Lord Jesus Christ"? Was this mere theological speculation? Surely not. Surely it was religion—warm, living religion. If this was not true religion, then where can religion ever be found? But the passages just quoted are not passages which deal with the details of Jesus' life; they are not passages which deal with general principles of love and grace, and fatherliness and brotherliness. On the contrary, they deal with just the thing most distasteful to the modern liberal Church; they deal with the atoning death of the Lord Jesus Christ, by which He took our sins upon Him and bare them in His own body on the tree. The matter is perfectly plain. Religion in Paul does not exist apart from theology, and theology does not exist apart from religion. Christianity, according to Paul, is both a life and a doctrine—but logically the doctrine comes first. The life is the expression of the doctrine and not vice versa. Theology, as it appears in Paul, is not a product of Christian experience, but a setting forth of those facts by which Christian experience has been produced. If, then, the theology of Paul was derived from extra-Christian sources, his religion must be abandoned also. The whole of Paulinism is based upon the redemptive work of Jesus Christ.

Thus Paul was a true follower of Jesus if Jesus was a divine Redeemer, come from heaven to die for the sins of men; he was not a true follower of Jesus if Jesus was a mere revealer of the fatherhood of God. Paulinism was not based upon a Galilean prophet. It was based either upon the Son of God who came to earth for men's salvation and still holds communion with those who trust Him, or else it was based upon a colossal error. But if the latter alternative be adopted, the error was not only colossal, but also unaccountable. It is made more unaccountable by all that has been said above, all that the liberal theologians have helped to establish, about the nearness of Paul to Jesus. If Paul really stood so near to Jesus, if he really came under Jesus' influence, if he really was intimate with Jesus' friends, how could he have misinterpreted so completely the significance of Jesus' person; how could he have substituted for the teacher of righteousness who had really lived in Palestine the heavenly Redeemer of the Epistles? No satisfactory answer has yet been given. In the relation between Jesus and Paul the historian discovers a problem which forces him on toward a Copernican revolution in all his thinking, which leads him to ground his own salvation and the hope of this world no longer in millions of acts of sinful men or in the gradual progress of civilization, but simply and solely in one redemptive act of the Lord of Glory.

CHAPTER V
THE JEWISH ENVIRONMENT

CHAPTER V

Of the three ways in which, upon naturalistic principles, the genesis of the religion of Paul has been explained, one has been examined, and has been found wanting. Paulinism, it has been shown, was not based upon the Jesus of modern liberalism. If Jesus was simply a teacher of righteousness, a revealer of God, then the religion of Paul was not derived from Him. For the religion of Paul was a religion of redemption.

But if the religion of Paul was not derived from the Jesus of modern liberalism, whence was it derived? It may, of course, have been derived from the divine Redeemer; the Jesus whom Paul presupposes may have been the Jesus who actually lived in Palestine. But that explanation involves the intrusion of the supernatural into the course of history; it is therefore rejected by "the modern mind." Other explanations, therefore, are being sought. These other explanations are alike in that they derive the religion of Paul from sources independent of Jesus of Nazareth. Two such explanations have been proposed. According to one, the religion of Paul was derived from contemporary Judaism; according to the other, it was derived from the paganism of the Greco-Roman world. The present chapter will deal with the former of these two explanations—with the explanation which derives the religion of Paul from contemporary Judaism.

This explanation is connected especially with the names of Wrede [1] and Brückner.[2] It has, however, seldom been maintained in any exclusive way, but enters into combination with other hypotheses. Indeed, in itself it is obviously insufficient; it will hardly explain the idea of redemption in the religion of Paul. But it is thought to explain, if not the idea of

---

[1] See p. 26, footnote 2.
[2] See p. 27, footnote 1.

redemption, at least the conception of the Redeemer's person, and from the conception of the Redeemer's person the idea of redemption might in some way be derived. The hypothesis of Wrede and Brückner, in other words, seeks to explain not so much the soteriology as the Christology of Paul; it derives from the pre-Christian Jewish conception of the Messiah the Pauline conception of the heavenly Christ. In particular, it seeks to explain the matter-of-oourse way in which in the Epistles the Pauline Christ is everywhere presupposed but nowhere defended. Apparently Paul was not aware that his Christology might provoke dissent. This attitude is very difficult to explain on the basis of the ordinary liberal reconstruction; it is difficult to explain if the Pauline Christology was derived by a process of development from the historical Jesus. For if it had been so derived, its newness and revolutionary character would naturally have appeared. As a matter of fact, however, Paul does not regard it as anything new; he treats his doctrine of Christ as though it were firmly established and required no defense. How shall this confident attitude of the apostle be explained? It is to be explained, Wrede says, by the theology of contemporary Judaism. Paul was so confident that his conception of Christ could not be regarded as an innovation because as a matter of fact it was not an innovation; it was nothing but the pre-Christian Jewish notion of the Messiah. The Pauline conception of Christ was thus firmly fixed in the mind of Paul and in the minds of many of his contemporaries long before the event on the road to Damascus; all that happened at that time was the identification of the Christ whom Paul had believed in all along with Jesus of Nazareth, and that identification, because of the meagerness of Paul's knowledge of Jesus, did not really bring any fundamental change in the Christology itself. After the conversion as well as before it, the Christ of Paul was simply the Christ of the Jewish apocalypses.

In order that this hypothesis may be examined, it will be advisable to begin with a brief general survey of the Jewish environment of Paul. The survey will necessarily be of the most cursory character, and it will not be based upon original research. But it may serve to clear the way for the real question at issue. Fortunately the ground has been covered rather thoroughly by recent investigators. In dependence upon Schürer and Charles and others, even a layman may hope to arrive at the most obvious facts. And it is only the most obvious facts which need now be considered.

Three topics only will be discussed, and they only in the most cursory way. These three topics are (1) the divisions within Judaism, (2) the Law, (3) the Messiah.

The most obvious division within the Judaism of Paul's day is the division between the Judaism of Palestine and that of the Dispersion. The Jews of Palestine, for the most part, spoke Aramaic; those of the Dispersion spoke Greek. With the difference of language went no doubt in some cases a difference in habits of thought. But exaggerations should be avoided. Certainly it is a serious error to represent the Judaism of the Dispersion as being universally or even generally a "liberal" Judaism, inclined to break down the strict requirements of the Law. The vivid descriptions of the Book of Acts point in the opposite direction. Opposition to the Gentile mission of Paul prevailed among the Hellenists of the Dispersion as well as among the Hebrews of Palestine. On the whole, although no doubt here and there individuals were inclined to modify the requirements imposed upon proselytes, or even were influenced by the thought of the Gentile world, the Jews of the first century must be thought of as being a strangely unified people, devoted to the Mosaic Law and jealous of their God-given prerogatives.

At any rate, it is a grave error to explain the Gentile mission of Paul as springing by natural development from a liberal Judaism of the Dispersion. For even if such a liberal Judaism existed, Paul did not belong to it. He tells us in no uncertain terms that he was a "Hebrew," not a Hellenist; inwardly, therefore, despite his birth in Tarsus, he was a Jew of Palestine. No doubt the impressions received from the Greek city where he was born were of great importance in his preparation for his life-work; it was no mere chance, but a dispensation of God, that the apostle to the Gentiles spent his earliest years in a seat of Gentile culture. But it was Jerusalem rather than Tarsus which determined Paul's outlook upon life. At any rate, however great or however little was the influence of his boyhood home, Paul was not a "liberal" Jew; for he tells us that he was a Pharisee, more exceedingly zealous than his contemporaries for the traditions of his fathers.

Birth in Tarsus, therefore, did not mean for Paul any adherence to a liberal Judaism, as distinguished from the strict Judaism of Palestine. According to Montefiore, a popular Jewish writer of the present day, it even meant the exact opposite; the Judaism of the Dispersion, Montefiore believes, was not more liberal, but less liberal, than the Judaism of Palestine; it was from Tarsus, Montefiore thinks, that Paul derived his gloomy view of sin, and his repellent conception of the wrath of God. Palestinian Judaism of the first century, according to Montefiore, was probably like the rabbinical Judaism of 500 A. D., and the rabbinical Judaism of 500 A. D., contrary to popular opinion, was a broad-minded regime which united devotion to the Law with confidence in the forgiveness of God.[1] This curious reversal of the usual opinion is of course open to serious objection. How does Montefiore know that the Judaism of the Dispersion was less liberal and held a gloomier view of sin than the Judaism of Palestine? The only positive evidence seems to be derived from 4 Ezra, which, with the other apocalypses, in an entirely unwarranted manner, is apparently made to be a witness to the Judaism of the Dispersion. And were the rabbinical Judaism of 500 A. D. and the Palestinian Judaism of 50 A. D. really characterized by that sweet reasonableness which Montefiore attributes to them? There is at least one testimony to the contrary—the testimony found in the words of Jesus.

Distinct from the question of fact is the question of value. But with regard to that question also, Montefiore's opinion may be criticized It may well be doubted whether the easygoing belief in the complacency of God, celebrated by Montefiore as characteristic of Judaism, was, if it ever existed, superior to the gloomy questionings of 4 Ezra. Certainly from the Christian point of view it was not superior. In its shallow view of sin, in its unwillingness to face the ultimate problems of sin and death, the Jewish liberalism of Montefiore is exactly like the so-called Christian liberalism of the modern Church.

[1] Montefiore, *Judaism and St. Paul*, 1914. Compare Emmet. "The Fourth Book of Esdras and St. Paul," in *Expository Times*, xxvii, 1915-1916, pp. 551-556.

And it is as far removed as possible from the Christianity of Paul. At one point, therefore, Montefiore is entirely correct. The gospel of Paul was based not upon a mild view of law, but upon a strict view; not upon a belief in the complacency of God, but upon the cross of Christ as a satisfaction of divine justice. Neither before his conversion nor after it was Paul a "liberal."

Besides the obvious division between the Judaism of Palestine and that of the Dispersion, other divisions may be detected, especially within Palestinian Judaism. Three principal Jewish sects are distinguished by Josephus; the Pharisees, the Sadducees, and the Essenes.[1] Of these, the first two appear also in the New Testament. The Essenes were separated from the ordinary life of the people by certain ascetic customs, by the rejection of animal sacrifice, and by religious practices which may perhaps be due to foreign influence. Apparently the Essenic order did not come into any close contact with the early Church. It is very doubtful, for example, whether Lightfoot was correct in finding Essenic influence in the errorists combated in Paul's Epistle to the Colossians. At any rate, there is not the slightest reason to suppose that Paul was influenced from this source.

The Sadducees were a worldly aristocracy, in possession of the lucrative priestly offices and reconciled to Roman rule. Their rejection of the doctrine of resurrection is attested not only by the New Testament but also by Josephus. They were as far removed as possible from exerting influence upon the youthful Paul.

The Pharisees represented orthodox Judaism, with its devotion to the Law. Their popularity, and their general, though not universal, control of education, made them the real leaders of the people. Certainly the future history of the nation was in their hands; for when the Temple was destroyed the Law alone remained, and the Pharisees were the chief interpreters of the Law. It was this party which claimed the allegiance of Paul. So he testifies himself. His testimony is often forgotten, or at least the implications of it ignored. But it is unequivocal. Saul of Tarsus was not a liberal Jew, but a Pharisee.

[1] Josephus, *Antiq.* XVIII. i. 2-5.

The mention of the Pharisees leads naturally to the second division of our sketch of pre-Christian Judaism—namely, the Law. According to Baldensperger, the two foci around which Judaism moved were the Law and the Messianic hope.[1] These two foci will here be touched upon very briefly in order.

Unquestionably post-exilic Judaism was devoted to the Law. The Law was found in the Old Testament, especially in the books of Moses. But around the written Law had grown up a great mass of oral interpretations which really amounted to elaborate additions. By this "tradition of the elders" the life of the devout Jew was regulated in its minutest particulars. Morality thus became a matter of external rules, and religion became a credit-and-debit relationship into which a man entered with God. Modern Jews are sometimes inclined to contradict such assertions, but the evidence found both in rabbinical sources and in the New Testament is too strong. Exaggerations certainly should be avoided; there are certainly many noble utterances to be found among the sayings of the Jewish teachers; it is not to be supposed that formalism was unrelieved by any manifestations whatever of the goodness of the heart. Nevertheless, the Jewish writings themselves, along with flashes of true insight, contain a great mass of fruitless casuistry; and the New Testament confirms the impression thus produced. In some quarters, indeed, it is customary to discredit the testimony of Jesus, reported in the Gospels, as being the testimony of an opponent. But why was Jesus an opponent? Surely it was because of something blameworthy in the life of those whom He denounced. In the sphere of moral values, the testimony of Jesus of Nazareth is worth having; when He denounces the formalism and hypocrisy of the scribes, it is very difficult for any student of the history of morals not to be impressed. Certainly the denunciation of Jesus was not indiscriminate. He "loved" the rich young ruler, and said to the lawyer, "Thou art not far from the kingdom of God." Thus the Gospels in their choice of the words of Jesus which they record have not been prejudiced by any hatred of the Jews; they have faithfuly set down various elements in Jesus' judgment of His contemporaries. But

[1] Baldensperger, *Die Messianisch-apokalyptischen Hoffnungen des Judentums*, 3te Aufl., 1903, pp. 88, 89.

the picture which they give of Jewish legalism cannot be put out of the world; it seems clear that the religion of the Pharisees at the time of Paul was burdened with all the defects of a religion of merit as distinguished from a religion of grace.

The legalism of the Pharisees might indeed seem to possess one advantage as a preparation for the gospel of Paul; it might seem likely to produce the consciousness of sin and so the longing for a Saviour. If the Law was so very strict as the Pharisees said it was, if its commands entered so deep into every department of life, if the penalty which it imposed upon disobedience was nothing less than loss of the favor of a righteous God, would not the man who was placed under such a régime come to recognize the imperfection of his obedience to the countless commands and so be oppressed by a sense of guilt? Paul said that the Law was a schoolmaster to bring the Jews to Christ, and by that he meant that the Law produced the consciousness of sin. But if the Law was a schoolmaster, was its stern lesson heeded? Was it a schoolmaster to bring the Jews to Christ only in its essential character, or was it actually being used in that beneficent way by the Jews of the age of Paul?

The answer to these questions, so far as it can be obtained, is on the whole disappointing. The Judaism of the Pauline period does not seem to have been characterized by a profound sense of sin. And the reason is not far to seek. The legalism of the Pharisees, with its regulation of the minute details of life, was not really making the Law too hard to keep; it was really making it too easy. Jesus said to His disciples, "Except your righteousness shall exceed the righteousness of the scribes and Pharisees, ye shall in no wise enter into the kingdom of heaven." The truth is, it is easier to cleanse the outside of the cup than it is to cleanse the heart. If the Pharisees had recognized that the Law demands not only the observance of external rules but also and primarily mercy and justice and love for God and men, they would not have been so readily satisfied with the measure of their obedience, and the Law would then have fulfilled its great function of being a schoolmaster to bring them to Christ. A low view of law leads to legalism in religion; a high view of law makes a man a seeker after grace.

Here and there, indeed, voices are to be heard in the Judaism of the New Testament period which attest a real sense of sin. The Fourth Book of Ezra,[1] in particular, struggles seriously with the general reign of evil in the lives of men, and can find no solution of the terrible problem. "Many have been created, but few shall be saved!" (4 Ezra viii. 3). "Or who is there that has not transgressed thy covenant?" (vii. 46). Alas for the "evil heart" (vii. 48)! In a very interesting manner 4 Ezra connects the miserable condition of humanity with the fall of Adam; the fall was not Adam's alone but his descendants' (vii. 118). At this point, it is interesting to compare 2 Baruch,[2] which occupies a somewhat different position; "each of us," declares 2 Baruch, "has been the Adam of his own soul." And in general, 2 Baruch takes a less pessimistic view of human evil, and (according to Charles' estimate, which may be correct) is more self-complacent about the Law. But the profound sense of guilt in 4 Ezra might conceivably be a step on the way to saving faith in Christ. "O Lord above us, if thou wouldst . . . give unto us the seed of a new heart!" (4 Ezra viii. 6). This prayer was gloriously answered in the gospel of Paul.[3]

It must be remembered, however, that 4 Ezra was completed long after the Pauline period; its attitude to the problem of evil certainly cannot be attributed with any confidence to Saul of Tarsus, the pupil of Gamaliel. It is significant that when, after the conversion, Paul seeks testimonies to the universal sinfulness of man, he looks not to contemporary Judaism, but to the Old Testament. At this point, as elsewhere, Paulinism is based not upon later developments but upon the religion of the Prophets and the Psalms. On the whole, therefore, especially in the light of what was said above, it cannot be supposed that Saul the Pharisee held a spiritual view of law, or was possessed of a true conviction of sin. Paul

[1] See Box, in Charles, *Apocrypha and Pseudepigrapha of the Old Testament*, 1913, ii, pp. 542-624; Schürer, *Geschichte des jüdischen Volkes*, 3te und 4te Aufl., iii, 1909, pp. 315-335 (English Translation, *A History of the Jewish People*, Division II, vol. iii, 1886, pp. 93-104). The work of Charles has been used freely, without special acknowledgment, for the citations from the Jewish apocalypses.

[2] See Charles, *op. cit.*, ii, pp. 470-526; Schürer, *op. cit.*, iii, pp. 305-315 (English Translation, Division II, vol. iii, pp. 83-93).

[3] Compare Box, in Charles, *op. cit.*, p. 593. See also Emmet, *loc. cit.*

was convicted of his sin only when the Lord Jesus said to him, "I am Jesus whom thou persecutest."

The other focus about which pre-Christian Judaism, according to Baldensperger, revolved was the Messianic hope. This hope had its roots in the Old Testament. A complete introduction to the subject would of course deal first with the Old Testament background. Here, however, the background will have to be dismissed with a word.

According to the ordinary "critical" view, the doctrine of an individual Messiah, and especially that of a transcendent Messiah, arose late in the history of Israel. At first, it is maintained, there was the expectation of a blessed line of Davidic kings; then the expectation of a line of kings gave way in some quarters to the expectation of an individual king; then the expectation of an earthly king gave way in some quarters to the expectation of a heavenly being like the "Son of Man" who is described in 1 Enoch. This theory, however, has been called in question in recent years, for example by Gressmann.[1] According to Gressmann, the doctrine of an individual transcendent Saviour is of hoar antiquity, and antedates by far the expectation of a blessed line of Davidic kings and that of an individual earthy king. Gressmann is not, of course, returning to the traditional view of the Old Testament. On the contrary, he believes that the ancient doctrine of a heavenly Saviour is of extra-Israelitish origin and represents a widespread myth. But in the details of exegesis, the radicalism of Gressmann, as is also the case with many forms of radicalism in connection with the New Testament, involves a curious return to the traditional view. Many passages of the Old Testament, formerly removed from the list of Messianic passages by the dominant school of exegesis, or else regarded as late interpolations, are restored by Gressmann to their original significance. Thus the suffering servant of Jehovah of Is. liii (a passage which the dominant school of exegesis has interpreted in a collective sense, as referring to the nation of Israel or to the righteous part of the nation) is regarded by Gressmann as being an individual (mythical) figure to whose death and resurrection is attributed saving significance.

[1] *Der Ursprung der israelitisch-jüdischen Eschatologie,* 1905.

The supernaturalistic view of the Old Testament [1] agrees with Gressmann in his individualistic interpretation of such passages as Is. liii, but differs from him in that it attributes objective validity to the representation thus obtained. According to the supernaturalistic view, Israel was from the beginning the people of the Promise. The Promise at first was not fully defined in the minds of all the people. But even at the beginning there were glorious revelations, and the revelations became plainer and plainer as time went on. The various elements in the Promise were not indeed kept carefully distinct, and their logical connections were not revealed. But even long before the Exile there was not only a promise of blessing to David's line, with occasional mention of an individual king, but also a promise of a Redeemer and King who should far exceed the limits of humanity. Thus God had sustained His people through the centuries with a blessed hope, which was finally fulfilled, in all its aspects, by the Lord Jesus Christ.

Discussion of these various views would exceed the limits of the present investigation. All that can here be done is to present briefly the Messianic expectations of the later period, in which Paul lived.

But were those expectations widely prevalent? Was the doctrine of a coming Messiah firmly established among the Jews of the time of Paul? The answer to these questions might seem to be perfectly plain. The common impression is that the Judaism of the first century was devoted to nothing if not to the hope of a king who was to deliver God's people from the oppression of her enemies. This impression is derived from the New Testament. Somewhat different is the impression which might be derived from the Jewish sources if they were taken alone. The expectation of a Messiah hardly appears at all in the Apocrypha, and even in the Pseudepigrapha it appears by no means in all of the books. Even when the thought of the future age is most prominent, that age does not by any means appear in inevitable connection with a personal Messiah. On the contrary, God Himself, not His instrument the Messiah, is often represented as ushering in the new era when Israel should be blessed.

Despite this difference between the New Testament and the

[1] See Beecher, *The Prophets and the Promise*, 1905.

Jewish literature, it is generally recognized that the testimony
of the New Testament must be essentially correct. The picture which is given in the Gospels of the intensity of the Messianic hope among the Jews must be founded upon fact even
if Jesus Himself did not claim to be the Messiah. Indeed, it
is just in that latter case that the testimony in some respects
would become strongest of all. For if Jesus did not claim to
be the Messiah, the attribution of Messiahship to Him by His
disciples could be explained only by the intensity of their own
Messianic expectations. As a matter of fact, however, Jesus
did claim to be the Messiah; the elimination of His Messianic
consciousness has not won the assent of any large body of
historians. He did claim to be the Messiah, and He died because the Jews regarded Him as a false claimant. But His
opponents, no less than His disciples, were expecting a "King
of the Jews." The New Testament throughout, no matter
what view may be held as to the historicity of the individual
narratives, is quite inexplicable unless the Jews both in Palestine and in the Dispersion had a doctrine of "the Christ."

This New Testament representation is confirmed here and
there by other writers. Even Philo,[1] as Brückner remarks,
pays his tribute, though in an isolated passage, to the common
Messianic doctrine.[2] Josephus,[3] also, despite his effort
to avoid offending his Roman readers, is obliged to mention
the Messianic hope as one cause of the great war, and can
only make the reference harmless by finding the Messiah in
the Emperor Vespasian![4] On the whole, the fact may be
regarded as certain that in the first century after Christ the
expectation of the Messiah was firmly established among the
Jews. The silence of great sections of the Apocrypha may
then be explained partly by the date of some of the books.
It may well be that there was a period, especially during the
Maccabean uprising, when because of the better present condition of the nation the Messianic hope was less in the forefront
of interest, and that afterwards, under the humiliation of
Roman rule, the thoughts of the people turned anew to the
expected Deliverer. But however that may be, it is altogether

---

[1] *De praem et poen.* 16 (ed. Cohn, 1902, iv, p. 357).
[2] Brückner, *Die Entstehung der paulinischen Christologie,* 1903, pp. 102f.
[3] *Bell. Jud.* VI. v. 4.
[4] Schürer, *op. cit.,* ii, 1907, p. 604 (English Translation, Division II,
vol. ii, 1885, p. 149).

probable that the expectation of a Messiah was everywhere cherished in the Judaism of the time of Paul.

If then the hope of a Messiah was prevalent in the Judaism of the first century, what was the nature of that hope? Two forms of Messianic expectation have ordinarily been distinguished. In the first place, it is said, there was an expectation of an earthly king of David's line, and in the second place, there was the notion of a heavenly being already existing in heaven. The former of these two lines of expectation is usually thought to represent the popular view, held by the masses of the people; and the latter is regarded as an esoteric doctrine held by a limited circle from which the apocalypses have sprung.

At this point, Brückner is somewhat in opposition to the ordinary opinion; he denies altogether the presence in first-century Judaism of any distinctive doctrine of a purely human Messiah.[1] The Messiah, he says, appears in all the sources distinctly as a supernatural figure. Even in the Psalms of Solomon, he insists, where the Messiah is represented as a king reigning upon earth, He is nevertheless no ordinary king, for He destroys His enemies not by the weapons of war but "by the breath of His mouth." In the Gospels, moreover, although the people are represented as looking for a king who should break the Roman rule, yet they demand of this king works of superhuman power.

Undoubtedly there is a measure of truth in this contention of Brückner. It may perhaps be admitted that the Messiah of Jewish expectation was always something more than an ordinary king; it may perhaps be admitted that He was endowed with supernatural attributes. Nevertheless, the view of Brückner is exaggerated. There is still to be maintained the distinction between the heavenly being of 1 Enoch and the Davidic king. The latter might perhaps be regarded as possessed of miraculous powers, but still He was in the essentials of His person an earthly monarch. He was to be born like other men; He was to rule over an earthly kingdom; He was to conquer earthly armies; presumably He was to die. It is significant that John the Baptist, despite the fact that he had as yet wrought no miracles, was apparently thought by some to be the Messiah (Lk. iii. 15; John i. 19-27). Even

[1] Brückner, op. cit., pp. 104-112.

if this representation of the Gospels of Luke and of John should be regarded as quite unhistorical, still it does show that the writers of these two Gospels, neither of whom was by any means ignorant of Jewish conditions, regard it as no incongruity that some should have supposed such a man as John to be the Messiah. The Messiah, therefore, could not have been regarded always as being like the heavenly Son of Man of 1 Enoch. But it is unnecessary to appeal to details. The whole New Testament, whatever view may be taken of the historicity of its narratives in detail, attests the prevalence in the first century of a Messianic expectation according to which the Messiah was to be an earthly king of David's line.

This view of Messiahship becomes explicit in Justin Martyr's Dialogue with Trypho, which was written at about the middle of the second century. In this book, the Jewish opponent of Justin represents the Messiah as a "mere man." [1] No doubt this evidence cannot be used directly for the earlier period in which Paul lived. There does seem to have been a reaction in later Jewish expectations against that transcendent view of Messiahship which had been adopted by the Christian Church. Thus the apocalypses passed out of use among the Jews, and, in some cases at least, have been preserved only by the Church, and only because of their congruity with Christian views. It is possible, therefore, that when Trypho in the middle of the second century represents the Messiah as a "mere man," he is attesting a development in the Jewish doctrine which was subsequent to the time of Paul. But even in that case his testimony is not altogether without value. Even if Trypho's doctrine of a merely human Messiah be a later development, it was probably not without some roots in the past. If the Jews of the first century possessed both the doctrine of an earthly king and that of a heavenly "Son of Man," it is possible to see how the latter doctrine might have been removed and the former left in sole possession of the field; but if in the first century the transcendent doctrine alone prevailed, it is unlikely that a totally different view could have been produced so quickly to take its place. [2]

[1] ψιλὸς ἄνθρωπος.
[2] Indeed Brückner himself (op. cit., p. 110) admits that there were two lines of thought about the Messiah in pre-Christian Judaism. But he denies that the two were separated, and insists that the transcendent conception had transformed the conception of an earthly king.

Thus it must be insisted against Brückner that in the first century the transcendent conception of Messiahship attested by the apocalypses was not the only conception that prevailed. Despite its dominance in the apocalypses, it was probably not the doctrine of the masses of the people. Probably the ordinary view of the matter is essentially correct; probably the Jews of the first century were eagerly awaiting an earthly king of David's line who should deliver them from Roman rule.

If, however, the transcendent conception of Messiahship which is found in the apocalypses was not the only conception held by pre-Christian Judaism, it is none the less of special interest, and will repay examination. It is found most fully set forth in the "Similitudes" of 1 Enoch,[1] but appears also in 4 Ezra and in 2 Baruch.

In the Similitudes, the heavenly being, who is to appear at the end of the age and be the instrument of God in judgment, is usually called the Elect One, Mine Elect One, the Son of Man, or that Son of Man. He is also called the Righteous One, and twice he is called Messiah or Anointed One (xlviii. 10; lii. 4). This latter title would seem to connect him with the expected king of David's line, who was the Anointed One or the Messiah. Lake and Jackson, however, would deny all connection. The heavenly Son of Man, they maintain, was never in pre-Christian Judaism identified with the expected king of David's line—that is, with the "Messiah" in the technical sense—so that it is a mistake to speak of "Messianic" passages in the Book of Enoch.[2] But after all, the heavenly figure of 1 Enoch is represented as fulfilling much the same functions as those which are attributed in the Psalms of Solomon, for example, to the Messiah. It would be difficult to conceive of the same writer as expecting two deliverers—one the Messiah of the Psalms of Solomon, and the other the Son of Man of 1 Enoch. On the whole, therefore, it is correct, despite the protest of Lake and Jackson, to speak of the passages in 1 Enoch as Messianic, and of

---

[1] All parts of 1 Enoch are now usually thought to be of pre-Christian origin. The Similitudes (chaps. xxxvii-lxxi) are usually dated in the first century before Christ. See Charles, *op. cit.*, ii, pp. 163-281; Schürer, *op. cit.*, iii, pp. 268-290 (English Translation, Division II, vol. iii, pp. 54-73).

[2] Lake and Jackson, *The Beginnings of Christianity*, Part I, vol. i, 1920, pp. 373f.

the Son of Man as the "Messiah." In 4 Ezra xii. 32, more-over, the transcendent being, who is set forth under the figure of the lion, is distinctly identified with the Messiah "who shall spring from the seed of David." Of course, the late date of 4 Ezra may be insisted upon, and it may be maintained that the Davidic descent of the Messiah in 4 Ezra is a mere tradi-tional detail, without organic connection with the rest of the picture. But it is significant that the writer did feel it neces-sary to retain the detail. His doing so proves at least that the heavenly being of the apocalypses was not always thought of as distinct from the promised king of David's line. All that can be granted to Lake and Jackson is that the future Deliverer was thought of in pre-Christian Judaism in widely diverse ways, and that there was often no effort to bring the different representations into harmony. But it is correct to speak of all the representations as "Messianic." For the coming Deliverer in all cases (despite the variety of the ex-pectations) was intended to satisfy at least the same religious needs.

The title "Son of Man," which is used frequently in the Similitudes, has given rise to a great deal of discussion, espe-cially because of its employment in the Gospels as a self-designation of Jesus. It has been maintained by some scholars that "Son of Man" never could have been a Messianic title, since the phrase in Aramaic idiom means simply "man." Thus the Greek phrase, "the Son of Man," in the Gospels would merely be an over-literal translation of an Aramaic phrase which meant simply "the man," and the use of "Son of Man" as a title would not extend back of the time when the tradition about the words of Jesus passed over into Greek. But in recent years this extreme position has for the most part been abandoned. In the first place, it is by no means clear that the Aramaic phrase from which the phrase "the Son of Man" in the Gospels is derived was simply the ordinary phrase mean-ing simply "the man." Opposed to this view is to be put, for example, the weighty opinion of Dalman.[1] In the second place, it has been shown that the linguistic question is not so important as was formerly supposed. For even if "the son

---

[1] Dalman, *Die Worte Jesu*, i, 1898, pp. 191-197 (English Translation, *The Words of Jesus*, i, 1902, pp. 234-241); Bousset, *Kyrios Christos*, 1913, pp. 13, 14.

of man" in Aramaic meant simply "the man," it might still be a title. The commonest noun may sometimes become a title, and a title of highly specialized significance. For example, the word "day" is a very common word, but "The Day" in certain connections, like the German, "Der Tag," altogether without the help of any adjectives, comes to designate one particular day. So "the Man" or "that Man" could become a very lofty title, especially if it refers to some definite scene in which He who is the "Man" *par excellence* is described.

In the Similitudes, such is actually the case; the phrase "Son of Man," whatever be its exact meaning, plainly refers to the "one like unto a son of man" who in Daniel vii. 13 appears in the presence of "the Ancient of Days." This reference is made perfectly plain at the first mention of the Son of Man (1 Enoch xlvi. 1, 2), where the same scene is evidently described as the scene of Dan. vii. 13. The "Son of Man" is not introduced abruptly, but is first described as a "being whose countenance had the appearance of a man," and is then referred to in the Similitudes not only as "the Son of Man," but also as "that Son of Man." Charles and others suppose, indeed, that the Ethiopic word translated "that" is merely a somewhat false representation, in the Ethiopic translation, of the Greek definite article, so that the Greek form of the book from which the extant Ethiopic was taken had everywhere "the Son of Man," and nowhere "that Son of Man." The question is perhaps not of very great importance. In any case, the phrase "son of man" derives its special significance from the reference to the scene of Dan. vii. 13. Not any ordinary "man" or "son of man" is meant, but the mysterious figure who came with the clouds of heaven and was brought near to the Ancient of Days.

The Son of Man, or the Elect One, in the Similitudes, appears clothed with the loftiest attributes. He existed before the creation of the world (xlviii. 3, 6). When he finally appears, it is to sit in glory upon the throne of God (li. 3, etc.), and judge not only the inhabitants of earth but also the fallen angels (lv. 4). For the purposes of judgment he is endued with righteousness and wisdom. He is concerned, moreover, not only with the judgment but also with the execution of the judgment; he causes "the sinners to pass away and be destroyed from off the face of the earth" (lxix. 27). For the righteous, on the other hand, the judgment results in blessing and in communion with the Son of Man. "And the righteous and elect shall be saved in that day, and they shall never thenceforward see the face of the sinners and the unrighteous. And the Lord of Spirits will abide over them, and with that Son of Man shall they eat and lie down and rise up for ever and ever" (lxii. 13, 14).

The entire representation in the Similitudes is supernatural; the Son of Man is a heavenly figure who appears suddenly in the full blaze of his glory. Yet the connection with earth is not altogether broken off. It is upon a glorified earth that the righteous are to dwell. Indeed, despite the cosmic extent of the drama, the prerogatives of Israel are preserved; the Gentile rulers are no doubt referred to in "the Kings and the Mighty" who are to suffer punishment because of their former oppression of "the elect." On the other hand, mere connection with Israel is not the only ground for a man's acceptance by the Son of Man; the judgment will be based upon a real understanding of the secrets of individual lives.

In 4 Ezra vii. 26-31, the rule of the Messiah is represented as distinctly temporary. The Messiah will rejoice the living for four hundred years; then, together with all human beings, he will die; then after the world has returned to primeval silence for seven days, the new age, with the final resurrection, will be ushered in. It may be doubted whether this representation harmonizes with what is said elsewhere in 4 Ezra about the Messiah, indeed whether even in this passage the representation is thoroughly consistent. Box, for example, thinks that there are contradictions here, which are to be explained by the composite nature of the book and by the work of a redactor. But at any rate the result, in the completed book, is clear. The Messiah is to die, like all the men who are upon the earth, and is not connected with the new age. This death of the Messiah is as far as possible from possessing any significance for the salvation of men. Certainly it is not brought into any connection with the problem of sin, which, as has been observed above, engages the special attention of the writer of 4 Ezra. "It is important to observe how the Jewish faith knew of a Saviour for external ills, but not for sin and condemnation; and how the Christ is able only to create a brief earthly joy, which passes away with the destruction of the world." [1]

In the "Testaments of the Twelve Patriarchs," [2] although Brückner is no doubt right in saying that the Messiah here as well as in 1 Enoch is a supernatural figure, the connection of the Messiah with the tribe of Levi introduces the reader into a somewhat different circle of ideas. The difference becomes more marked in the "Psalms of Solomon," [3] where the Messiah is a king of David's line. It is no doubt true that even here the Messiah is no ordinary human being; he destroys his enemies, not by the weapons of warfare and not by the help of Israelitish armies, but by the breath of his mouth. Yet the local, earthly character of the Messiah's reign—what may even be called, perhaps, its political character—is more clearly marked than in the apocalypses. Also there is stronger emphasis upon the ethical qualities of the Messianic king; the righteousness of his people is celebrated in lofty terms, which, however, do not exclude a strong element of Jewish and Pharisaic particularism.

No complete exposition of the Jewish belief about the Messiah has here been attempted. But enough has perhaps been said to indicate at least some features of the Messianic expectation in the period just preceding the time of Paul. Evidently, in certain circles at least, the Messianic hope was transcendent, individualistic, and universalistic. The scene of Messiah's kingdom was not always thought of merely as the earthly Jerusalem; at least the drama by which that kingdom is ushered in was thought of as taking place either in heaven or upon an earth which has been totally transformed. With this transcendent representation went naturally a tendency towards individualism. Not merely nations were to be judged, but also the secrets of the individual life; and individuals were to have a part in the final blessing or the final woe. Of course, for those who should die before the end of the age, this participation in the final blessedness or the final woe would be possible only by a resurrection. And the doctrine of resurrection, especially for the righteous, is in the apoca-

---

[1] Volz, *Jüdische Eschatologie von Daniel bis Akiba*, 1903, pp. 202f.

[2] See Charles, *op. cit.*, ii, pp. 282-367; Schürer, *op. cit.*, iii, pp. 339-356 (English Translation, Division II, vol. iii, pp. 114-124).

[3] See Gray, in Charles, *op. cit.*, ii, pp. 625-652; Schürer, *op. cit.*, iii, pp. 205-212 (English Translation, Division II, vol. iii, pp. 17-23).

lypses clearly marked. In 2 Baruch, indeed, there is an interesting discussion of the relation between the resurrection state and the present condition of man; the righteous will first rise in their old bodies, but afterwards will be transformed (2 Baruch xlix-li). Finally, the apocalypses exhibit a tendency toward universalism. The coming of the Messianic kingdom is regarded as an event of cosmic significance. The Gentiles are even sometimes said to share in the blessing. But they are to share in the blessing only by subordination to the people of God.

Despite the importance of the later period, it is interesting to observe that all the essential features of later Jewish eschatology have their roots in the canonical books of the Old Testament. In the first place, the transcendence of the later representation has an Old Testament basis. In Isaiah ix and xi the Messiah appears clearly as a supernatural figure, and in Isaiah lxv. 17 there is a prophecy of new heavens and a new earth. The heavenly "Son of Man" is derived from Dan. vii. 13, and the individualistic interpretation of that passage, which makes the Son of Man, despite verse 18, something more than a mere collective symbol for the people of Israel, is to-day in certain quarters coming to its rights. Not only in the Psalms of Solomon, but also in the apocalypses, the Old Testament language is used again and again to describe the heavenly Messiah. There is, in the second place, an Old Testament basis for the individualism of the later representation. The doctrine of resurrection, with its consequences for an individualistic hope, appears in Daniel. And, finally, the universalism of the apocalypses does not transcend that of the great Old Testament prophets. In the prophets also, the nations are to come under the judgment of God and are to share in some sort in the blessings of Israel.

If, therefore, the apostle Paul before his conversion believed in a heavenly Messiah, supernatural in origin and in function, he was not really unfaithful to the Old Testament.

But was his pre-Christian notion of the Messiah really the source of the Christology of the Epistles? Such is the contention of Wrede and Brückner. Wrede and Brückner believe that the lofty Christology of Paul, inexplicable if it was derived from the man Jesus, may be accounted for if it was merely the pre-Christian conception of the Messiah brought into loose connection with the prophet of Nazareth. This hypothesis must now be examined.

At the beginning of the investigation, it may be questioned whether Paul before his conversion held the apocalyptic view of the Messiah. It might, indeed, even be questioned whether he was particularly interested in the Messianic hope at all. If Baldensperger is correct in saying that the Messianic dogma was in some sort a substitute for the Law, and the Law a substitute for the Messianic dogma, so that finally rabbinical interest in the Law tended to dampen interest in the Messiah,[1] then the pre-Christian life of Paul was presumably not dominated by Messianic expectations. For Paul himself, as Baldensperger observes,[2] does not, in speaking of his pre-Christian life, reckon himself with the Messianists. He reckons himself, rather, with those who were zealous for the Law. Such considerations are interesting. But their importance should not be exaggerated. It must be remembered that according to the testimony of the whole New Testament the doctrine of the Messiah was firmly established in the Judaism of Paul's day. It is hardly likely that Paul the Pharisee dissented from the orthodox belief. In all probability, therefore, Paul before his conversion did hold some doctrine of the Messiah.

It is not so certain, however, that the pre-conversion doctrine of Paul presented a transcendent Messiah like the heavenly Son of Man of the apocalypses. Certainly there is in the Pauline Epistles no evidence whatever of literary dependence upon the apocalyptic descriptions of the Messiah. The characteristic titles of the Messiah which appear in the Similitudes of Enoch, for example, are conspicuously absent from Paul. Paul never uses the title "Son of Man" or "Elect One" or "Righteous One" in speaking of Christ. And in the apocalypses, on the other hand, the Pauline terminology is almost equally unknown. The apocalypses, at least 1 Enoch, use the title "Messiah" only very seldom, and the characteristic Pauline title, "Lord," never at all. It is evident, therefore, that the Pauline Christology was not derived from the particular apocalypses that are still extant. All that can

---

[1] Baldensperger, *Die Messianisch-apocalyptischen Hoffnungen des Judentums*, 3te Aufl., 1903, pp. 88, 207f., 216f.
[2] Baldensperger, *op. cit.*, pp. 216f.

possibly be maintained is that it was derived from apocalypses which have been lost, or from an apocalyptic oral tradition. But dependence upon lost sources, direct comparison not being possible, is always very difficult to establish.

Thus the terminology of the Epistles and of the apocalypses is rather unfavorable to the view which attributes to the youthful Paul the apocalyptic doctrine of the Messiah. No literary relation can be established between the Epistles and the extant apocalypses. But will general considerations serve to supply the lack of direct evidence of dependence? On the whole, the reverse is the case. General considerations as to the pre-Christian opinions of Paul point rather to a less transcendent and more political conception than the conception which is found in the apocalypses. No doubt the Messiah whom Paul was expecting possessed supernatural attributes; it seems to have been generally expected in New Testament times that the Messiah would work miracles. But the supernatural attributes of the Messiah would not necessarily involve a conception like that which is presented in the Similitudes of Enoch. Possibly it is rather to the Psalms of Solomon that the historian should turn. The Psalms of Solomon were a typical product of Pharisaism in its nobler aspects. Their conception of the Messiah, therefore, may well have been that of the pupil of Gamaliel. And the Messiah of the Psalms of Solomon, though possessed of supernatural power and wisdom, is thought of primarily as a king of David's line, and there is no thought of his preëxistence. He is very different from the Son of Man of 1 Enoch.

It is, therefore, not perfectly clear that Paul before the conversion believed in a heavenly, preëxistent Messiah like the Messiah of the apocalypses. There is some reason for supposing that the apocalyptic Messiah was the Messiah, not of the masses of the people and not of the orthodox teachers, but of a somewhat limited circle. Did Paul belong to that limited circle? The question cannot be answered with any certainty.

The importance of such queries must not, indeed, be exaggerated. It is not being maintained here that Paul before his conversion did not believe in the Messiah of the apocalypses; all that is maintained is that it is not certain that he did. Possibly the diffusion of apocalyptic ideas in pre-Christian Judaism was much wider than is sometimes supposed; possibly the youthful Paul did come under the influence of such ideas. But Wrede and Brückner are going too far if they assert that Paul must necessarily have come under such influences. The truth is that the pre-Christian life of Paul is shrouded in the profoundest obscurity. Almost the only definite piece of information is what Paul himself tells us—that he was zealous for the Law. He says nothing about his conception of the Messiah. The utmost caution is therefore in place. Brückner is going much further than the sources will warrant when he makes Paul before his conversion a devotee of the apocalyptic Messiah, and bases upon this hypothesis an elaborate theory as to the genesis of the Pauline Christology.

But even if Paul before his conversion was a devotee of the apocalyptic Messiah, the genesis of the Pauline Christology has not yet been explained. For the apocalyptic Messiah is different in important respects from the Christ of the Epistles.

In the first place, there is in the apocalypses no doctrine of an activity of the Messiah in creation, like that which appears in 1 Cor. viii. 6; Col. i. 16. The Messiah of the apocalypses is preëxistent, but He is not thought of as being associated with God in the creation of the world. This difference may seem to be only a difference in detail; but it is a difference in detail which concerns just that part of the Pauline Christology which would seem to be most similar to the apocalyptic doctrine. It is the Pauline conception of the preëxistent Christ, as distinguished from the incarnate or the risen Christ, which Wrede and Brückner find it easiest to connect with the apocalypses. But even in the preëxistent period the Christ of Paul is different from the apocalyptic Messiah, because the Christ of Paul, unlike the apocalyptic Messiah, has an active part in the creation of the world.

In the second place, there is in the apocalypses no trace of the warm, personal relation which exists between the believer and the Pauline Christ.[1] The Messiah of the apocalypses is hidden in heaven. He is revealed only as a great mystery, and only to favored men such as Enoch. Even after the judgment, although the righteous are to be in company with Him, there is no such account of His person as would make conceivable a living, personal relationship with Him. The heavenly Messiah of the apocalypses is a lifeless figure,

[1] Compare especially Olschewski, *Die Wurzeln der paulinischen Christologie*, 1909.

clothed in unapproachable light. The risen Christ of Paul, on the other hand, is a person whom a man can love; indeed He is a person whom as a matter of fact Paul did love. Whence was derived the concrete, personal character of the Christ of Paul? It was certainly not derived from the Messiah of the apocalypses. Whence then was it derived?

The natural answer would be that it was derived from Jesus of Nazareth. The fact that the risen Christ of Paul is not merely a heavenly figure but a person whom a man can love is most naturally explained by supposing that Paul attributed to the Messiah all the concrete traits of the striking personality of Jesus of Nazareth. But this supposition is excluded by Wrede's hypothesis. Indeed, Wrede supposes, if Paul had come into such close contact with the historical Jesus as to have in his mind a full account of Jesus' words and deeds, he could not easily have attached to Him the supernatural attributes of the heavenly Son of Man; only a man who stood remote from the real Jesus could have regarded Jesus as the instrument in creation and the final judge of all the world. Thus the hypothesis of Wrede and Brückner faces a quandary. In order to explain the supernatural attributes of the Pauline Christ, Paul has to be placed near to the apocalypses and far from the historical Jesus; whereas in order to explain the warm, personal relation between Paul and his Christ, Paul would have to be placed near to the historical Jesus and far from the apocalypses.

This quandary could be avoided only by deriving the warm, personal relation between Paul and his Christ from something other than the character of the historical Jesus. Wrede and Brückner might seek to derive it from the one fact of the crucifixion. All that Paul really derived from the historical Jesus, according to Wrede and Brückner, was the fact that the Messiah had come to earth and died. But that one fact, it might be maintained, was sufficient to produce the fervent Christ-religion of Paul. For Paul interpreted the death of the Messiah as a death suffered for the sins of others. Such a death involved self-sacrifice; it must have been an act of love. Hence the beneficiaries were grateful; hence the warm, personal relationship of Paul to the one who had loved him and given Himself for him.[1]

[1] Compare Brückner, *Die Entstehung der paulinischen Christologie*, 1903, p. 237.

But how did the death of Jesus ever come to be interpreted by Paul as a vicarious death of the Messiah? The natural answer would be that it was because of something that Jesus had said or because of an impression derived from His character. That answer is excluded by Wrede's hypothesis. How then did Paul come to regard the death of Jesus as a vicarious death of the Messiah? It could only have been because Paul already had a doctrine of the vicarious death of the Messiah before his conversion. But nothing is more unlikely. There is in late pre-Christian Jewish literature not a trace of such a doctrine.[1] The Messiah in 4 Ezra is represented, indeed, as dying, but His death is of benefit to no one. He dies, along with all the inhabitants of earth, simply in order to make way for the new world.[2] In Justin Martyr's Dialogue with Trypho, the Jew Trypho is represented as admitting that the Messiah was to suffer. But the suffering is not represented as vicarious. And since the Dialogue was written in the middle of the second century after Christ, the isolated testimony of Trypho cannot be used as a witness to first-century conditions. It is perfectly possible, as Schürer suggested, that certain Jews of the second century were only led to concede the suffering of the Messiah in the light of the Scriptural arguments advanced by the Christians. The rabbinical evidence as to sufferings of the Messiah is also too late to be used in reconstructing the pre-Christian environment of Paul. And of real evidence from the period just before Paul's day there is none. In 4 Maccabees vi. 28, 29, indeed (less clearly in xvii. 21, 22), the blood of the righteous is represented as bringing purification for the people. The dying martyr Eleazar is represented as praying:[3] "Be merciful unto thy people, and let our punishment be a satisfaction in their behalf. Make my blood their purification, and take my soul to ransom their souls." This passage, however, is entirely isolated. There is no evidence whatever that the vicarious suffering of the righteous was anything like an established doctrine in the Judaism of Paul's day, and in particular there is no evidence that in pre-Christian Judaism the idea of vicarious suffering was applied to the Messiah. Un-

[1] See Schürer, *op. cit.*, ii, pp. 648-651 (English Translation, Division II, vol. ii, pp. 184-187).

[2] It will be remembered, moreover, that 4 Ezra, at least in its completed form, dates from long after the time of Paul.

[3] Townshend, in Charles, *op. cit.*, ii, p. 674.

doubtedly Isaiah liii might have formed a basis for such an application; it may even seem surprising that that glorious passage was not more influential. But as a matter of fact, Judaism was moving in a very different direction; the later doctrine of the Messiah had absolutely no place for a vicarious death or for vicarious suffering. All the sources are here in agreement. Neither in the apocalypses nor in what is presupposed in the New Testament about Jewish belief is there any trace of a vicarious death of the Messiah. Indeed, there is abundant evidence that such an idea was extremely repulsive to the Jewish mind. The Cross was unto the Jews a stumbling-block.[1]

Thus the warm, personal relation of love and gratitude which Paul sustains to the risen Christ is entirely unexplained by anything in his Jewish environment. It is not explained by the Jewish doctrine of the Messiah; it is not explained by reflection upon the vicarious death of the Messiah. For the Messiah in Jewish expectation was not to suffer a vicarious death. Such a relation of love and gratitude could be sustained only toward a living person. It could be sustained toward Jesus of Nazareth, if Jesus continued to live in glory, but it could not be sustained toward the Messiah of the apocalypses.

The third difference between the Pauline Christ and the Messiah of the apocalypses concerns the very center of the Pauline conception—there is in the apocalypses no doctrine

---

[1] B. W. Bacon (*Jesus and Paul*, 1921, pp. 45-49) seeks to bridge the gulf between Jesus and Paul by supposing that Jesus himself, somewhat like the Maccabean hero, finally attained, after the failure of His original program and at the very close of His life, the conception that His approaching death was to be in some sort an expiation for His people. But the idea of expiation which Bacon attributes to Jesus is no doubt very different from the Pauline doctrine of the Cross of Christ. The gulf between Jesus and Paul is therefore not really bridged. Moreover, it cannot be said that Bacon's hypothesis of successive stages in the experience of Jesus, culminating in the idea of expiation attained at the last supper, has really helped at all to solve the problem presented to every historian who proceeds upon naturalistic presuppositions by Jesus' lofty claims. At least, however, this latest investigator of the problem of "Jesus and Paul" has betrayed a salutary consciousness of the fact that the Pauline conception of Jesus' redemptive work is inexplicable unless it find some justification in the mind of Jesus Himself. Only, the justification which Bacon himself has found—particularly his account of the way in which the idea of expiation is supposed to have arisen in Jesus' mind—is entirely inadequate.

of the divinity of the Messiah. In Paul, the divinity of
Christ is presupposed on every page. The word "divinity" is
indeed often being abused; in modern pantheizing liberalism,
it means absolutely nothing. But the divinity of Christ in
the Pauline Epistles is to be understood in the highest possible sense. The Pauline doctrine of the divinity of Christ is
not dependent upon individual passages; it does not depend
upon the question whether in Rom. ix. 5 Paul applies the term
"God" to Christ. Certainly he does so by any natural interpretation of his words. But what is far more important is
that the term "Lord" in the Pauline Epistles, the characteristic Pauline name of Christ, is every whit as much a designation of deity as is the term "God." [1] Everywhere in the
Epistles, moreover, the attitude of Paul toward Christ is not
merely the attitude of man to man, or scholar to master; it
is the attitude of man toward God.

Such an attitude is absent from the apocalyptic representation of the Messiah. For example, the way in which God
and Christ are linked together regularly at the beginnings of
the Pauline Epistles—God our father and the Lord Jesus
Christ [2]—this can find no real parallel in 1 Enoch. The
isolated passages (1 Enoch xlix. 10; lxx. 1) where in 1 Enoch
the Lord of Spirits and the Son of Man or the Elect One are
linked together by the word "and," do not begin to approach
the height of the Pauline conception. It is not surprising
and not particularly significant that the wicked are designated in one passage as those who have "denied the Lord of
Spirits and His anointed" (1 Enoch xlix. 10). Such an expression would be natural even if the Anointed One were, for
example, merely an earthly king of David's line. What is
characteristic of Paul, on the other hand, is that God the
Father and the Lord Jesus Christ are not merely united by
the conjunction "and" in isolated passages—that might happen even if they belonged to different spheres of being—but
are united regularly and as a matter of course, and are just
as regularly separated from all other beings except the Holy
Spirit. Moreover, God and Christ, in Paul, have attributed
to them the same functions. Grace and peace, for example,

[1] See Warfield, " 'God our Father and the Lord Jesus Christ,' " in
Princeton Theological Review, xv, 1917, pp. 1-20.
[2] Warfield, *loc. cit.*

come equally from both. Such a representation would be quite incongruous in 1 Enoch. Equally incongruous in 1 Enoch would be the Pauline separation of the Christ from ordinary humanity and from angels. The author of 1 Enoch could hardly have said, "Not from men nor through a man but through the Elect One and the Lord of Spirits," as Paul says, "Not from men nor through a man but through Jesus Christ and God the Father who raised him from the dead" (Gal. i. 1). On the other hand, the way in which 1 Enoch includes the Elect One in the middle of a long list of beings who praise the Lord of Spirits (1 Enoch lxi. 10, 11) would be absolutely inconceivable in Paul.

This stupendous difference is established not by isolated passages, but by every page of the Pauline Epistles. The Pauline Christ is exalted to an infinite height above the Messiah of the apocalypses. How did He reach this height? Was it because He was identified with Jesus of Nazareth? But that identification, if Jesus of Nazareth were a mere man, would have dragged Him down rather than lifted Him up. There lies the unsolved problem. Even if Paul before his conversion believed in the heavenly Messiah of the apocalypses, he had to exalt that Messiah far beyond all that had ever been attributed to Him in the boldest visions of the Jewish seers, before he could produce the Christ of the Epistles. Yet the only new thing that had entered Paul's life was identification of the Messiah with Jesus. Why did that identification lift the Messiah to the throne of God? Who was this Jesus, who by His identification with the Messiah, lifted the Messiah even far above men's wildest dreams?

Thus the Messianic doctrine of the apocalypses is an insufficient basis for the Pauline Christology. Its insufficiency is admitted by Hans Windisch.[1] But Windisch seeks to supply what is lacking in the apocalyptic Messiah by appealing to the Jewish doctrine of "Wisdom." The apocalyptic doctrine of the Messiah, Windisch admits, will not explain the origin of the Pauline Christology; for example, it will not explain Paul's doctrine of the activity of Christ in creation. But "Wisdom" is thought to supply the lack.

In Prov. viii, "wisdom" is celebrated in lofty terms, and

[1] "Die göttliche Weisheit der Juden und die paulinische Christologie," in *Neutestamentliche Studien Georg Heinrici dargebracht*, 1914, pp. 220-234.

is said to have existed before the creation of the world. "Wisdom" is here boldly personified in a poetic way. But she is not regarded as a real person separate from God. In later books, however, notably in the Alexandrian "Wisdom of Solomon," the personification is developed until it seems to involve actual personality. Wisdom seems to be regarded as an "hypostasis," a figure in some sort distinct from God. This hypostasis, Windisch believes, was identified by Paul with Christ, and the result was the Pauline Christology.

The figure of Wisdom, Windisch believes, will supply two elements in the Pauline Christ-religion which are lacking in the Messiah of the apocalypses. In the first place, it will account for the Pauline notion that Christ was active in creation, since Wisdom in Jewish belief is repeatedly represented as the assessor or even the instrument of the Creator. In the second place, it will account for the intimate relation between Paul and his Christ, since Wisdom is represented in the "Wisdom of Solomon" as entering into the wise man, and the wise man seems to be represented in Proverbs viii and in Ecclesiasticus as the mouthpiece of Wisdom.[1]

But when was the identification of the Messiah with Wisdom accomplished? Was it accomplished by Paul himself after his conversion? Or was it received by Paul from pre-Christian Jewish doctrine? If it was accomplished by Paul himself after his conversion, then absolutely no progress has been made toward the explanation of the Pauline Christology. How did Paul come to identify Jesus of Nazareth with the divine figure of Wisdom? It could only have been because Jesus was such a person as to make the identification natural. But that supposition is of course excluded by the naturalistic principles with which Windisch is operating. The identification of Jesus with Wisdom at or after the conversion is, therefore, absolutely inexplicable; in substituting Wisdom for the apocalyptic Messiah as the basis of the Pauline Christology, Windisch has destroyed whatever measure of plausibility the theory of Wrede and Brückner possessed. For it is really essential to Wrede's theory that Paul before his conversion had not only believed in the existence of a heavenly being like the Son of Man of 1 Enoch, but had also expected that heavenly being to appear. Since he had expected the heavenly being to

[1] Windisch, *op. cit.*, p. 226.

appear, it might seem to be not so absolutely inexplicable that he came to think that that being had actually appeared in the person of Jesus. But no one expected Wisdom to appear, in any more definite way than by the entrance which she had already accomplished into the hearts of wise men. The thought of an incarnation or a parousia of Wisdom is absolutely foreign to Jewish thought. What possible reason was there, then, for Paul to think that Wisdom actually had appeared and would finally appear again in the person of Jesus?

Thus the theory of Windisch can be maintained only if the identification of Wisdom with the Messiah was accomplished not by Paul after the conversion but by pre-Christian Judaism. If Paul's pre-Christian doctrine of the Messiah already contained vital elements drawn from the doctrine of Wisdom, then and then only might it be held that the Pauline Christ, with His activity in creation and His spiritual indwelling in the believer, was merely the pre-Christian Messiah. But was the pre-Christian Messiah ever identified with the hypostasis Wisdom? Upon an affirmative answer to this question depends the whole structure of Windisch's theory. But Windisch passes the question over rather lightly. He tries, indeed, to establish certain coincidences between the doctrine of the Messiah in 1 Enoch and in the Septuagint translation of Micah v. 2 and Ps. cx. 3 on the one hand, and the descriptions of Wisdom on the other; but the coincidences apparently amount to nothing except the ascription of preëxistence to both figures. But the fundamental trouble is that Windisch has an entirely inadequate conception of what really needs to be proved. What Windisch really needs to do is to ascribe to the pre-Christian doctrine of the Messiah two elements—activity in creation and spiritual indwelling—which in the extant sources are found not at all in the descriptions of the Messiah but only in the descriptions of Wisdom. Even if he succeeded in establishing verbal dependence of the descriptions of the Messiah upon the descriptions of Wisdom, that would not really prove his point at all. Such verbal dependence as a matter of fact has not been established, but if it were established it would be without significance. It would be far more completely devoid of significance than is the similarity between the descriptions of the heavenly Messiah as judge and the descriptions of God as judge. This latter similarity may be significant, when taken in connection with other evidence, as being a true anticipation of the Christian doctrine of the deity of Christ, but in itself it will hardly be held (at least it will hardly be held by Windisch) to establish the complete personal identity, in Jewish thinking, of the Messiah and God, so that everything that is said about God in pre-Christian Jewish sources can henceforth be applied to the Messiah. Why then should similarity in language between the descriptions of the Wisdom of God as preëxistent and the descriptions of the Messiah as preëxistent (even if that similarity existed) establish such identity between the Messiah and Wisdom that what is attributed to Wisdom (notably spiritual indwelling) can henceforth be attributed to the Messiah? There is really no evidence whatever for supposing that the Messiah was conceived of in pre-Christian Judaism either as being active in creation or as dwelling in the hearts of men. Indeed, with regard to the latter point, there is decisive evidence of the contrary. The figure of the Messiah in the apocalypses is as incongruous as anything can possibly be with the idea of spiritual indwelling. Wisdom is conceived of as dwelling in the hearts of men only because Wisdom in Jewish literature is not really or completely a concrete person, but is also an abstract quality. The Messiah is a concrete person and hence is not thought of as indwelling. It was something absolutely without precedent, therefore, when Paul regarded his Christ—who is nothing if not a person, and a person who may be loved—as dwelling in the heart of the believer.

Objection will no doubt be raised against this treatment of the idea of personality. Wisdom, we have argued, was never in Jewish literature regarded consistently as a person distinct from God; whereas the Messiah was always regarded as a person. Against this argument it will be objected that the ancient world possessed no idea of personality at all, so that the difference between Wisdom and the Messiah disappears. But what is meant by the objection? If it is meant only that the ancient world possessed no definition of personality, the point may perhaps be conceded. But it is quite irrelevant. If, on the other hand, what is meant is that the ancients had no way of distinguishing between a person and a mere quality, no way of feeling the difference even if the difference could not be put into words, then an emphatic denial is in place. Without such a power of practical, if not theoretical, distinction, no mental or moral life at all, to say nothing of the highly developed life of the Hellenistic age, would have been possible. It is highly important, therefore, to observe that Wisdom in Jewish literature hardly becomes regarded as a person in any consistent way. Undoubtedly the hypostasizing has gone to considerable lengths, but it is always possible for the writers to hark back to the original sense of the word "wisdom"—to play at least upon the original meaning. Wisdom seems to be treated not merely as a person but also as an attribute of God.

Thus Windisch is entirely unjustified when he uses passages which represent the Messiah as possessing "wisdom" to prove that the Messiah was regarded as identical with Wisdom. A striking example of this mistake is found in the treatment of 1 Enoch xlix. 3, where it is said that in the Elect One "dwells the spirit of wisdom, and the spirit which gives insight, and the spirit of understanding and of might and the spirit of those who have fallen asleep in righteousness." A still more striking example is found in the use of 1 Cor. i. 24, 30, where Christ crucified is called the power of God and the wisdom of God, and is said to have become to believers wisdom and justification and sanctification and redemption. Windisch actually uses these passages as evidence for the application to the apocalyptic Messiah and to the Pauline Christ of the attributes of the hypostasis Wisdom. Could anything be more utterly unwarranted? The inclusion of "wisdom" in a considerable list of what the Son of Man possesses or of what Christ means to the believer, far from proving that 1 Enoch or Paul identified the Messiah with the hypostasized Wisdom, rather proves, if proof be necessary, that they did not make the identification. It is a very different thing to say that Christ possesses wisdom (along with other qualities) or brings wisdom to the believer (along with other gifts) from saying that Christ is so identical with the hypostasis Wisdom of the "wisdom literature" that what is there said about Wisdom is to be attributed to Him. Windisch himself observes, very significantly, that Paul could not actually designate Christ as "Wisdom" because the word wisdom is of feminine gender in Greek. The difference of gender is here the symbol of a profound difference in essential character. The figure of Wisdom in Jewish literature, with its curious vacillation between personality and abstraction, is absolutely incongruous with the warm, living, concrete, personal figure of the Pauline Christ. The two belong to totally different circles of ideas. No wonder that even Bousset (as Windisch complains) has not ventured to bring them into connection. The Pauline Christology was certainly not based upon the pre-Christian doctrine of Wisdom.

Thus the first great objection to Wrede's derivation of the Pauline Christology is that it is simply insufficient. The Messiah of the Jewish apocalypses is not great enough to have been the basis of the Pauline Christ. If before the conversion Paul had believed in the apocalyptic Messiah, then when he was converted he lifted his conception to far greater heights than it had before attained. But what caused him to do so? Apparently he ought to have done exactly the reverse. If Jesus was a mere man, then the identification of the Messiah with Him ought to have pushed the conception of the Messiah down instead of lifting it up. As Baldensperger significantly remarks, the Jewish apocalyptists faced less difficulty in presenting a transcendent Messiah than did their successors, the exponents of a metaphysical Christology in the Christian Church, since the Jewish apocalyptists could give free course to their fancy, whereas the Christians were hampered by the recollections of the earthly Jesus.[1] This observation, on the basis of Baldensperger's naturalistic presuppositions, is entirely correct. But the strange thing is that the recollections of Jesus, far from hampering the Christians in their ascription of supernatural attributes to the Messiah, actually had just the opposite effect. Paul furnishes a striking example. Before he identified the Messiah with Jesus, he did not really think of the Messiah as divine—not even if he believed in the transcendent Messiah of 1 Enoch. But after he identified the Messiah with Jesus, he said "not by man but by Christ." Why was it that identification with Jesus, instead of bringing the apocalyptic Messiah down to earth, lifted Him rather to the throne of God? Was it, after all, because of something in Jesus? If it was, then the eternal Son of God walked upon earth, and suffered for the sins of men. If it was not, then the fundamental historical problem of Christianity is still entirely unsolved.

[1] Baldensperger, *op. cit.*, p. 126.

But another objection faces the solution proposed by Wrede and Brückner. Suppose the apocalyptic doctrine of the Messiah were really adequate to the strain which is placed upon it. Suppose it really represented the Messiah as active in creation and as indwelling in the hearts of the faithful and as exalted to the throne of God. These suppositions are entirely without warrant in the facts; they transcend by far even the claims of Wrede and Brückner themselves. But suppose they were correct. Even then the genesis of Paul's religion would not be explained. Suppose the Pauline doctrine of the Messiah really was complete in his mind before he was converted. Even then, another problem remains. How did he come to identify his exalted Messiah with a Jew who had lived but a few years before and had died a shameful death? The thing might be explained if Jesus was what He is represented in all of the extant sources as being—a supernatural person whose glory shone out plain even through the veil of flesh. It might be explained if Paul before his conversion really believed that the heavenly Christ was to come to earth before His final parousia and die an accursed death. But the former alternative is excluded by the naturalistic presuppositions of the modern man. And the latter is excluded by an overwhelming weight of evidence as to pre-Christian Judaism and the pre-Christian life of Paul. How then did Paul come to identify his heavenly Messiah with Jesus of Nazareth? It could only have been through the strange experience which he had near Damascus. But what, in turn, caused that experience? No answer, on the basis of naturalistic presuppositions, has yet been given. In removing the supernatural from the earthly life of Jesus, modern naturalism has precluded the only possible naturalistic explanation of the conversion of Paul. If Jesus had given evidence of being the heavenly Son of Man, then Paul might conceivably, though still not probably, have become convinced against his will, and might, conceivably though still not probably, have experienced an hallucination in which he thought he saw Jesus living in glory. But if Jesus was a mere man, the identification of Him with the heavenly apocalyptic Messiah becomes inconceivable, and the experience through which that identification took place is left absolutely uncaused. Thus the hypothesis of Wrede and Brückner defeats itself. In arguing that Paul's pre-conversion conception of the Messiah was not a conception of a mere earthly being or the like, but that of a transcendent being, Wrede and Brückner are really digging the grave of their own theory. For the more exalted was the Messiah in whom Paul believed before his conversion, the more inexplicable becomes the identification of that Messiah with a crucified malefactor.

But still another objection remains. Suppose the Pauline Christ were simply the Messiah of the Jewish apocalypses; suppose Paul knew so little about the historical Jesus that he could even identify the exalted Messiah with Him. Even then another fact requires explanation. How did Paul come to be so strikingly similar to the historical Jesus both in teaching and in character? Wrede was audacious enough to explain the similarity as due to a common dependence upon Judaism.[1] But at this point few have followed him. For the striking fact is that Paul agrees with Jesus in just those matters to which Judaism was most signally opposed. It would be more plausible to say that Paul agrees with Jesus because both of them abandoned contemporary Judaism and returned to the Old Testament prophets. But even that explanation would be quite inadequate. The similarity between Jesus and Paul goes far beyond what both hold in common with the Prophets and the Psalms. And why did two men return to the Prophets and Psalms at just the same time and in just the same way? The similarity between Jesus and Paul might then be regarded as due to mere chance. Paul, it might be supposed, developed the ideal of Christian love from the death of the Messiah, which he interpreted as an act of self-sacrifice.[2] This ideal of love happened to be just the same as that which Jesus of Nazareth exemplified in a life of service—to which life of service, however, Paul was completely indifferent. Such, essentially, is what the hypothesis of Wrede really amounts to. The hypothesis is really absurd. But its absurdity is instructive. It is an absurdity to which the naturalistic account of the origin of Christianity is driven by an inexorable logic. Paul, it must be supposed, could not have regarded Jesus as a divine being if he had really known Jesus. The similarity of

---

[1] Wrede, *Paulus*, 1904, pp. 90, 91 (English Translation, *Paul*, 1907, pp. 157, 158).
[2] See Brückner, *op. cit.*, p. 237.

his life and teaching to that of Jesus cannot, therefore, be due to knowledge of Jesus. It must therefore be due to chance. In other words, it is dangerous, on naturalistic principles, to bring Paul into contact with Jesus. For if he is brought into contact with Jesus, his witness to Jesus will have to be heard. And when his witness is heard, the elaborate modern reconstructions of the "liberal Jesus" fall to the ground. For according to Paul, Jesus was no mere Galilean prophet, but the Lord of Glory.

CHAPTER VI

THE RELIGION OF THE HELLENISTIC AGE

CHAPTER VI

IT has been shown in the last chapter that the religion of Paul was not derived from the pre-Christian Jewish doctrine of the Messiah. If, therefore, the derivation of Paulinism from the historical Jesus is still to be abandoned, recourse must be had to the pagan world. And as a matter of fact, it is in the pagan world that the genesis of Paulinism is to-day more and more frequently being sought. The following chapters will deal with that hypothesis which makes the religion of Paul essentially a product of the syncretistic pagan religion of the Hellenistic age.

This hypothesis is not only held in many different forms, but also enters into combination with the view which has been considered in the last chapter. For example, M. Brückner, who regards the Pauline Christology as being simply the Jewish conception of the Messiah, modified by the episode of the Messiah's humiliation, is by no means hostile to the hypothesis of pagan influence. On the contrary, he brings the Jewish conception of the Messiah upon which the Pauline Christology is thought to be based, itself into connection with the widespread pagan myth of a dying and rising saviour-god.[1] Thus Brückner is at one with the modern school of comparative religion in deriving Paul's religion from paganism; only he derives it from paganism not directly but through the medium of the Jewish conception of the Messiah. On the other hand, most of those who find direct and not merely mediate pagan influence at the heart of the religion of Paul are also willing to admit that some important influences came through pre-Christian Judaism—notably, through the Messianic expectations of the apocalypses. The division between the subject of the present chapter and that of the preceding chapter is therefore difficult to carry out. Nevertheless, that division will be

[1] Brückner, *Der sterbende und auferstehende Gottheiland*, 1908.

found convenient. It will be well to consider separately the
hypothesis (now in the very forefront of interest) which derives Paulinism, not from the historical Jesus, and not from
pre-Christian Judaism, but from the pagan religion of the
Greco-Roman world.

Here, as in the last chapter, the discussion may begin
with a brief review of that type of religion from which Paulinism is thought to have been derived. The review will again
have to be of a most cursory character, and will make free
use of recent researches.[1] Those researches are becoming
more and more extensive in recent years. The Hellenistic age is
no longer regarded as a period of hopeless decadence, but is
commanding a larger and larger share of attention from philo-
logians and from students of the history of religion. The
sources, however, so far as the sphere of popular religion is concerned, are rather meager. Complete unanimity of opinion,
therefore, even regarding fundamental matters, has by no
means been attained.

At the time of Paul, the civilized world was unified,
politically, under the Roman Empire. The native religion of
Rome, however, was not an important factor in the life of the
Empire—certainly not in the East. That religion had been
closely bound up with the life of the Roman city-state. It
had been concerned largely with a system of auguries and religious ceremonies intended to guide the fortunes of the city
and insure the favor of the gods. But there had been little
attempt to enter into any sort of personal contact with the
gods or even to produce any highly differentiated account of
their nature. The native religion of Rome, on the whole,
seems to have been rather a cold, unsatisfying affair. It
aroused the emotions of the people only because it was an expression of stern and sturdy patriotism. And it tended to
lose its influence when the horizon of the people was broadened
by contact with the outside world.

The most important change was wrought by contact with
Greece. When Rome began to extend her conquests into the
East, the eastern countries, to a very considerable extent,

[1] For example, Rohde, *Psyche*, 2 Bde, 3te Aufl., 1903; Farnell, *Cults of
the Greek States*, vol. iii, 1907; Wendland, *Die hellenistisch-römische Kultur*,
2te u. 3te Aufl., 1912; Anrich, *Das antike Mysterienwesen*, 1894; Cumont,
Les religions orientales dans le paganisme romain, 2ième éd., 1909 (English Translation, *The Oriental Religions in Roman Paganism*, 1911).

had already been Hellenized, by the conquests of Alexander
and by the Greek kingdoms into which his short-lived empire
had been divided. Thus the Roman conquerors came into contact with Greek civilization, not only in the Greek colonies
in Sicily and southern Italy, not only in Greece proper and on
the Ægean coast of Asia Minor, but also to some extent everywhere in the eastern world. No attempt was made to root out
the Greek influences. On the contrary, the conquerors to a
very considerable extent were conquered by those whom they
had conquered; Rome submitted herself, in the spiritual sphere,
to the dominance of Greece.

The Greek influence extended into the sphere of religion.
At a very early time, the ancient Roman gods were identified
with the Greek gods who possessed roughly analogous functions
—Jupiter became Zeus, for example, and Venus became Aphrodite. This identification brought an important enrichment into
Roman religion. The cold and lifeless figures of the Roman
pantheon began to take on the grace and beauty and the
clearly defined personal character which had been given to their
Greek counterparts by Homer and Hesiod and the dramatists
and Phidias and Praxiteles. Thus it is not to the ancient official religion of Rome but to the rich pantheon of Homer that
the student must turn in order to find the spiritual ancestry of
the religion of the Hellenistic world.

Even before the time of Homer, Greek religion had undergone development. Modern scholarship, at least, is no longer
inclined to find in Homer the artless simplicity of a primitive
age. On the contrary, the Homeric poems, it is now supposed,
were the product of a highly developed, aristocratic society,
which must be thought of as standing at the apex of a social
order. Thus it is not to be supposed that the religion of
Homer was the only Hellenic religion of Homer's day. On the
contrary, even in the Homeric poems, it is said, there appear
here and there remnants of a popular primitive religion—
human sacrifice and the like—and many of the rough, primitive conceptions which crop out in Greek life in the later
centuries were really present long before the Homeric age,
and had been preserved beneath the surface in the depths of
a non-literary popular religion. However much of truth there
may be in these contentions, it is at any rate clear that the
Homeric poems exerted an enormous influence upon subsequent

generations. Even if they were the product of a limited circle, even if they never succeeded in eradicating the primitive conceptions, at least they did gain enormous prestige and did become the most important single factor in molding the religion of the golden age of Greece.

As determined by the Homeric poems, the religion of Greece was a highly developed polytheism of a thoroughly anthropomorphic kind. The Greek gods were simply men and women, with human passions and human sins—more powerful, indeed, but not more righteous than those who worshiped them. Such a religion was stimulating to the highest art. Anthropomorphism gave free course to the imagination of poets and sculptors. There is nothing lifeless about the gods of Greece; whether portrayed by the chisel of sculptors or the pen of poets, they are warm, living, breathing, human figures. But however stimulating to the sense of beauty, the anthropomorphic religion of Greece was singularly unsatisfying in the moral sphere. If the gods were no better than men, the worship of them was not necessarily ennobling. No doubt there was a certain moral quality in the very act of worship. For worship was not always conceived of as mere prudent propitiation of dangerous tyrants. Sometimes it was conceived of as a duty, like the pious reverence which a child should exhibit toward his parent. In the case of filial piety, as in the case of piety toward the gods, the duty of reverence is independent of the moral quality of the revered object. But in both cases the very act of reverence may possess a certain moral value. This admission, however, does not change the essential fact. It remains true that the anthropomorphic character of the gods of Greece, just because it stimulated the fancy of poets by attributing human passions to the gods and so provided the materials of dramatic art, at the same time prevented religion from lifting society above the prevailing standards. The moral standards of snowy Olympus, unfortunately, were not higher than those of the Athenian market place.

In another way also, the polytheistic religion of Greece was unsatisfying. It provided little hope of personal communion between the gods and men. Religion, in Greece scarcely less than in ancient Rome, was an affair of the state. A man was born into his religion. An Athenian citizen, as such, was a worshiper of the Athenian gods. There was little place for individual choice or for individual devotion. Moreover, there was little place for the mystical element in religion. The gods of Greece were in some sort, indeed, companionable figures; they were similar to men; men could understand the motives of their actions. But there was no way in which companionship with them could find expression. There was a time, indeed, when the gods had come down to earth to help the great heroes who were their favorites or their sons. But such favors were not given to ordinary mortals. The gods might be revered, but direct and individual contact with them was for the most part not to be attained.

These limitations, however, were not universal; and for purposes of the present investigation the exceptions are far more important than the rule. It is not true that the religion of Greece, even previous to the golden age, was entirely devoid of enthusiasm or individualism or mystic contact with the gods. The polytheism of Homer, the polytheism of the Olympic pantheon, despite its wide prevalence was not the only form of Greek religion. Along with the worship of the Olympic gods there went also religious practices of a very different kind. There was a place even in Greece for mystical religion.

This mystical or enthusiastic element in the religion of Greece is connected especially with the worship of Dionysus. Dionysus was not originally a Greek god. He came from Thrace and is very closely related to the Phrygian Sabazius. But, at an early time, his worship was widely adopted in the Greek world. No doubt it was not adopted entirely without modification; no doubt it was shorn of some of those features which were most repulsive to the Greek genius. But enough remained in order to affect very powerfully the character of Greek religion.

The worship of Dionysus supplied, to some extent at least, just those elements which were lacking in the religion of the Greek city-state. In the first place, there was direct contact with the god. The worshipers of Dionysus sought to attain contact with the god partly by a divine frenzy, which was induced by wild music and dancing, and partly by the cruss method of eating the raw flesh of the sacred animal, the bull. No doubt these savage practices were often modified when they were introduced into Greece. It has been thought, for example, that the frenzied dances and nightly excursions to the wilds of the mountains, which originally had been carried on in true self-forgetfulness, became in Greece rather parts of an established cult. But on the whole, the influence of Dionysus-worship must be regarded as very great. An element of true mysticism or enthusiasm was introduced into the Greek world.

In the second place, the worship of Dionysus stimulated interest in a future life. The Homeric poems had represented the existence of the soul after death—at least the soul of an ordinary mortal—as being a mere shadow-existence which could not be called life at all. It is indeed questionable whether at this point Homer truly represented the original Hellenic belief, or the popular belief even of the time when the poems were written. Modern scholars have detected in the Iliad and the Odyssey here and there remnants of a more positive doctrine of a future life. But at any rate, the worship of Dionysus brought such positive beliefs—if they existed in Greece before—more to the surface. Thracian religion, apparently, had concerned itself to a very considerable extent with the future condition of the soul; the introduction of the Thracian Dionysus, therefore, stimulated a similar interest in Greece.

Finally, the worship of Dionysus tended to separate religion from the state and make it partly at least an affair of the individual man. Such individualism is connected of course with the enthusiastic character of the worship; a state religion as such is not likely to be enthusiastic. The whole body of citizens cannot be possessed of a divine frenzy, and if not, then those who have the experience are likely to separate themselves to some extent from their countrymen. It is not surprising, therefore, that the worshipers of Dionysus, here and there, were inclined to unite themselves in sects or brotherhoods.

The most important of these brotherhoods were connected with the name of Orpheus, the mythical musician and seer. The origin of the Orphic sects is indeed very obscure. Apparently, however, they sprang up or became influential in the sixth century before Christ, and were connected in some way with Dionysus. They seem to have represented a reform of Dionysiac practice. At any rate, they continued that interest in the future life which the worship of Dionysus had already cultivated. Orphism is especially important because it taught men to expect in the future life not only rewards but also punishments. The soul after death, according to Orphic doctrine, was subject to an indefinite succession of reincarnations, not only in the bodies of men, but also in those of animals. These reincarnations were regarded as an evil, because the body was thought of as a prison-house of the soul. At last, however, the righteous soul attains purification, and, escaping from the succession of births, enters into a blessed existence.

Related in some way to the Orphic sects were the brotherhoods that owned Pythagoras as their master. But the relation between the two movements is not perfectly plain.

At any rate, both Orphism and Pythagoreanism stand apart from the official cults of the Greek states. Even within those cults, however, there were not wanting some elements which satisfied more fully than the ordinary worship of the Olympic gods the longing of individual men for contact with the higher powers and for a blessed immortality. Such elements were found in the "mysteries," of which far the most important were the mysteries of Eleusis.[1] The Eleusinian Mysteries originated in the worship of Demeter that was carried on at Eleusis, a town in Attica some fifteen miles from Athens. When Eleusis was conquered by Athens, the Eleusinian cult of Demeter, far from suffering eclipse, was adopted by the conquerors and so attained unparalleled influence. Characteristic of the cult as so developed was the secrecy of its central rites; the Eleusinian cult of Demeter became (if it was not one already) a mystery-cult, whose secrets were divulged only to the initiates. The terms of admission, however, were very broad. All persons of Greek race, even slaves—except those persons who were stained with bloodguiltiness or the like— could be admitted. As so constituted, the Eleusinian Mysteries were active for some ten centuries; they continued until the very end of pagan antiquity.

Initiation into the mysteries took place ordinarily in three stages; the candidate was first initiated into the "lesser mysteries" at Agræ near Athens in the spring; then into a first stage of the "great mysteries" at Eleusis in the following autumn; then a year later his initiation was completed at Eleusis by the reception of the mystic vision. The mysteries of Eleusis were prepared for by a succession of acts about

[1] On the Eleusinian Mysteries and the cult of Demeter and Kore-Persephone, see especially Farnell, *op. cit.*, iii, pp. 29-279.

which some information has been preserved. These acts were extended over a period of days. First the sacred objects were brought from Eleusis to Athens. Then the candidates for initiation, who had purified themselves by abstinence from certain kinds of food and from sexual intercourse, were called upon to assemble. Then, at the cry, "To the sea, O mystæ!" the candidates went to the sea-coast, where they made sacrifice of a pig, and purified themselves by washing in the sea water. Then came the solemn procession from Athens to Eleusis, interrupted by ribald jests at the passage of the river Cephissus. The initiation itself took place in the "telesterion." What happened there is obscure; antiquity has well observed the secrecy which was essential to the mysteries. Certainly, however, the ceremony was accompanied, or rather, perhaps, preceded, by the drinking of the "kykeon," a mixture composed of water and barley-meal and other ingredients. The significance of this act is not really known. It would be very rash, for example, to assert that the partaking of the kykeon was sacramental, or was thought of as imparting a new nature to the recipients. Apparently the kykeon did not have a part in the mysteries themselves, for if it had, it could hardly have been spoken of so openly by pagan writers. The mysteries seem to have consisted in some sort of sacred drama, representing the search of Demeter for her daughter Persephone who had been carried off to the lower world, and in the exhibition of sacred emblems or of images of the gods. Hippolytus scornfully says that the supreme object of mystic awe was a cut corn-stalk.[1] His testimony is variously estimated. But it is quite possible that he has here given us genuine information. Since Demeter was the goddess of the fertility of the soil, the corn-stalk was not ill fitted to be her sacred emblem.

It has been supposed that the cult of Demeter at Eleusis was originally an agrarian cult, intended to celebrate or to induce the fertility of the soil. But the chief significance of the mysteries was found in another sphere. In the mysteries, the cult goddesses, Demeter and Persephone, were thought of chiefly as goddesses of the nether world, the abode of the dead; and the mysteries were valued chiefly as providing a guarantee of a blessed immortality. How the guarantee was given is quite obscure. But the fact is well attested. Those who had been

[1] Hippolytus, *Ref. omn. haer.*, V, viii, 39 (ed. Wendland, 1916).

initiated into the mysteries were able to expect a better lot in the future life than the lot of the generality of men.

The mysteries at Eleusis were not the only mysteries which were practised in the golden age of Greece. There were not only offshoots of the Eleusinian mysteries in various places, but also independent mysteries like those of the Kabeiri on the island of Samothrace. But the mysteries at Eleusis were undoubtedly the most important, and the others are even less fully known. The moral value of the mysteries, including those at Eleusis, should not be exaggerated. Slight allusions in pagan writers seem to point here and there to a purifying moral effect wrought by initiation. But the indications are not very clear. Certainly the secrets of Eleusis did not consist in any body of teaching, either religious or ethical. The effect was produced, not upon the intellect, but upon the emotions and upon the imagination.

Thus the religion of the golden age of Greece was an anthropomorphic polytheism, closely connected with the life of the city-state, but relieved here and there by practices intended to provide more direct contact with the divine or bestow special blessing upon individuals.

The religion of Greece was finally undermined by at least three agencies.

In the first place, philosophy tended to destroy belief in the gods. The philosophic criticism of the existing religion was partly theoretical and partly ethical. The theoretical criticism arose especially through the search for a unifying principle operative in the universe. If the manifold phenomena of the universe were all reduced to a single cause, the gods might indeed still be thought of as existing, but their importance was gone. There was thus a tendency either toward monotheism or else toward some sort of materialistic monism. But the objections which philosophy raised against the existing polytheism were ethical as well as theoretical. The Homeric myths were rightly felt to be immoral; the imitation of the Homeric gods would result in moral degradation. Thus if the myths were still to be retained they could not be interpreted literally, but had to be given some kind of allegorical interpretation.

This opposition of philosophy to the existing religion was often not explicit, and it did not concern religious practice. Even those philosophers whose theory left no room for the existence or at least the importance of the gods, continued to engage loyally in the established cults. But although the superstructure of religion remained, the foundation, to some extent at least, was undermined.

In the second place, since religion in ancient Greece had been closely connected with the city-states, the destruction of the states brought important changes in religion. The Greek states lost their independence through the conquests of Philip of Macedon and Alexander the Great. Those conquests meant, indeed, a wide extension of Greek culture throughout the eastern world. But the religion of Alexander's empire and of the kingdoms into which it was divided after his death was widely different from the religion of Athens in her glory. Cosmopolitanism brought mighty changes in religion, as in the political sphere.

In the third place, the influence of the eastern religions made itself more and more strongly felt. That influence was never indeed dominant in the life of Greece proper so completely as it was in some other parts of the world. But in general it was very important. When the Olympic gods lost their place in the minds and hearts of men, other gods were ready to take their place.

Before any account can be given of the eastern religions taken separately, and of their progress toward the west, it may be well to mention certain general characteristics of the period which followed the conquests of Alexander. That period, which extended several centuries into the Christian era, is usually called the Hellenistic age, to distinguish it from the Hellenic period which had gone before.

The Hellenistic age was characterized, in the first place, by cosmopolitanism. Natural and racial barriers to an astonishing extent were broken down; the world, at least the educated world of the cities, was united by the bonds of a common language, and finally by a common political control. The common language was the Koiné, the modified form of the Attic dialect of Greek, which became the vehicle of a world-civilization. The common political control was that of the Roman Empire. On account of the union of these two factors, intercommunication between various nations and races was safe and easy; the nations were united both in trade and in intellectual activity.

With the cosmopolitanism thus produced there went naturally a new individualism, which extended into the religious sphere. Under the city-state of ancient Greece the individual was subordinated to the life of the community. But in the world-empire the control of the state, just because it was broader, was at the same time looser. Patriotism no longer engrossed the thoughts of men. It was impossible for a subject of a great empire to identify himself with the life of the empire so completely as the free Athenian citizen of the age of Pericles had identified himself with the glories of his native city. Thus the satisfactions which in that earlier period had been sought in the life of the state, including the state-religion, were in the Hellenistic age sought rather in individual religious practice.

The ancient religions of the city-state did indeed find a successor which was adapted to the changed condition. That successor was the worship of the Emperors. The worship of the Emperors was more than a mere form of flattery. It expressed a general gratitude for the reign of peace which was introduced by Augustus, and it had its roots, not only in Greek religion, but also, and far more fundamentally, in the religions of the East. The worship of the rulers was firmly established in the kingdoms into which Alexander's empire was divided, and from there it was transmitted very naturally to the new and greater empire of Rome. Very naturally it became a dangerous enemy of the Christian Church; for the refusal of the Christians to worship the Emperor seemed inexplicable to an age of polytheism, and gave rise to the charge of political disloyalty. At first, however, and so during the period of Paul's missionary journeys, the Church shared more or less in the special privileges which were granted to the Jews. Christianity at first seemed to be a variety of Judaism, and Judaism in Roman practice was a *religio licita*.

But the worship of the Emperors, important as it was, was not practised in any exclusive way; it did not at all exclude the worship of other gods. It remains true, therefore, that in the Hellenistic age, far more than under the ancient Greek city-state, there was room for individual choice in religious practice.

It is not surprising that such an age was an age of religious propaganda. Since religion was no longer an affair of the nation as such, but addressed itself to men as men, free scope was offered for the extension to the whole world of religions which originally had been national in character. The golden age of such religious propaganda, it is true, did not begin until the second century; and that fact is of very great importance in dealing with certain modern theories of dependence so far as Pauline Christianity is concerned. Nevertheless the cosmopolitanizing of national religions had begun to some extent in an early period and was rendered natural by the entire character of the Hellenistic age. Even before the fall of the Greek city-state, little communities of the worshipers of eastern gods had established themselves here and there in Greece; a 1 in other parts of the world the barriers against religious propaganda were even less effective. In the Hellenistic age such barriers were almost everywhere broken down. When any religion ceased to be an affair of the nation, when it could no longer count on the devotion of the citizens or subjects as such, it was obliged, if it desired to subsist, to seek its devotees through an appeal to the free choice of individuals.

This religious propaganda, however, was not carried on in any exclusive way; the adoption of one god did not mean the abandonment of another. On the contrary, the Hellenistic age was the age of syncretism *par excellence*. Gods of different nations, originally quite distinct, were identified almost as a matter of course. One example of such identification has already been noted; at an early time the gods of Rome were identified with those of Greece. But in the later portion of the Hellenistic age the process went on in more wholesale fashion. And it was sometimes justified by the far-reaching theory that the gods of different nations were merely different names of one great divinity. This theory received classic expression in the words of the goddess Isis which are contained in the "Metamorphoses" of Apuleius: "For the Phrygians that are the first of all men call me the Mother of the gods at Pessinus; the Athenians, which are sprung from their own soil, Cecropian Minerva; the Cyprians, which are girt about by the sea, Paphian Venus; the Cretans which bear arrows, Dictynnian Diana; the Sicilians, which speak three tongues, infernal Proserpine; the Eleusians their ancient goddess Ceres; some Juno, other Bellona, other Hecate, other Rhamnusia, and principally both sort of the Ethiopians which dwell in the Orient and are enlightened by the morning rays of the sun, and the Egyptians, which are excellent in all kind of ancient doctrine, and by their proper ceremonies accustom to worship me, do call me by my true name, Queen Isis." [1]

But what is perhaps the most important feature of the religion of the Hellenistic age has not yet been mentioned. It is found in the widespread desire for redemption. In the golden age of Greece men had been satisfied with the world. Who could engage in gloomy questionings, who could face the under-lying problem of evil, when it was possible to listen with keen appreciation to an ode of Pindar or to a tragedy of Æschylus? The Greek tragic poets, it is true, present in terrible fashion the sterner facts of life. But the glorious beauty of the pres-entation itself produces a kind of satisfaction. In the age of Pericles, life was rich and full; for the Athenian citizen it was a joy to live. The thought of another world was not needed; this world was large and rich enough. Joyous development of existing human faculties was, in the golden age of Greece, the chief end of man.

But the glorious achievements of the Greek genius were fol-lowed by lamentable failure. There was failure in political life. Despite the political genius of Athenian statesmen, Athens soon lay prostrate, first before her sister states and then before the Macedonian conqueror. There was failure in intellectual life. The glorious achievements of Athenian art were followed by a period of decline. Poets and sculptors had to find their in-spiration in imitation of the past. Human nature, once so proud, was obliged to confess its inadequacy; the Hellenistic age was characterized by what Gilbert Murray, borrowing a phrase of J. B. Bury, calls a "failure of nerve." [2]

This failure of nerve found expression, in the religious sphere, in the longing for redemption. The world was found not to be so happy a place as had been supposed, and human nature was obliged to seek help from outside. Thus arose the desire for "salvation." The characteristic gods of the Hellenistic age are in some sort saviour-gods—gods who could give help in the miseries of life. Asclepius finally became more important than

[1] Apuleius, *Metam.* xi. 5, Addington's translation revised by Gaselee, in Apuleius, *The Golden Ass*, in the *The Loeb Classical Library*, p. 547.
[2] Gilbert Murray, *Four Stages of Greek Religion*, 1912, pp. 8, 103-154. Compare, however, Rohde (*op. cit.*, ii, pp. 298-300). who calls attention to an opposite aspect of the Hellenistic age.

Zeus. Dissatisfied with the world of sense, men turned their thoughts to another world; dissatisfied with the achievements of human nature, they sought communion with higher powers.

Opinions may differ as to the value of this development. To the humanist of all ages, it will seem to be a calamity. From the glories of Pindar to the morbid practices of the Hellenistic mysteries, how great a fall! But there is another way of regarding the change. Possibly the achievements of ancient Greece, glorious as they were, had been built upon an insecure foundation. Scrutiny of the foundation was no doubt painful, and it dulled the enthusiasm of the architects. But perhaps it was necessary and certainly it was inevitable. Perhaps also it might become a step toward some higher humanism. The Greek joy of living was founded upon a certain ruthlessness toward human misery, a certain indifference toward moral problems. Such a joy could not be permanent. But how would it be if the underlying problem could be faced, instead of being ignored? How would it be if human nature could be founded upon some secure rock, in order that then the architect might start to build once more, and build, this time, with a conscience void of offense? Such is the Christian ideal, the ideal of a loftier humanism—a humanism as rich and as joyful as the humanism of Greece, but a humanism founded upon the grace of God.

But however "the failure of nerve" which appears in the Hellenistic age be appreciated by the student of the philosophy of history, the fact at least cannot be ignored. The Hellenistic age was characterized by a widespread longing for redemption—a widespread longing for an escape from the present world of sense to some higher and better country. Such longing was not satisfied by the ancient religion of Greece. It caused men, therefore, to become seekers after new gods.

But what was the attitude of philosophy? Philosophy had contributed to the decline of the ancient gods. Had it been equally successful on the positive side? Had it been able to fill the void which its questionings had produced? The answer on the whole must be rendered in the negative. On the whole, it must be said that Greek philosophy was unsuccessful in its efforts to solve the riddle of the universe. The effort which it made was indeed imposing. Plato in particular endeavored to satisfy the deepest longings of the human soul; he attempted to provide an escape from the world of sense to the higher world of ideas. But the way of escape was open at best only to the few philosophical souls; the generality of men were left hopeless and helpless in the shadow-existence of the cave. And even the philosophers were not long satisfied with the Platonic solution. The philosophy of the Hellenistic age was either openly skeptical or materialistic, as is the case, for example, with Epicureanism, or at any rate it abandoned the great theoretical questions and busied itself chiefly with practical affairs. Epicureans and Stoics and Cynics were all interested chiefly, not in ontology or epistemology, but in ethics. At this point the first century was like the twentieth. The distrust of theory, the depreciation of theology, the exclusive interest in social and practical questions—these tendencies appear now as they appeared in the Hellenistic age. And now as well as then they are marks of intellectual decadence.

But if the philosophy of the Hellenistic age offered no satisfactory solution of the riddle of the universe and no satisfaction for the deepest longings of the soul, it presented, on the other hand, no effective opposition to the religious current of the time. It had helped bring about that downfall of the Olympic gods, that sad neglect of Zeus and his altars which is described by Lucian in his wonderfully modern satires. But it was not able to check the rising power of the eastern religions. Indeed it entered into a curious alliance with the invaders. As early as the first century before Christ, Posidonius seems to have introduced an element of oriental mysticism into the philosophy of the Stoics, and in the succeeding centuries the process went on apace. The climax was reached, at the close of pagan antiquity, in that curious mixture of philosophy and charlatanism which is found in the neo-Platonic writers.

The philosophy of the Hellenistic age, with its intense interest in questions of conduct, constitutes, indeed, an important chapter in the history of the human race, and can point to certain noteworthy achievements. The Stoics, for example, enunciated the great principle of human brotherhood; they made use of the cosmopolitanism and individualism of the Hellenistic age in order to arouse a new interest in man as man. Even the slaves, who in the theory of an Aristotle had been treated as chattels, began to be looked upon here and there as members of a great human family. Men of every race and of every social grade came to be the object of a true humanitarian interest.

But the humanitarian efforts of Stoicism, though proceeding from an exalted theory of the worth of man as man, proved to be powerless. The dynamic somehow was lacking. Despite the teaching of Seneca and Marcus Aurelius, despite the beginnings of true humanitarian effort here and there, the later Empire with its cruel gladiatorial shows and its heartless social system was sinking into the slough of savagery. What Stoicism was unable to do, Christianity to some extent at least accomplished. The ideal of Christianity was not the mere ideal of a human brotherhood. Pure humanitarianism, the notion of "the brotherhood of man," as that phrase is usually understood, is Stoic rather than Christian. Christianity did make its appeal to all men; it won many of its first adherents from the depths of slavery. It did inculcate charity toward all men whether Christians or not. And it enunciated with an unheard-of seriousness the doctrine that all classes of men, wise and unwise, bond and free, are of equal worth. But the equality was not found in the common possession of human nature. It was found, instead, in a common connection with Jesus Christ. "There can be neither Jew nor Greek, there can be neither bond nor free, there can be no male and female"—so far the words of Paul can find analogies (faint analogies, it is true) in the Stoic writers. But the Pauline grounding of the unity here enunciated is the very antithesis of all mere humanitarianism both ancient and modern—"For ye are all one person," says Paul, "in Christ Jesus." Christianity did not reveal the fact that all men were brothers. Indeed it revealed the contrary. But it offered to make all men brothers by bringing them into saving connection with Christ.

The above sketch of the characteristics of the Hellenistic age has been quite inadequate. And even a fuller presentation could hardly do justice to the complexity of the life of that time. But perhaps some common misconceptions have been corrected. The pagan world at the time when Paul set sail from Seleucia on his first missionary journey was not altogether without religion. Even the ancient polytheism was by no means altogether dead. It was rather a day of religious unrest. The old faiths had been shaken, but they were making room for the new. The Orontes, to use the figure of Juvenal, was soon to empty into the Tiber. The flow of eastern superstition and eastern mystical religion was soon to spread over the whole world.

But what were the eastern religions which in the second century after Christ, if not before, entered upon their triumphal march toward the west? [1] They were of diverse origin and diverse character. But one feature was common to a number of the most important of them. Those eastern religions which became most influential in the later Roman Empire were mystery religions—that is, they had connected with them secret rites which were thought to afford special blessing to the initiates. The mysteries did not indeed constitute the whole of the worship of the eastern gods. Side by side with the mysteries were to be found public cults to which every one was admitted. But the mysteries are of special interest, because it was they which satisfied most fully the longing of the Hellenistic age for redemption, for "salvation," for the attainment of a higher nature.

It will be well, therefore, to single out for special mention the chief of the mystery religions—those eastern religions which although they were by no means altogether secret did have mysteries connected with them.

The first of these religions to be introduced into Rome was the religion of the Phrygian Cybele, the "Great Mother of the Gods." [2] In 204 B.C., in the dark days of the Carthaginian invasion, the black meteoric stone of Pessinus was brought, by command of an oracle, to Rome. With the sacred stone came the cult. But Rome was not yet ready for the barbaric worship of the Phrygian goddess. For several hundred years the cult of Cybele was kept carefully isolated from the life of the Roman people. The foreign rites were supported by the authority of the state, but they were conducted altogether by a foreign priesthood; no Roman citizen was allowed to participate in them. It was not until the reign of Claudius (41-54 A.D.) that the barrier was finally broken down.

The myth of Cybele is narrated in various forms. Ac-

[1] The sketch which follows is indebted especially to Cumont, *Les religions orientales dans le paganisme romain*, 2ième éd., 1909 (English translation, *The Oriental Religions in Roman Paganism*, 1911).

[2] For the religion of Cybele and Attis, see Showerman, *The Great Mother of the Gods*, 1901; Hepding, *Attis*, 1903.

cording to the most characteristic form, the youthful Attis, beloved by Cybele, is struck with madness by the jealous goddess, deprives himself of his virility, dies through his own mad act, and is mourned by the goddess. The myth contains no account of a resurrection; all that Cybele is able to obtain is that the body of Attis should be preserved, that his hair should continue to grow, and that his little finger should move.

The cult was more stable than the myth. No doubt, indeed, even the cult experienced important changes in the course of the centuries. At the beginning, according to Hepding and Cumont, Cybele was a goddess of the mountain wilds, whose worship was similar in important respects to that of Dionysus. With Cybele Attis was associated at an early time. The Phrygian worship of Cybele and Attis was always of a wild, orgiastic character, and the frenzy of the worshipers culminated even in the act of self-mutilation. Thus the eunuch-priests of Cybele, the "Galli," became a well-known feature of the life of the Empire. But the Phrygian cult of Cybele and Attis cannot be reconstructed by any means in detail; extensive information has been preserved only about the worship as it was carried on at Rome. And even with regard to the Roman cult, the sources of information are to a very considerable extent late. It is not certain, therefore, that the great spring festival of Attis, as it was celebrated in the last period of the Roman Empire, was an unmodified reproduction of the original Phrygian rites.

The Roman festival was conducted as follows:[1] On March 15, there was a preliminary festival. On March 22, the sacred pine-tree was felled and carried in solemn procession by the "Dendrophori" into the temple of Cybele. The pine-tree appears in the myth as the tree under which Attis committed his act of self-mutilation. In the cult, the felling of the tree is thought by modern scholars to represent the death of the god. Hence the mourning of the worshipers was connected with the tree. March 24 was called the "day of blood"; on this day the mourning for the dead Attis reached its climax. The Galli chastised themselves with scourges and cut themselves with knives—all to the wild music of the drums and cymbals which were connected especially with the worship of the Phrygian Mother. On this day also, according to Hep-

[1] See Hepding, *op. cit.*, pp. 147-176.

ding's conjecture, the new Galli dedicated themselves to the
service of the goddess by the act of self-mutilation. Finally,
the resurrection or epiphany of the god Attis was celebrated.
This took place perhaps during the night between March 24
and March 25. But Hepding admits that the time is not directly attested. It is also only conjecture when a famous
passage of Firmicus Maternus (fourth century after Christ)
is applied to the worship of Attis and to this part of it.[1]
But the conjecture may well be correct. Firmicus Maternus [2]
describes a festival in which the figure of a god rests upon a
bier and is lamented, and then a light is brought in and the
priest exclaims, "Be of good courage, ye initiates, since the
god is saved; for to us there shall be salvation out of
troubles." [3] Apparently the resurrection of the god is here
regarded as the cause of the salvation of the worshipers;
the worshipers share in the fortunes of the god. At any
rate, March 25 in the Roman Attis festival was the "Hilaria,"
a day of rejoicing. On this day, the resurrection of the god
was celebrated. March 26 was a day of rest; and finally, on
March 27, there was a solemn washing of the sacred images
and emblems.

As thus described, the worship of Cybele and Attis was,
for the most part at least, public. But there were also mysteries connected with the same two gods. These mysteries apparently were practised in the East before the cult was brought
to Rome. But the eastern form of their celebration is quite obscure, and even about the Roman form very little is known.
Connected with the mysteries was some sort of sacred meal.[4]
Firmicus Maternus has preserved the formula: "I have eaten
from the drum; I have drunk from the cymbal; I have become
an initiate of Attis." [5] And Clement of Alexandria (about
200 A. D.) also connected a similar formula with the Phrygian
mysteries: "I ate from the drum; I drank from the cymbal;

---

[1] Loisy (*Les mystères païens et le mystère chrétien*, 1919, p. 104) prefers
to attach the passage to Osiris rather than to Attis.

[2] See Hepding, *op. cit.*, pp. 166, 167.

[3] Firmicus Maternus, *De error. prof. rel.*, xxii (ed. Ziegler, 1907):
θαρρεῖτε μύσται τοῦ θεοῦ σεσωσμένου·
ἔσται γὰρ ἡμῖν ἐκ πόνων σωτηρία.

[4] See Hepding, *op. cit.*, pp. 184-190.

[5] Firmicus Maternus, *op. cit.*, xviii: ἐκ τυμπάνου βέβρωκα, ἐκ κυμβάλου πέπωκα,
γέγονα μύστης Ἄττεως.

I carried the 'kernos'; I stole into the bridal chamber." [1]
The significance of this ritual eating and drinking is not clear.
Certainly it would be rash to find in it the notion of new birth
or sacramental union with the divine nature. Hepding suggests that it meant rather the entrance of the initiate into the
circle of the table-companions of the god.

The actual initiation is even more obscure in the Attis
mysteries than it is in those of Eleusis; Hepding admits that
his reconstruction of the details of the mysteries is based
largely on conjecture. Possibly in the formula quoted above
from Clement of Alexandria, the words, "I stole into the bridal
chamber," indicate that there was some sort of representation
of a sacred marriage; but other interpretations of the Greek
words are possible. Hepding suggests that the candidate
entered into the grotto, descended into a ditch within the
grotto, listened to lamentations for the dead god, received a
blood-bath, then saw a wonderful light, and heard the joyful
words quoted above: "Be of good courage, ye initiates, since
the god is saved; for to us shall there be salvation out of
troubles," and finally that the candidate arose out of the ditch
as a new man ("reborn for eternity") or rather as a being
identified with the god. [2]

According to this reconstruction, the initiation represented
the death and the new birth of the candidate. But the reconstruction is exceedingly doubtful, and some of the most important features of it are attested in connection with the Attis
mysteries if at all only in very late sources. Hepding is particularly careful to admit that there is no direct documentary
evidence for connecting the blood-bath with the March festival.

This blood-bath, which is called the taurobolium, requires
special attention. The one who received it descended into a pit
over which a lattice-work was placed. A bull was slaughtered
above the lattice-work, and the blood was allowed to run
through into the pit, where the recipient let it saturate his
clothing and even enter his nose and mouth and ears. The
result was that the recipient was "reborn forever," or else
reborn for a period of twenty years, after which the rite had
to be repeated. The taurobolium is thought to have signified

[1] Clem. Al., *Protrepticus,* ii. 15 (ed. Stählin, 1905): ἐκ τυμπάνου ἔφαγον· ἐκ
κυμβάλου ἔπιον· ἐκερνοφόρησα· ὑπὸ τὸν παστὸν ὑπέδυν.

[2] Hepding, *op. cit.,* pp. 196ff.

a death to the old life and a new birth into a higher, divine existence. But it is not perfectly clear that it had that significance in the East and in the early period. According to Hepding, the taurobolium was in the early period a mere sacrifice, and the first man who is said to have received it in the sense just described was the Emperor Heliogabalus (third century after Christ). Other scholars refuse to accept Hepding's distinction between an earlier and a later form of the rite. But the matter is at least obscure, and it would be exceedingly rash to attribute pre-Christian origin to the developed taurobolium as it appears in fourth-century sources. Indeed, there seems to be no mention of any kind of taurobolium whatever before the second century,[1] and Hepding may be correct in suggesting that possibly the fourth-century practice was influenced by the Christian doctrine of the blood of Christ.[2]

No less important than the religion of Cybele and Attis was the Greco-Egyptian religion of Isis and Osiris. Isis and Osiris are both ancient Egyptian gods, whose worship, in modified form, was carried over first into the Greek kingdom of the Ptolemies, and thence into the remotest bounds of the Roman Empire. The myth which concerns these gods is reported at length in Plutarch's treatise, "Concerning Isis and Osiris." Briefly it is as follows: Osiris, the brother and husband of Isis, after ruling in a beneficent manner over the Egyptians, is plotted against by his brother Typhon. Finally Typhon makes a chest and promises to give it to any one who exactly fits it. Osiris enters the chest, which is then closed by Typhon and thrown into the Nile. After a search, Isis finds the chest at Byblos on the coast of Phœnicia, and brings it back to Egypt. But Typhon succeeds in getting possession of the body of Osiris and cuts it up into fourteen parts, which are scattered through Egypt. Isis goes about collecting the parts. Osiris becomes king of the nether world, and helps his son Horus to gain a victory over Typhon.

The worship of Isis and Osiris was prominent in ancient Egyptian religion long before the entrance of Greek influence. Osiris was regarded as the ruler over the dead, and as such was naturally very important in a religion in which supreme attention was given to a future life. But with the establish-

---

[1] Showerman, op. cit., p. 280.
[2] Hepding, op. cit., p. 200, Anm. 7.

ment of the Ptolemaic kingdom at about 300 B. C., there was
an important modification of the worship. A new god, Serapis,
was introduced, and was closely identified with Osiris. The
origin of the name Serapis has been the subject of much discussion and is still obscure. But one motive for the introduction of the new divinity (or of the new name for an old divinity) is perfectly plain. Ptolemy I desired to unify the
Egyptian and the Greek elements in his kingdom by providing
a cult which would be acceptable to both and at the same
time intensely loyal to the crown. The result was the Greco-
Egyptian cult of Serapis (Osiris) and Isis. Here is to be
found, then, the remarkable phenomenon of a religion deliberately established for political reasons, which, despite its arti-
ficial origin, became enormously successful. Of course, the
success was obtained only by a skillful use of existing beliefs,
which had been hallowed in Egyptian usage from time imme-
morial, and by a skillful clothing of those beliefs in forms
acceptable to the Greek element in the population.

The religion of Isis and Serapis was, as Cumont observes,
entirely devoid of any established system of theology or any
very lofty ethics. It was effective rather on account of its
gorgeous ritual, which was handed down from generation to
generation with meticulous accuracy, and on account of the
assurance which it gave of a blessed immortality, the worshipers being conceived of as sharing in the resuscitation
which Osiris had obtained. The worship was at first repulsive
to Roman ideals of gravity, but effected an official entrance
into the city in the reign of Caligula (37-41 A. D.). In the
second and third centuries it was extended over the whole Empire. In alliance with the religion of Mithras it became finally
perhaps the most serious rival of Christianity.

The cult was partly public and partly private. Prominent
in the public worship were the solemn opening of the temple
of Isis in the morning and the solemn closing in the afternoon.
Elaborate care was taken of the images of the gods—the gods
being regarded as dependent upon human ministrations. Besides the rites that were conducted daily, there were special
festivals like the spring festival of the "ship of Isis" which is
brilliantly described by Apuleius.

But it is the mysteries which arouse the greatest interest,
especially because of the precious source of information about

them which is found in the eleventh book of the Metamorphoses of Apuleius (second century after Christ). In this book, although the secrets of the mysteries themselves are of course not revealed, Apuleius has given a more complete and orderly account of the events connected with an initiation than is to be found anywhere else in ancient literature. The hero Lucius is represented first as waiting for a summons from the goddess Isis, which comes with miraculous coincidence independently to him and to the priest who is to officiate in his initiation. Then Lucius is taken into the temple and made acquainted with certain mysterious books, and also washes his body at the nearest baths. This washing has as little as possible the appearance of a sacrament; evidently it was not intended to produce "regeneration" or anything of the sort.[1] The purpose of it seems to have been cleanliness, which was naturally regarded as a preparation for the holy rite that was to follow. There follows a ten days' period of fasting, after which the day of initiation arrives. Lucius is taken into the most secret place of the temple. Of what happens there he speaks with the utmost reserve. He says, however: "I came to the limits of death, and having trod the threshold of Proserpine and been borne through all the elements I returned; at midnight I saw the sun shining with a bright light; I came into the presence of the upper and nether gods and adored them near at hand."[2] It is often supposed that these words indicate some sort of mysterious drama or vision, which marked the death of the initiate, his passage through the elements, and his rising to a new life. But certainly the matter is very obscure. The next morning Lucius is clothed with gorgeous robes, and is presented to the gaze of the multitude. Apparently he is regarded as partaking of the divine nature. Two other initiations of Lucius are narrated, one of them being an initiation into the mysteries of Osiris, as the first had been into the mysteries of Isis. But little is added by the account of these later experiences, and it has even been suggested that the multiplication of the initiations was due to the self-interest

---

[1] But compare Kennedy, *St. Paul and the Mystery-Religions,* 1913, p. 229.
[2] Apuleius, *Metam.,* xi. 23 (ed. Van der Vliet, 1897, p. 270): "Accessi confinium mortis et calcato Proserpinae limine per omnia vectus elementa remeavi; nocte media vidi solem candido coruscantem lumine; deos inferos et deos superos accessi coram et adoravi de proxumo."

of the priests rather than to any real advantage for the initiate.

Similar in important respects to the Egyptian Osiris was the Adonis of Phœnicia, who may therefore be mentioned in the present connection, even though little is known about mysteries connected with his worship. According to the well-known myth, the youth Adonis, beloved by Aphrodite, was killed by a wild boar, and then bemoaned by the goddess. The cult of Adonis was found in various places, notably at Byblos in Phœnicia, where the death and resurrection of the god were celebrated. With regard to this double festival, Lucian says in his treatise "On the Syrian Goddess": "They [the inhabitants of Byblos] assert that the legend about Adonis and the wild boar is true, and that the facts occurred in their country, and in memory of this calamity they beat their breasts and wail every year, and perform their secret ritual amid signs of mourning through the whole countryside. When they have finished their mourning and wailing, they sacrifice in the first place to Adonis, as to one who has departed this life: after this they allege that he is alive again, and exhibit his effigy to the sky." [1] The wailing for Adonis at Byblos is similar to what is narrated about the worship of the Babylonian god Tammuz. Even the Old Testament mentions in a noteworthy passage "the women weeping for Tammuz" (Ezek. viii. 14). But the Tammuz-worship does not seem to have contained any celebration of a resurrection.

Attis, Osiris, and Adonis are alike in that all of them are apparently represented as dying and coming to life again. They are regarded by Brückner [2] and many other modern scholars as representing the widespread notion of a "dying and rising saviour-god." But it is perhaps worthy of note that the "resurrection" of these gods is very different from what is meant by that word in Christian belief. The myth of Attis, for example, contains no mention of a resurrection; though apparently the cult, in which mourning is followed by gladness, did presuppose some such notion. In the myth of Osiris also, there is nothing that could be called resurrection; after his passion the god becomes ruler, not over the liv-

---

[1] Lucian, *De dea syria*, 6, translation of Garstang (*The Syrian Goddess*, 1913, pp. 45f.).

[2] *Der sterbende und auferstehende Gottheiland*, 1908.

ing, but over the dead. In Lucian's description of the worship of Adonis at Byblos, there is perhaps as clear an account as is to be found anywhere of the celebration of the dying and resuscitation of a god, but even in this account there is not strictly speaking a resurrection. A tendency is found in certain recent writers to exaggerate enormously the prevalence and the clarity of the pagan ideas about a dying and rising god.

According to a common opinion, Attis, Osiris, and Adonis are vegetation-gods; their dying and resuscitation represent, then, the annual withering and revival of vegetation. This hypothesis has attained general, though not universal, acceptance. Certainly the facts are very complex. At any rate, the celebration of the principle of fecundity in nature was not of a purely agrarian character, but found expression also in the gross symbols and immoral practices which appear in connection with the gods just mentioned at various points in the ancient world.

The most important of the religions which have just been examined had their rise in Asia Minor and in Egypt. No less important, at least in the last period of pagan antiquity, was the religious influence of Syria. The Syrian gods, called "Baals" ("Lords"), were not, according to Cumont, distinguished from one another by any clearly defined characteristics. Every locality had its own Baal and a female divinity as the Baal's consort, but the attributes of these local gods were of the vaguest character. The female divinity Atargatis, whose temple at Hierapolis is described by Lucian, and the male divinity Hadad, of Heliopolis, are among the best-known of the Syrian gods. The Syrian worship was characterized by especially immoral and revolting features, but seems to have become ennobled by the introduction of the Babylonian worship of the heavenly bodies, and thus contributed to the formation of the solar monotheism which was the final form assumed by the pagan religion of the Empire before the triumph of Christianity.

In point of intrinsic worth, the Persian mystery religion of Mithras is easily superior to any of the religions which have thus far been mentioned, but it is of less importance than some of the others for the purposes of the present investigation, since it became influential in the Roman Empire only

after the time of Paul. Great stress has indeed been laid upon
the fact that Plutarch attests the practice of Mithraic mysteries by the pirates whom Pompey conquered in the middle
of the first century before Christ, and says furthermore that
the Mithraic rites begun by the pirates were continued until
the writer's own day.[1]   The pirates practised their rites
at Olympus, which is on the southern coast of Asia Minor. But
the Olympus which is meant is in Lycia, some three hundred
miles from Tarsus. It is a mistake, therefore, to bring the
Mithraic mysteries of the pirates into any close geographical
connection with the boyhood home of Paul. Against the
hypothesis of any dependence of Paul upon the mysteries of
Mithras is to be placed the authority of Cumont, the chief
investigator in this field, who says: "It is impossible to suppose that at that time [the time of Paul] there was an imitation of the Mithraic mysteries, which then had not yet attained
any importance." [2]   Attempts have often been made to explain away this judgment of Cumont, but without success. The
progress of Mithraism in the Empire seems to have been due
to definite political causes which were operative only after
Paul's day.

The Persian religion, from which Mithraism was descended,
was superior to the others which have just been considered in
its marked ethical character. It presented the doctrine of a
mighty conflict between light and darkness, between good and
evil. And Mithraism itself regarded religion under the figure
of a warfare. It appealed especially to the soldiers, and only
men (not women) were admitted to its mysteries. There were
seven grades of initiation, each with its special name. The
highest grade was that of "father." The Mithras cult was
always celebrated underground, in chambers of very limited
extent. There was a sacred meal, consisting of bread and
water, which Justin Martyr, in the middle of the second century, regards as having been instituted through demoniac imitation of the Christian Eucharist.[3] This religion of Mithras
finally became, with the religion of Isis, the most serious rival
of Christianity. But at the time of Paul it was without im-

---

[1] Plutarch, *Vita Pompei*, 24.
[2] Cumont, *op. cit.*, p. xvi (English Translation, p. xx).
[3] Justin Martyr, *Apol.* 66.

portance, and could not have exerted any influence upon the apostle.

But the religion of the Hellenistic age was not limited to the individual cults which have just been considered, and it is not chiefly to the individual cults that recourse is had by those modern scholars who would derive Paulinism from pagan sources. Mention has already been made of the syncretism of the age; various religions were mingled in a limitless variety of combinations. And there was also a mingling of religion with philosophy. It is in the manifold products of this union between Greek philosophy and oriental religion that the genesis of Paulinism is now often being sought. Not oriental religion in its original state, but oriental religion already to some extent Hellenized, is thought to have produced the characteristic features of the religion of Paul.

The hypothesis is faced by one obvious difficulty. The difficulty appears in the late date of most of the sources of information. In order to reconstruct that Hellenized oriental mysticism from which the religion of Paul is to be derived, the investigator is obliged to appeal to sources which are long subsequent to Paul's day. For example, in reproducing the spiritual atmosphere in which Paul is supposed to have lived, no testimony is more often evoked than the words of Firmicus Maternus, "Be of good courage, ye initiates, since the god is saved; for to us there shall be salvation out of troubles." [1] Here, it is thought, is to be found that connection between the resurrection of the god and the salvation of the believers which appears in the Pauline idea of dying and rising with Christ. But the trouble is that Firmicus Maternus lived in the fourth century after Christ, three hundred years later than Paul. With what right can an utterance of his be used in the reconstruction of pre-Christian paganism? What would be thought, by the same scholars who quote Firmicus Maternus so confidently as a witness to first-century paganism, of a historian who should quote a fourth-century Christian writer as a witness to first-century Christianity?

This objection has been met by the modern school of comparative religion somewhat as follows. In the first place, it is said, the post-Christian pagan usage which at any time

[1] See above, p. 229, with footnote 3.

may be under investigation is plainly not influenced by Christianity. But, in the second place, it is too similar to Christian usage for the similarity to be explained by mere coincidence. Therefore, in the third place, since it is not dependent upon Christian usage, Christian usage must be dependent upon it, and therefore despite its late attestation it must have existed in pre-Christian times.

A little reflection will reveal the precarious character of this reasoning. Every step is uncertain. In the first place, it is often by no means clear that the pagan usage has not been influenced by Christianity. The Church did not long remain obscure; even early in the second century, according to the testimony of Pliny, it was causing the heathen temples to be deserted. What is more likely than that in an age of syncretism the adherents of pagan religion should borrow weapons from so successful a rival? It must be remembered that the paganism of the Hellenistic age had elevated syncretism to a system; it had absolutely no objection of principle against receiving elements from every source. In the Christian Church, on the other hand, there was a strong objection to such procedure; Christianity from the beginning was like Judaism in being exclusive. It regarded with the utmost abhorrence anything that was tainted by a pagan origin. This abhorrence, at least in the early period, more than overbalanced the fact that the Christians for the most part had formerly been pagans, so that it might be thought natural for them to retain something of pagan belief. Conversion involved a passionate renunciation of former beliefs. Such, at any rate, was clearly the kind of conversion that was required by Paul.

In the second place, the similarity between the pagan and the Christian usages is often enormously exaggerated; sometimes a superficial similarity of language masks the most profound differences of underlying meaning. Illustrations will be given in Chapter VII.

Thus the conclusion is, to say the least, precarious. It is by no means so easy as is sometimes supposed to prove that a pagan usage attested only long after the time of Paul is really the source of Pauline teaching. And it will not help to say that although there is no direct dependence one way or the other yet the pagan and the Pauline teaching have a common source. For to say that a usage has a pagan source several centuries earlier than the time at which the usage is first attested is really to assume the point that is to be proved. We are not here dealing with a question of literary dependence, where the unity of the books which are being compared is assumed. In such a question the independence of the two writers may be proved by the general comparison of the books; it may be shown, in other words, that if one author had used the other author's work at all he would have had to use it a great deal more than as a matter of fact the similarity would indicate. In such cases, striking verbal similarity in one place may prove that both books were dependent upon a common source. But if a pagan usage of the fourth century is similar to a Christian usage, the fact that in general the paganism of the fourth century is independent of Christianity does not disprove dependence of paganism upon Christianity at this one point.

It is not surprising, therefore, that the reasoning just outlined is usually supplemented by a further consideration. It is maintained, namely, that the mystic piety of paganism forms to some extent a unit; it was not a mere fortuitous collection of beliefs and practices, but was like an enveloping spiritual atmosphere of which, despite variations of humidity and temperature, the fundamental composition was everywhere the same. If, therefore, the presence of this atmosphere of mystical piety can be established here and there in sources of actually pre-Christian date, the investigator has a right to determine the nature of the atmosphere in detail by drawing upon later sources. In other words, the mystical religion of the Hellenistic age is reconstructed in detail by the use of post-Christian sources, and then (the essential unity of the phenomenon being assumed) the early date of this oriental mystical religion is established by the scanty references in pre-Christian times. It is admitted, perhaps, that the elements of oriental mysticism actually found in pre-Christian sources would not be sufficient to prove dependence of Paul upon that type of religion; but the elements found in later sources are thought to be so closely allied to those which happen to have early attestation that they too must be supposed to have been present in the early period, and since they are similar to Paulinism they must have exerted a formative influence upon Paul's religion. To put the matter briefly, the nature of Hellenized oriental religion is established by post-Pauline sources; whereas the early origin of that religion is established by the scanty pre-Christian references.

This procedure constitutes a curious reversal of the procedure which is applied by the very same scholars to Christianity. Christianity is supposed to have undergone kaleidoscopic changes in the course of a few years or even months, changes involving a transformation of its inmost nature; yet pagan religion is apparently thought to have remained from age to age the same. When Paul, only a few years after the origin of the Church, says that he "received" certain fundamental elements in his religion, the intimate connection of those elements with the rest of the Pauline system is not allowed to establish the early origin of the whole, yet the paganism of the third and fourth centuries is thought to have constituted such a unity that the presence of certain elements of it in the pre-Christian period is regarded as permitting the whole system to be transplanted bodily to that early time.

Of course, the hypothesis which is now being examined is held in many forms, and is being advocated with varying degrees of caution. Some of its advocates might defend themselves against the charge of transplanting post-Christian paganism bodily into the pre-Christian period. They might point to special evidence with regard to many details. Such evidence would have to be examined in any complete investigation. But the objection just raised, despite possible answers to it in detail, is not without validity. It remains true, despite all reservations, that adherents of the "comparative-religion school" are entirely too impatient with regard to questions of priority. They are indeed very severe upon those who raise such questions. They do not like having the flow of their thought checked by so homely a thing as a date. But dates sometimes have their importance. For example, the phrase, "reborn for eternity," occurs in connection with the blood-bath of the taurobolium. How significant, it might be said, is this connection of regeneration with the shedding of blood! How useful as establishing the pagan origin of the Christian idea! From the confident way in which the phrase "reborn for eternity" is quoted in discussions of the origin of Christianity, one would think that its pre-Christian origin were established beyond peradventure. It may come as a shock, therefore, to readers of recent discussions to be told that as a matter of fact the phrase does not appear until the fourth century, when Christianity was taking its place as the established religion of the Roman world. If there is any dependence, it is certainly dependence of the taurobolium upon Christianity, and not of Christianity upon the taurobolium.

The same lordly disregard of dates runs all through the modern treatment of the history of religion in the New Testament period. It is particularly unfortunate in popular expositions. When the lay reader is overwhelmed by an imposing array of citations from Apuleius and from Lucian, to say nothing of Firmicus Maternus and fourth-century inscriptions, and when these late citations are confidently treated by men of undoubted learning as witnesses to pre-Christian religion, and when the procedure is rendered more plausible by occasional references to pre-Christian writers which if looked up would be found to prove nothing at all, and when there is a careful avoidance of anything like temporal arrangement of the material, but citations derived from all countries and all ages are brought together for the reconstruction of the environment of Paul—under such treatment the lay reader often receives the impression that something very important is being proved. The impression would be corrected by the mere introduction of a few dates, especially in view of the fact that oriental religion undoubtedly entered upon a remarkable expansion shortly after the close of the New Testament period, so that conditions prevailing after that expansion are by no means necessarily to be regarded as having existed before the expansion took place.

This criticism is here intended to be taken only in a provisional way. The justice of it can be tested only by a detailed examination of the hypothesis against which the criticism is directed.

How, then, is the pre-Christian mystical religion of the Hellenistic world to be reconstructed? What sources are to be used? Some of the sources have already been touched upon in the review of the individual oriental cults. And incidentally the unsatisfactory character of some of these sources has already appeared. But it is now necessary to examine other sources which are not so definitely connected with any clearly defined cult.

Increasing attention has been paid in recent years to the complex of writings which goes under the name of Hermes Trismegistus. These Hermetic writings embrace not only a corpus of some fourteen tractates which has been preserved in continuous Greek manuscript form, but also fragments contained in the works of Stobæus and other writers, and finally the "Asclepius" attributed to Apuleius. It is not usually maintained that the Hermetic literature was completed before about 300 A.D.; no one claims anything like pre-Christian origin for the whole. The individual elements of the literature—for example, the individual tractates of the Hermetic corpus—are usually regarded as having been produced at various times; but no one of them is generally thought to have been written before the beginning of the Christian era. With regard to the most important tractate, the "Poimandres," which stands at the beginning of the corpus, opinions differ somewhat. J. Kroll, for example, the author of the leading monograph on the Hermetic writings, regards the Poimandres as the latest of the tractates in the corpus, and as having appeared not before the time of Numenius (second half of the second century);[1] whereas Zielinski regards it as the earliest writing of the corpus.[2] By an ingenious argument, Reitzenstein attempts to prove that the Christian "Shepherd of Hermes" (middle of the second century) is dependent upon an original form of the "Poimandres."[3] But his argument has not obtained any general consent. It is impossible to push the material of the Poimandres back into the first century—certainly impossible by any treatment of literary relationships.

With regard to the origin of the ideas in the Hermetic writings, there is considerable difference of opinion. Reitzenstein allows a large place to Egyptian and Persian elements; other scholars emphasize rather the influence of Greek philosophy, which of course is in turn thought to have been modified by its contact with oriental religion. J. Kroll,[4] W. Kroll,[5] Reitzenstein,[6] and others deny emphatically the

[1] J. Kroll, *Die Lehren des Hermes Trismegistos*, 1914, in *Beiträge zur Geschichte der Philosophie des Mittelalters*, xii. 2-4, pp. 388, 389.
[2] Zielinski, "Hermes und die Hermetik," in *Archiv für Religionswissenschaft*, viii, 1905, p. 323.
[3] Reitzenstein, *Poimandres*, 1904, pp. 10-13.
[4] *Op. cit.*
[5] Article "Hermes Trismegistos," in Pauly-Wissowa, *Real-Encyclopädie der classischen Altertumswissenschaft*, xv, 1912, pp. 791-823.
[6] *Op. cit.*

presence of any considerable Christian influence in Hermes; but at this point Heinrici, after particularly careful researches, differs from the customary view.[1] Windisch is enough impressed by Heinrici's arguments to confess that Christian literature may have influenced the present form of the Hermetic writings here and there, but insists that the Christian influence upon Hermes is altogether trifling compared to the influence upon primitive Christianity of the type of religion of which Hermes is an example.[2] The true state of the case, according to Windisch, is probably that Christianity first received from oriental religion the fundamental ideas, and then gave back to oriental religion as represented by Hermes certain forms of expression in which those ideas had been clothed. At the same time Windisch urges careful attention to Heinrici's argument for Christian influence upon Hermes for three reasons: (1) all Hermetic writings are later than the New Testament period, (2) the Hermetic writings are admittedly influenced by Judaism, (3) at least the latest stratum in the Hermetic writings has admittedly passed through the Christian sphere. These admissions, coming from one who is very friendly to the modern method of comparative religion, are significant. When even Windisch admits that the form of expression with regard to the new birth in the Poimandres may possibly be influenced by the Gospel tradition, and that the author of the fourth Hermetic tractate, for example, was somewhat familiar with New Testament writings or Christian ideas and "assimilated Christian terminology to his gnosis," and that the term "faith" has possibly come into Hermes (iv and ix) from Christian tradition—in the light of these admissions it may appear how very precarious is the employment of Hermes Trismegistus as a witness to pre-Christian paganism.

Opinions differ, moreover, as to the importance of the Hermetic type of thought in the life of the ancient world. Reitzenstein exalts its importance; he believes that back of the Hermetic writings there lies a living religion, and that this Hermetic type of religion was characteristic of the Hellenistic age. At this point Cumont and others are in sharp disagreement; Cumont believes that in the West Hermetism had nothing more than a literary existence and did not pro-

---

[1] Heinrici, *Die Hermes-Mystik und das Neue Testament*, 1918.
[2] Windisch, "Urchristentum und Hermesmystik," in *Theologisch Tijdschrift*, lii, 1918, pp. 186-240.

duce a Hermetic sect, and that in general Reitzenstein has greatly exaggerated the Hermetic influence.[1]   With regard to this controversy, it can at least be said that Reitzenstein has failed to prove his point.

Detailed exposition of the Hermetic writings will here be impossible.   A number of recent investigators have covered the field with some thoroughness.   Unfortunately a complete modern critical edition of the Hermetic corpus is still lacking; the student is obliged to have recourse to the edition of Parthey (1854),[2] which is not complete and does not quite measure up to modern standards.   Reitzenstein has included in his "Poimandres" (1904) a critical edition of Tractates I, XIII, XVI, XVII, XVIII.   There has been no collection, in the original languages, of all the Hermetic writings (including those outside of the corpus), though Ménard has provided a French translation,[3] and Mead an English translation with elaborate introduction and notes.[4]   The work of Mead, which is published by the Theosophical Publishing Society, is not usually regarded as quite satisfactory.   But the translation at least will be found exceedingly useful.   The systematic exposition of the thought of the Hermetic writings by J. Kroll is clear and instructive;[5] and Heinrici, who differs from Kroll in treating the individual writings separately, has also made a valuable contribution to the subject.[6]

In the Hermetic tractates I and XIII, upon which Reitzenstein lays the chief emphasis, there is presented a notion of the transformation of the one who receives divine revelation.   The transformation, as in the Hermetic writings generally, is for the most part independent of ceremonies or sacraments.   An experience which in the mysteries is connected with an initiation involving an appeal to the senses here seems to have been spiritualized under the influence of philosophy; regeneration comes not through a mystic drama or the like but through an inner experience.   Such at least is a common

[1] Cumont, op. cit., pp. 340, 341 (English Translation, pp. 233, 234, note 41).
[2] Parthey, Hermetis Trismegisti Poemander, 1854.
[3] Ménard, Hermès Trismégiste, 1910.
[4] Mead, Thrice-Greatest Hermes, three volumes, 1906.
[5] Op. cit. Cf. the review by Bousset, in Göttingische gelehrte Anzeigen, clxxvi, 1914, pp. 697-755.
[6] Op. cit.

modern interpretation of the genesis of the Hermetic doctrine. At any rate, it seems to be impossible to reduce that doctrine to anything like a consistent logical scheme. Reitzenstein has tried to bring order out of chaos by distinguishing in the first tractate two originally distinct views as to the origin of the world and of man, but his analysis has not won general acceptance. It must probably be admitted, however, that the Hermetic literature has received elements from various sources and has not succeeded in combining them in any consistent way.

The student who will first read Tractates I and XIII for himself will probably be surprised when he is told (for example by Reitzenstein) that here is to be found the spiritual atmosphere from which Paulinism came. For there could be no sharper contrast than that between the fantastic speculations of the Poimandres and the historical gospel of Paul. Both the Poimandres and Paul have some notion of a transformation that a man experiences through a divine revelation. But the transformation, according to Paul, comes through an account of what had happened but a few years before. Nothing could possibly be more utterly foreign to Hermes. On the other hand, the result of the transformation in Hermes is deification. "This," says Hermes (Tractate I, 26), "is the good end to those who have received knowledge, to be deified." [1] Paul could never have used such language. For, according to Paul, the relation between the believer and the Christ who has transformed him is a personal relation of love. The "Christ-mysticism" of Paul is never pantheistic. It is indeed supernatural; it is not produced by any mere influence brought to bear upon the old life. But the result, far from being apotheosis, is personal communion of a man with his God.

In connection with Hermes Trismegistus may be mentioned the so-called Oracula Chaldaica, which apparently sprang from the same general type of thought.[2] These Oracula Chaldaica, according to W. Kroll, constitute a document of heathen gnosis, which was produced about 200 A. D. Although Kroll believes that there is here no Christian influence, and that Jewish influence touches not the center but only the circumference, yet for the reasons already noticed it would be

---

[1] τοῦτο ἐστι τὸ ἀγαθὸν τέλος τοῖς γνῶσιν ἐσχηκόσι, θεωθῆναι.
[2] See W. Kroll, *De Oraculis Chaldaicis*, 1894; "Die chaldäischen Orakel," in *Rheinisches Museum für Philologie*, l, 1895, pp. 636-639.

precarious to use a document of 200 A.D. in reconstructing pre-Pauline paganism.

A very important source of information about the Greco-oriental religion of the Hellenistic age is found by scholars like Dieterich and Reitzenstein in the so-called "magical" papyri. Among the many interesting papyrus documents which have recently been discovered in Egypt are some that contain formulas intended to be used in incantations. At first sight these formulas look like hopeless nonsense; it may perhaps even be said that they are intended to be nonsense. That is, the effect is sought, not from any logical understanding of the formulas either on the part of those who use them or on the part of the higher powers upon whom they are to be used, but simply and solely from the mechanical effect of certain combinations of sounds. Thus the magical papyri include not only divine names in foreign languages (the ancient and original name of a god being regarded as exerting a coercive effect upon that god), but also many meaningless rows of letters which do not form words at all. But according to Dieterich and Reitzenstein and others, these papyri, nonsensical as they are in their completed form, often embody materials which belong not to magic but to religion; in particular, they make use, for a magical purpose, of what was originally intended to be used in a living religious cult. Indeed the distinction between magic and religion is often difficult to draw. In religion there is an element of interest, on the part of the worshiper, in the higher powers as such, some idea of propitiating them, of winning their favor; whereas in magic the higher powers are made use of as though they were mere machines through the use of incantations and spells. But when this distinction is applied to the ancient mystery religions, sometimes these religions seem to be little more than magic, so external and mechanical is the way in which the initiation is supposed to work. It is not surprising, therefore, if the composers of magical formulas turned especially, in seeking their materials, to the mystery cults; for they were drawn in that direction by a certain affinity both of purpose and of method. At any rate, whatever may be the explanation, the existing magical papyri, according to Dieterich and others, do contain important elements derived from the oriental religious cults; it is only necessary, Dieterich maintains, to subtract the obviously later elements—the nonsensical rows of letters and the like—in order to obtain important sources of information about the religious life of the Hellenistic age.

This method has been applied by Dieterich especially to a Paris magical papyrus, with the result that the underlying religious document is found to be nothing less than a liturgy of the religion of Mithras.[1] Dieterich's conclusions have not escaped unchallenged; the connection of the document with Mithraism has been denied, for example, by Cumont.[2] Of course, even if the document be not really a "Mithras liturgy," it may still be of great value in the reconstruction of Hellenistic gnosis. With regard to date, however, it is not any more favorably placed than the documents which have just been considered. The papyrus manuscript in which the "liturgy" is contained was written at the beginning of the fourth century after Christ; and the composition of the "liturgy" itself cannot be fixed definitely at any very much earlier date. [3] Dieterich supposes that the beginning was made in the second century, and that there were successive additions afterward. At any rate, then, not only the papyrus manuscript, but also the liturgy which it is thought to contain, was produced long after the time of Paul. Like the Hermetic writings, moreover, Dieterich's Mithras liturgy presents a conception of union with divinity which is really altogether unlike the Pauline gospel.

But information about pre-Christian paganism is being sought not only in ostensibly pagan sources; it is also being sought in the Gnosticism which appears in connection with the Christian Church. Gnosticism used to be regarded as a "heresy," a perversion of Christian belief. Now, on the contrary, it is being regarded as essentially non-Christian, as a manifestation of Greco-oriental religion which was brought into only very loose connection with Christianity; the great Gnostic systems of the second century, it is said, when they are stripped of a few comparatively unimportant Christian elements are found to represent not a development from Christianity but rather the spiritual atmosphere from which Christianity itself sprang.

If this view of the case be correct, it is at least significant

[1] Dieterich, *Eine Mithrasliturgie*, 2te Aufl., 1910.
[2] *Op. cit.*, p. 379 (English Translation, pp. 260f.).
[3] Dieterich, *op. cit.*, pp. 43f.

that pagan teachers of the second century (the Gnostics) should have been so ready to adopt Christian elements and so anxious to give their systems a Christian appearance. Why should a similar procedure be denied in the case, for example, of Hermes Trismegistus? If second-century paganism, without at all modifying its essential character, could sometimes actually adopt the name of Christ, why should it be thought incredible that the compiler of the Hermetic literature, who did not go quite so far, should yet have permitted Christian elements to creep into his syncretistic work? Why should similarity of language between Hermes and Paul, supposing that it exists, be regarded as proving dependence of Paul upon a type of paganism like that of Hermes, rather than dependence of Hermes upon Paul?

But the use of Gnosticism as a witness to pre-Christian paganism is faced with obvious difficulties. Gnosticism has admittedly been influenced by Christianity. Who can say, then, exactly how far the Christian influence extends? Who can say that any element in Gnosticism, found also in the New Testament, but not clearly contained in pagan sources, is derived from paganism rather than from Christianity? Yet it is just exactly such procedure which is advocated by Reitzenstein and others.

The dangers of the procedure may be exhibited by an example. In Hermes Trismegistus the spirit is regarded as the garment of the soul.[1] This doctrine is the exact reverse of Pauline teaching, since it makes the soul appear higher than the spirit, whereas in Paul the Spirit, in the believer, is exalted far above the soul. In Hermes the spirit appears as a material substratum of the soul; in Paul the Spirit represents the divine power. There could be no sharper contradiction. And the matter is absolutely central in Reitzenstein's hypothesis, for it is just the Pauline doctrine of the Spirit which he is seeking to derive from pagan religion. The difficulty for Reitzenstein, then, is that in Hermes the spirit appears as the garment of the soul, whereas in the interests of his theory the soul ought to appear rather as the garment of the spirit. But Reitzenstein avoids the difficulty by appealing to Gnosticism. The Hermetic doctrine, he says, is nothing but the neces-

[1] *Corp. Herm.* x. 13.

sary philosophic reversal of the Gnostic doctrine that the soul is the garment of the spirit.[1] Thus Gnosticism is here made to be a witness to pre-Christian pagan belief, in direct defiance of pagan sources. Is it not more probable that the difference between Gnosticism on the one hand and pagan gnosis as represented by Hermes on the other, is due to the influence upon the former of the Christian doctrine? It is interesting to observe that J. Kroll, from whom the above illustration is obtained, insists against Reitzenstein that the Gnostic doctrine, as over against the doctrine of Hermes, is here clearly secondary.[2] At any rate, then, the reconstruction of a pre-Christian pagan doctrine of the soul as the garment of the spirit is a matter of pure conjecture.

Similar difficulties appear everywhere. It is certainly very hazardous to use Gnosticism, a post-Pauline phenomenon appealing to Paul as one of its chief sources, as a witness to pre-Pauline paganism. Certainly such use of Gnosticism should be carefully limited to those matters where there is some confirmatory pagan testimony. But such confirmatory testimony, in the decisive cases, is significantly absent.

The use of Gnosticism as a source of information about pre-Christian paganism might be less precarious if the separation of the pagan and Christian elements could be carried out by means of literary criticism. Such a method is employed by Reitzenstein in connection with an interesting passage in Hippolytus. In attacking the Gnostic sect of the Naassenes, Hippolytus says that the sect has been dependent upon the pagan mysteries, and in proof he quotes a Naassene writing. This quotation, as it now exists in the work of Hippolytus, is, according to Reitzenstein, "a pagan text with Gnostic-Christian scholia (or in a Gnostic-Christian revision), which has been taken over by an opponent who did not understand this state of the case, and so, in this form, has been used by Hippolytus."[3] Reitzenstein seeks to reproduce the pagan document.[4]

Unquestionably the passage is interesting, and unques-

---

[1] Reitzenstein, *Hellenistische Mysterienreligionen*, 2te Aufl., 1920, p. 183.
[2] J. Kroll, *op. cit.*, pp. 286-289, especially p. 288, Anm. 1.
[3] Reitzenstein, *Poimandres*, p. 82.
[4] *Op. cit.*, pp. 83-98.

tionably it contains important information about the pagan mysteries. But it does not help to establish influence of the mysteries upon Paul. It must be observed that what is now being maintained against Reitzenstein is not that the Gnostics who appear in the polemic of the anti-heretical, ecclesiastical writers of the close of the second century and the beginning of the third were not influenced by pre-Christian paganism, or even that they did not derive the fundamentals of their type of religion from pre-Christian paganism. All that is being maintained is that it is very precarious to use the Gnostic systems in reconstructing pre-Christian paganism in detail—especially where the Gnostic systems differ from admittedly pagan sources and agree with Paul. In reconstructing the origin of Paulinism it is precarious to employ the testimony of those who lived after Paul and actually quoted Paul.

All the sources of information about Greco-oriental religion which have thus far been discussed belong to a time subsequent to Paul. If the type of religion which they attest is to be pushed back into the pre-Christian period, it can be done only by an appeal to earlier sources. Such earlier sources are sometimes found in passages like Livy's description of the Bacchanalian rites of the second century before Christ in Italy, and in writers such as Posidonius and Philo. But the presence of Bacchanalian rites in Italy in the second century before Christ is not particularly significant, and the details of those rites do not include the features which in the later sources are thought to invite comparison with Paul. Posidonius, the Stoic philosopher of the first century before Christ, seems to have been a man of very great influence; and no doubt he did introduce oriental elements into the Stoic philosophy. But his works, for the most part, have been lost, and so far as they have been reconstructed by the use of writers who were dependent upon him, they do not seem to contain those elements which might be regarded as explaining the genesis of Paulinism. With regard to Philo, who was an older contemporary of Paul, the investigator finds himself in a much more favorable position, since voluminous works of the Alexandrian philosopher have been preserved. There is a tendency in recent investigation to make Philo an important witness to Greco-oriental religion as it found expression in the mysteries.[1] But the bearing of the evidence does not seem to be absolutely unequivocal. At any rate, the relation between Paul and Philo has been the subject of investigation for many years, and it cannot be said that the results have accomplished anything toward explaining the genesis of Paul's religion. Direct dependence of Paul upon Philo, it is admitted, has not been proved, and even dependence of both upon the same type of thought is highly problematical. The state of the evidence is not essentially altered by designating as the type of thought upon which both are supposed to have been dependent the Greco-oriental religion of the mysteries. The real question is whether the testimony of Philo establishes as of pre-Christian origin that type of mystical piety from which Paulinism is being derived—the type of religion which is attested, for example, by Firmicus Maternus or by the fourth-century inscriptions that deal with the taurobolium, or by Hermes Trismegistus, or by Dieterich's "Mithras liturgy," or by the pagan elements which are supposed to lie back of second-century Gnosticism. And so far as can be judged on the basis of the evidence which is actually being adduced by the comparative-religion school, the question must be answered in the negative. Even the living connection of Philo with the mysteries of his own day does not seem to be definitely established. And if it were established, the further question would remain as to whether the mystery religions of Philo's day contained just those elements which in the mystery religions of the post-Pauline period are supposed to show similarity to Paul. If the mystical piety which is attested by Philo is sufficient to be regarded as the basis of Paulinism, why should the investigator appeal to Firmicus Maternus? And if he does appeal to Firmicus Maternus, with what right can he assume that the elements which he thus fads existed in the days of Philo and of Paul?

---

[1] Helbig, review of "Philo von Alexandrien; Werke, in deut. Uebersetzg. hrsg. v. Prof. Dr. Leop. Cohn. 3. Tl.," in *Theologische Literaturzeitung*, xlv, 1920, column 30: "Here one perceives with all requisite clearness that Philo did not merely imitate the language of the mystery religions, but had been himself a μύστης."

CHAPTER VII

REDEMPTION IN PAGAN RELIGION AND
IN PAUL

CHAPTER VII

REDEMPTION IN PAGAN RELIGION AND IN PAUL

IT has been observed thus far that in comparing Paul with Hellenistic pagan religion, the question of priority cannot be ruled out so easily as is sometimes supposed. Another preliminary question, moreover, remains. Through what channels did the supposed influence of the mystery religions enter into the life of Paul? The question is somewhat perplexing. In view of the outline of Paul's life which was set forth in Chapters II and III, it would seem difficult to find a place for the entrance of pagan religious thought.

One suggestion is that pagan thought came to Paul only through the medium of Judaism. That suggestion would explain the consciousness that Paul attests of having been, before his conversion, a devout Jew. If pagan religion had already entered into the warp and woof of Judaism, and if the throes of the process of assimilation had already been forgotten before the time of Paul, then Paul might regard himself as a devout Jew, hostile to all pagan influence, and yet be profoundly influenced by the paganism which had already found an entrance into the Jewish stronghold.

But the trouble is that with regard to those matters which are thought to be necessary for the explanation of Paul's religion there is no evidence that paganism had entered into the common life of the Jews. It has been shown in Chapter V that the Judaism of the first century, as it can be reconstructed by the use of the extant sources, is insufficient to account for the origin of Paulinism. That fact is admitted by those scholars who are having recourse to the hypothesis of pagan influence. Therefore, if the pagan influence came to Paul through the medium of Judaism, the historian must first posit the existence of a Judaism into which the necessary pagan elements had entered. There is no evidence for the existence of such a Judaism; in fact the extant Jewish sources point

255

clearly in an opposite direction. It is exceedingly difficult, therefore, to suppose, in defiance of the Jewish sources, and in the mere interests of a theory as to the genesis of Paulinism, that the Pharisaic Judaism from which Paul sprang was imbued with a mystical piety like that of the mystery religions or of Hermes Trismegistus. In fact, in view of the known character of Pharisaic Judaism, the hypothesis is nothing short of monstrous.

Therefore, if Paul was influenced by the pagan mystery religions it could not have been simply in virtue of his connection with first-century Judaism; it must have been due to some special influences which were brought to bear upon him. Where could these influences have been exerted? One suggestion is that they were exerted in Tarsus, his boyhood home. Stress is thus laid upon the fact that Paul was born not in Palestine but in the Dispersion. As he grew up in Tarsus, it is said, he could not help observing the paganism that surrounded him. At this point, some historians, on entirely insufficient evidence, are inclined to be specific; they are tempted, for example, to speak of mysteries of Mithras as being practised in or near Tarsus in Paul's early years. The hypothesis is only weakened by such incautious advocacy; it is much better to point merely to the undoubted fact that Tarsus was a pagan city and was presumably affected by the existing currents of pagan life. But if Paul grew up in a pagan environment, was he influenced by it? An affirmative answer would seem to run counter to his own testimony. Although Paul was born in Tarsus, he belonged inwardly to Palestine; he and his parents before him were not "Hellenists" but "Hebrews." Moreover, he was a Pharisee, more exceedingly zealous than his contemporaries for his paternal traditions. The evidence has been examined in a previous chapter. Certainly then, Paul was not a "liberal" Jew; far from being inclined to break down the wall of partition between Jews and Gentiles he was especially zealous for the Law. It is very difficult to conceive of such a man—with his excessive zeal for the Mosaic Law, with his intense hatred of paganism, with his intense consciousness of the all-sufficiency of Jewish privileges—as being susceptible to the pagan influences that surrounded his orthodox home.

The hypothesis must, therefore, at least be modified to

the extent that the pagan influence exerted at Tarsus be regarded as merely unconscious. Paul did not deliberately accept the pagan religion of Tarsus, it might be said, but at least he became acquainted with it, and his acquaintance with it became fruitful after he entered upon his Gentile mission. According to this hypothesis, the attitude of Paul toward pagan religion was in the early days in Tarsus merely negative, but became more favorable (whether or no Paul himself was conscious of the real source of the pagan ideas) because of subsequent events. But what were the events which induced in Paul a more favorable attitude toward ideas which were really pagan? When did he overcome his life-long antagonism to everything connected with the worship of false gods? Such a change of attitude is certainly not attested by the Epistles.

It will probably be admitted that if pagan influence entered into the heart of Paul's religious life it could only have done so by some more subtle way than by the mere retention in Paul's mind of what he had seen at Tarsus. The way which finds special favor among recent historians is discovered in the pre-Pauline Christianity of cities like Damascus and Antioch. When Paul was converted, it is said, he was converted not to the Christianity of Jerusalem, but to the Christianity of Damascus and Antioch. But the Christianity of Damascus and Antioch, it is supposed, had already received pagan elements; hence the very fact of Paul's conversion broke down his Jewish prejudices and permitted the influx of pagan ideas. Of course Paul did not know that they were pagan ideas; he supposed that they were merely Christian; but pagan they were, nevertheless. The Hellenistic Jews who founded the churches at Damascus and Antioch, unlike the original apostles at Jerusalem, were liberal Jews, susceptible to pagan influence and desirous of attributing to Jesus all that the pagans attributed to their own cult-gods. Thus Jesus became a cult-god like the cult-gods of the pagan religions, and Christianity became similar, in important respects, to the pagan cults.

This hypothesis has been advocated brilliantly by Heitmüller and Bousset.[1] But what evidence can be adduced in favor of it? How may the Christianity of Damascus and An-

[1] See especially Heitmüller, "Zum Problem Paulus und Jesus," in *Zeitschrift für die neutestamentliche Wissenschaft*, xiii, 1912, pp. 320-337; "Jesus und Paulus," in *Zeitschrift für Theologie und Kirche*, xxv, 1915, pp. 156-179; Bousset, *Jesus der Herr*, 1916, pp. 30-37.

tioch, which is supposed to have been influenced by pagan religion, be reconstructed? Even Heitmüller and Bousset admit that the reconstruction is very difficult. The only unquestioned source of information about the pre-Pauline Christianity which is the subject of investigation is to b⁰ found in the Pauline Epistles themselves. But if the material is found in the Pauline Epistles, how can the historian be sure that it is not the product of Paul's own thinking? How can the specifically Pauline element in the Epistles be separated form the element which is supposed to have been derived from pre-Pauline Hellenistic Christianity?

The process of separation, it must be admitted, is difficult. But, according to Bousset and Heitmüller, it is not impossible. There are passages in the Epistles where Paul evidently assumes that certain things are known already to his readers. In churches where Paul himself had not already had the opportunity of teaching, notably at Rome, those elements assumed as already known must have been derived, it is said, from teachers other than Paul; they must have formed part of the pre-Pauline fund of Hellenistic Christianity.

But in order to reconstruct this pre-Pauline Hellenistic Christianity, it is not sufficient to separate what Paul had received from what he himself produced. Another process of separation remains; and this second process is vastly more difficult than the first. In order to reconstruct the Hellenistic Christianity of Antioch, upon which Paulinism is thought to be based, it is necessary not only to separate what Paul received from what he produced, but also to separate what he received from Antioch from what he received from Jerusalem. It is in connection with this latter process that the hypothesis of Heitmüller and Bousset breaks down. Unquestionably some elements in the Epistles can be established as having been received by Paul from those who had been Christians before him. One notable example is found in 1 Cor. xv. 1-7. In that all-important passage Paul distinctly says that he had "received" his account of the death, burial, and resurrection of Jesus. But how does Bousset know that he received it from the Church at Antioch or the Church at Damascus rather than from the Church at Jerusalem? Paul had been in intimate contact with Peter in Jerusalem; Peter is prominent in 1 Cor.

xv. 1-7. What reason is there, then, for deserting the common view, regarded almost as an axiom of criticism, to the effect that 1 Cor. xv. 1-7 represents the tradition of the Jerusalem Church which Paul received from Peter?

Moreover, what right have Bousset and Heitmüller to use the Epistle to the Romans in reconstructing the Christianity of Antioch? Even if in that Epistle the elements of specifically Pauline teaching can be separated from those things which Paul regards as already matter of course in the Roman Church, what reason is there to assume that the pre-Pauline Christianity of Rome was the same as the pre-Pauline Christianity of Antioch and Damascus? Information about the pre-Pauline Christianity of Antioch and Damascus is, to say the least, scanty and uncertain. And it is that Christianity only—the Christianity with which Paul came into contact soon after his conversion—and not the Christianity of Rome, which can be of use in explaining the origin of Paul's religion.

Finally, what reason is there for supposing that the Christianity of Damascus and Antioch was different in essentials from the Christianity of Jerusalem? An important step, it is said, was taken when the gospel was transplanted from its native Palestinian soil to the Greek-speaking world—the most momentous step in the whole history of Christianity, the most heavily fraught with changes. But it must be remembered that the primitive Jerusalem Church itself was bilingual; it contained a large Greek-speaking element. The transplanting of the gospel to Antioch was accomplished not by any ordinary Jews of the Dispersion, but by those Jews of the Dispersion who had lived at Jerusalem and had received their instruction from the intimate friends of Jesus. Is it likely that such men would so soon forget the impressions that they had received, and would transform Christianity from a simple acceptance of Jesus as Messiah with eager longing for His return into a cult that emulated the pagan cults of the surrounding world by worship of Jesus as Lord? The transition, if it occurred at all, occurred with astonishing rapidity. Paul was converted only two or three years after the crucifixion of Jesus. If, therefore, the paganizing Hellenistic Christianity of Damascus and Antioch was to be the spiritual soil in which Paul's religion was nurtured, it must have been formed in the very early days.

The pagan influences could hardly have begun to enter after the conversion of Paul [1] For then Paul would have been conscious of their entrance, and all the advantages of the hypothesis would disappear—the hypothesis would then be excluded by the self-testimony of Paul. But the formation of a paganizing Christianity at Antioch and Damascus, in the very early days and by the instrumentality of men who had come under the instruction of the intimate friends of Jesus, and despite the constant intercourse between Jerusalem and the cities in question, is very difficult to conceive. At any rate, the separation between what Paul received from Antioch and Damascus and what he received from Jerusalem is quite impossible. Heitmüller and Bousset have not really helped matters by trying to place an additional link in the chain between Paul and Jesus. The Hellenistic Christianity of Antioch, supposed to be distinct from the Christianity of Jerusalem, is to say the least a very shadowy thing.

But Bousset and Heitmüller probably will not maintain that all the pagan influences which entered the life of Paul entered through the gateway of pre-Pauline Hellenistic Christianity. On the contrary, it will probably be said that Paul lived all his life in the midst of a pagan religious atmosphere, which affected him directly as well as through the community at Antioch. But how was this direct pagan influence exerted? Some suppose that it was exerted through the reading of pagan religious literature; others suppose that it came merely through conversation with "the man in the street." Paul desired to become all things to all men (we are reminded), in order that by all means he might save some (1 Cor. ix. 22). But what was more necessary for winning the Gentiles than familiarity with their habits of thought and life? Therefore, it is said, Paul must have made some study of paganism in order to put his proclamation of the gospel in a form which would appeal to the pagans whom he sought to win.

A certain element of truth underlies this contention. It should not be supposed that Paul was ignorant of the pagan life that surrounded him. He uses figures of speech derived from the athletic games; here and there in his Epistles he makes reference to the former religious practices of his converts. It is not unnatural that he should occasionally have

[1] But compare Bousset, *op. cit.,* p. 32.

sought common ground with those to whom he preached, in accordance with the example contained in the seventeenth chapter of Acts. But on the whole, the picture of Paul making a study of paganism in preparation for his life-work is too modern to be convincing. It may seem natural to those modern missionaries who no longer regard Christianity as a positive religion, who no longer insist upon any sharp break on the part of the converts with their ancestral ways of thinking, who are perfectly content to derive help from all quarters and are far more interested in improving political and social conditions in the land for which they labor than they are in securing assent to any specific Christian message. The Christianity of such missionaries might consistently be hospitable to foreign influence; such missionaries might assign the central place in their preparation to the investigation of the religious life of mission lands. But the Christianity of Paul was entirely different. Paul was convinced of the exclusiveness and the all-sufficiency of his own message. The message had been revealed to him directly by the Lord. It was supported by the testimony of those who had been intimate with Jesus; it was supported by the Old Testament Scriptures. But throughout it was the product of revelation. To the Jews it was a stumbling-block, to the Greeks foolishness. But to those who were saved it was the power of God and the wisdom of God. "Where is the wise," says Paul, "where is the scribe, where is the disputer of this world? hath not God made foolish the wisdom of the world?" It is a little difficult to suppose that the man who wrote these words was willing to modify the divine foolishness of his message in order to make it conform to the religion of pagan hearers.

Two reservations, therefore, are necessary before the investigator can enter upon an actual comparison of the Pauline Epistles with Hermes Trismegistus and other similar sources. In the first place, it has not been proved that the type of religion attested by these sources existed at all in the time of Paul;[1] and in the second place, it is difficult to see how any pagan influence could have entered into Paul's life. But if despite these difficulties the comparison be instituted, it will show, as a matter of fact, not agreement, but a most striking divergence both of language and of spirit.

[1] See Chapter VI.

The investigation may be divided into three parts, although the three parts will be found to overlap at many points. Three fundamental elements in Paul's religion have been derived from Greco-oriental syncretism: first, the complex of ideas connected with the obtaining of salvation; second, the sacraments; third, the Christology and the work of Christ in redemption.[1]

The first of the three divisions just enumerated is connected especially with the name of R. Reitzenstein.[2] Reitzenstein lays great stress upon the lexical method of study; it may be proved, he believes, that Paul used terms which were derived from Hellenistic mystical religion, and with the terms went the ideas. The ideas, he admits, were not taken over without modification, but even after the Pauline modifications are subtracted, enough is thought to remain in order to show that the mystery religions exerted an important influence upon Paul.

Thus Reitzenstein attempts to exhibit in the Pauline Epistles a technical vocabulary derived from the Hellenized mystery religions. This supposed technical vocabulary embraces especially the terms connected with "knowledge"[3] and "Spirit."[4]

In the mystical religion of Paul's day, Reitzenstein says, "gnosis" (knowledge) did not mean knowledge acquired by processes of investigation or reasoning, but the knowledge that came by immediate revelation from a god. Such immediate revelation was given, in the mystery cults, by the mystic vision which formed a part of the experience of initiation; in the philosophizing derivatives of the mystery cults, like the type of piety which is attested in Hermes Trismegistus, the revela-

---

[1] For what follows, compare especially Kennedy, *St. Paul and the Mystery-Religions*, [1913]; Clemen, *Religionsgeschichtliche Erklärung des Neuen Testaments*, 1909 (English Translation, *Primitive Christianity and Its Non-Jewish Sources*, 1912), *Der Einfluss der Mysterienreligionen auf das älteste Christentum*, 1913. These writers deny for the most part any influence of the mystery religions upon the center of Paul's religion. For a thoroughgoing presentation of the other side of the controversy, see, in addition to the works of Bousset and Reitzenstein, Loisy, *Les mystères païens et le mystère chrétien*, 1919.

[2] *Poimandres*, 1904; *Die hellenistischen Mysterienreligionen*, 2te Aufl., 1920; "Religionsgeschichte und Eschatologie," in *Zeitschrift für die neutestamentliche Wissenschaft*, xiii, 1912, pp. 1-28.

[3] γνῶσις.

[4] πνεῦμα.

tion could be divorced from any external acts and connected with the mere reading of a book. But in any case, "gnosis" was not regarded as an achievement of the intellect; it was an experience granted by divine favor. The man who had received such favor was exalted far above ordinary humanity; indeed he was already deified.

This conception of gnosis, Reitzenstein believes, is the conception which is found in the Pauline Epistles; gnosis according to Paul was a gift of God, an experience produced by the divine Spirit. In the case of Paul, Reitzenstein continues, the experience was produced through a vision of the risen Christ. That vision had changed the very nature of Paul. It is true, Paul avoids the term "deification"; he does not say, in accordance with Hellenistic usage, that he had ceased to be a man and had become God. This limitation was required by his Jewish habits of thought. But he does say that through his vision he was illumined and received "glory." Thus, although the term deification is avoided, the idea is present. As one who has received gnosis, Paul regards himself as being beyond the reach of human judgments, and is not interested in tradition that came from other Christians. In short, according to Reitzenstein, Paul was a true "gnostic."

But this conclusion is reached only by doing violence to the plain meaning of the Epistles. "Gnosis" in the early Church (including Paul), as Von Harnack well observes,[1] is not a technical term; it is no more a technical term than is, for example, "wisdom." In 1 Cor. xii. 8 it appears, not by itself, but along with many other spiritual gifts of widely diverse nature. Gnosis, therefore, does not stand in that position of prominence which it ought to occupy if Reitzenstein's theory were correct. It is, indeed, according to Paul, important; and it is a direct gift from God. But what reason is there to have recourse to Hellenistic mystery religions in order to explain either its importance or its nature? Another explanation is found much nearer at hand—namely, in the Old Testament. The possibility of Old Testament influence in Paul does not have to be established by any elaborate arguments, and is not opposed by his own testimony. On the

[1] Von Harnack, "Die Terminologie der Wiedergeburt und verwandter Erlebnisse in der ältesten Kirche," in *Texte und Untersuchungen zur Geschichte der altchristlichen Literatur*, xlii, 1918, pp. 128f., Anm. 1.

contrary, he appeals to the Old Testament again and again in his Epistles. And the Old Testament contains all the elements of his conception of the knowledge of God. Even the Greek noun "gnosis" occurs in the Septuagint (though with comparative infrequency); but what is far more important is that the idea is expressed countless times by the verb. Let it not be said that the Septuagint is a Hellenistic book, and that therefore if the Septuagint idea of the knowledge of God affords the basis for Pauline teaching that does not disprove the influence of the Hellenistic mystery religions. For in its rendering of the passages dealing with the knowledge of God, whatever may be said of other matters, the Septuagint is transmitting faithfully the meaning of the Hebrew text. Knowledge of God in the Hebrew Old Testament is something far more than a mere intellectual achievement. It is the gift of God, and it involves the entire emotional nature.

But may it not be objected that the Pauline conception transcends that of the Old Testament in that in Paul the knowledge of God produces a transformation of human nature—the virtual deification of man? This question must be answered in the negative. Undoubtedly the Pauline conception does transcend that of the Old Testament, but not in the way which is here supposed. The intimate relation between the believer and the risen Christ, according to Paul, goes far beyond anything that was possible under the old dispensation. It involves a fuller, richer, more intimate knowledge. But the experience in which Paul saw the risen Christ near Damascus was not an end in itself, as it would have been in the milieu of the mystery religions; it was rather a means to an end.[1] It was the divinely appointed means by which Paul was convinced of an historical fact, the resurrection of Jesus, and was led to appropriate the benefits of that fact. Thus, as Oepke[2] has well observed, Paul does not expect his converts all to see Christ, or even to have experiences like that which is described in 2 Cor. xii. 2-4. It is sufficient for them to receive the historical account of Christ's redeeming work, through the testimony of Paul and of the other witnesses. That account, transmitted by ordinary word of mouth, is a sufficient basis for faith; and through faith comes the new life. At this

[1] Oepke, *Die Missionspredigt des Apostels Paulus,* 1920, p. 53.
[2] *Loc. cit.*

point is discovered an enormous difference between Paul and the mystery religions. In the mystery religions everything led up to the mystic vision; without that mystic vision there was no escape from the miseries of the old life. But according to Paul, the mighty change was produced by the acceptance of a simple story, an account of what had happened only a few years before, when Jesus died and rose again. From the acceptance of that story there proceeds a new knowledge, a gnosis. But this higher gnosis in Paul is not the means of salvation, as it is in the mystery religions; it is only one of the effects of salvation. This difference is no mere matter of detail. On the contrary, it involves a contrast between two entirely different worlds of thought and life.

The message of Paul, then, was a "gospel," a piece of news about something that had happened. As has well been observed,[1] the characteristic New Testament words are the words that deal with "gospel," "teaching," and the transmission of an historical message. Paul was not a "gnostic," but a witness; salvation, according to his teaching, came not through a mystic vision, but through the hearing of faith.[2]

Thus, so far as the idea of "knowledge" is concerned, Reitzenstein has not been successful in showing any dependence of Paul upon the mystery religions. But how is it with regard to the doctrine of the "Spirit"?

In 1 Cor. ii. 14, 15, the "spiritual man" is contrasted with the "psychic man." The spiritual man is the man who has the Spirit of God; the psychic man is the man who has only a human soul. It is not really correct to say that the spiritual man, according to Paul, is a man not who has the Spirit but who is the Spirit. Paul avoids such an expression for the same reason that prevents his speaking of the "deification" of the Christian. Everywhere in Paul the personal distinction between the believer and the Christ who dwells in him is carefully preserved. His "mysticism" (if the word may be used thus loosely) is never pantheistic. Here already is to be found a most vital difference between Paul and Hermes Trismegistus.

But this observation constitutes a digression. It is necessary to return to 1 Cor. ii. 14, 15. The spiritual man, ac-

---

[1] Heinrici, *Die Hermes-Mystik und das Neue Testament,* 1918, pp. 178-180.

[2] Compare Oepke, *op. cit.,* pp. 40ff.

cording to that passage, is the man who has the Spirit of God; the psychic man is the man who has only a human soul. Reitzenstein apparently insists that the "only" in this sentence should be left out. The psychic man, according to Paul, he says, has a soul; the spiritual man has no "soul" but has the divine Spirit instead. But such a representation is not really Pauline.[1] Paul clearly teaches that the human soul continues to exist even after the divine Spirit has entered in. "The Spirit himself," he says, "beareth witness with our spirit, that we are children of God" (Rom. viii. 16). Here "our spirit" clearly means "our soul," and is expressly distinguished from the divine Spirit. At every point, then, the attempt to find a pantheistic mysticism in Paul breaks down before the intensely personal character of his religion. The relation of Paul to the risen Christ, intimate as it is, mediated as it is by the all-pervasive Spirit, is a relation of one person to another.

But it is still necessary to return to the Pauline contrast between the "spiritual man" and the "psychic man." Reitzenstein lays great stress upon that contrast. He regards it as lying at the heart of Paul's religion, and he thinks that he can explain it from the Hellenistic mystery religions. Apparently the method of Reitzenstein can be tested at this point if it can be tested at all. If it does not succeed in explaining the Pauline doctrine of the Spirit, upon which the chief stress is laid, probably it will explain nothing at all.

At first sight the material adduced by Reitzenstein is impressive. It is impressive by its very bulk. The reader is led by the learned investigator into many new and entrancing fields. Surely after so long a journey the traveler must arrive at last at his desired goal. But somehow the goal is never reached. All of Reitzenstein's material, strange to say, seems to prove the exact opposite of what Reitzenstein desires.

Reitzenstein desires apparently to explain the Pauline use of the adjectives "psychic" and "spiritual"[2] in 1 Cor. ii. 14, 15; apparently he is quite sure that the usage finds its sufficient basis in Hermes Trismegistus and related sources.

[1] See especially Vos, "The Eschatological Aspect of the Pauline Conception of the Spirit," in *Biblical and Theological Studies by the Members of the Faculty of Princeton Theological Seminary*, 1912, pp. 248-250.
[2] ψυχικός and πνευματικός.

But the plain fact—almost buried though it is under the mass of irrelevant material—is that the adjective "psychic" and the adjective "spiritual" occur each only once in the sources which are examined, and that they never occur, as in 1 Cor. ii. 14, 15, in contrast with each other.[1] What is even far more disconcerting, however, is that the noun "spirit" [2] is not used (certainly not used ordinarily) in contrast with "soul," [3] as Paul uses it. Certainly it is not so used ordinarily in the Hermetic writings. On the contrary, in Hermes the spirit appears, in certain passages, not as something that is higher than the soul, but as something that is lower. Apparently the common Greek materialistic use of "pneuma" to indicate "breath" or "wind" or the like is here followed. At any rate, the terminology is as remote as could be imagined from that of Paul. There is absolutely no basis for the Pauline contrast between the human soul and the divine Spirit.[4]

It might be supposed that this fact would weaken Reitzenstein's devotion to his theory. But such is not the case. If, says Reitzenstein, "spirit" in Hermes Trismegistus does not indicate something higher than "soul," that is because the original popular terminology has here suffered philosophical revision. The popular term "spirit" has been made to give place to the more philosophical term "mind." [5] Where Hermes says "mind," therefore, it is only necessary to restore the term "spirit," and an admirable basis is discovered for the Pauline terminology. But how does Reitzenstein know that the popular, unphilosophical term in the mystery religions was "spirit," rather than "mind" or the like? The extant pagan sources do not clearly attest the term "spirit" in the sense which is here required. Apparently then the only reason for positing the existence of such a term in pagan mystery religion is that it must have existed in pagan mystery religion if the

---

[1] On the occurrence of ψυχικός at the beginning of Dieterich's "Mithras Liturgy" (line 24), see Bousset, *Kyrios Christos*, 1913, p. 141, Anm. 1. On the occurrence of πνευματικός, see Reitzenstein, *Hellenistische Mysterienreligionen*, 2te Aufl., 1920, p 162 Compare Bousset, *Jesus der Herr*, 1916, pp. 80f.

[2] πνεῦμα.

[3] ψυχή

[4] For this whole subject, see especially the comprehensive monograph of Burton (*Spirit, Soul, and Flesh*, [1918]), with the summary on pp 205-207.

[5] νοῦς.

Pauline use of it is to be explained. It looks, therefore, as though the learned argument of Reitzenstein had been moving all the time in a circle. After pursuing a roundabout course through many centuries and many races of men, after acquiring boundless treasures of curious information, after impressing the whole world with the learning thus acquired, the explorer arrives at last at the exact point where he started, and no richer than when he first set out! The Pauline terminology cannot be explained except as coming from the mystery religions; therefore, says Reitzenstein in effect, it must have had a place in the mystery religions even though the extant sources provide no sufficient evidence of the fact.[1]

But is there not some way out of the vicious circle? Is there not some witness to the terminology which is required? The investigator turns naturally to Philo. Philo is thought to be dependent upon the mysteries; perhaps he will attest the required mystical use of the term "spirit." But, alas, Philo apparently deserts his friends. Except where he is influenced by the Old Testament use of the word "spirit," he seems to prefer other terminology.[2] His terminology, then, like that of Hermes must be thought to have suffered philosophical reversal. And still the required mystery terminology eludes the eye of the investigator.

Of course there is one place where the terms "Spirit" and "spiritual" are exalted above the terms "psyche" and "psychic," in quite the manner that is desired. That place is found in the Christian Gnosticism of the second century. But the Gnostics of the second century are plainly dependent upon Paul; they vie with the Catholic Church in their appeal to the Pauline Epistles. The origin of their use of the terms "psychic" and "spiritual" is therefore only too plain. At least it might seem to be plain. But Reitzenstein rejects the common view.[3] According to Reitzenstein, the Gnostics have

---

[1] See Burton, *op. cit.*, p. 206: "For the Pauline exaltation of $\pi\nu\epsilon\tilde{\upsilon}\mu\alpha$ over $\psi\upsilon\chi\acute{\eta}$ there is no observed previous parallel. It marks an advance on Philo, for which there 'is no precedent in non-Jewish Greek, and only partial and imperfect parallels in the magical papyri. It is the reverse of Hermetic usage."

[2] See Bousset, *Kyrios Christos*, pp. 138, 140, 141 (Anm. 2).

[3] Also Bousset, *op. cit.*, pp. 140f. According to Bousset, it is unlikely that "the few and difficult terminological explanations of Paul . . . should have exerted such extensive influence upon the most diverse Gnostic systems." But is the teaching of Paul about the Spirit as higher than the soul really obscure? Does it not appear plainly all through the Epistles?

derived their usage not from Paul but from the pre-Pauline mystery religions; and the Gnostic usage of "Spirit" as higher than "soul" is the source of the Hermetic usage of "soul" as higher than "spirit," which, Reitzenstein believes, has been derived from it by philosophical revision. But the argument is beyond the reach even of J. Kroll, who cannot be accused of theological interest. As has already been observed, Kroll insists that the Gnostic usage is here secondary.[1]

One argument remains. The trouble, from Reitzenstein's point of view, is that when the Hermetic writings ought, in the interests of the theory, to say "spirit" they actually say "mind." It becomes necessary, therefore, to prove that "mind" means the same thing as "spirit." A proof is found by Reitzenstein in Paul himself, in 1 Cor. ii. 15, 16. "But the spiritual man," says Paul, "examines all things, but he himself is examined by none. For 'who hath known the mind of the Lord, that he should instruct Him?' But we have the mind of Christ." Here, says Reitzenstein,[2] the possession of the "mind" of Christ makes a man a "spiritual" man, that is, a man who has the "Spirit." Hence "mind" is the same thing as "spirit." Hence —such, at least, would seem to be the only inference from the passage in 1 Corinthians which would really establish Reitzenstein's theory—when Hermes Trismegistus says "mind," it is legitimate to substitute "spirit" in order thus to find the basis for the ordinary Pauline terminology.

But it is by no means clear that "mind" in 1 Cor. ii. 16b is the same as "spirit." If a man has the Spirit of Christ, he also has the mind of Christ; the Spirit gives him an understanding of the thoughts of Christ. Conversely, the possession of the mind of Christ is a proof that the man has the Spirit of Christ; it is only the Spirit who could have given him his understanding of Christ's thoughts. But it does not follow by any means that the term "mind" means the same thing as the term "spirit." Moreover, the passage is entirely isolated; and the choice of the unusual word "mind" may be due to the form of the Septuagint passage which Paul is citing.

At any rate, the plain fact is that the terminology in Hermes Trismegistus and related sources is strikingly different from that of Paul. Reitzenstein finds himself in the peculiar position of proving that Paul is dependent upon pagan

[1] See above, p. 249, with footnote 2.
[2] *Hellenistische Mysterienreligionen*, 2te Aufl., 1920, pp. 189f.

sources by the fact that the Pauline terminology does not occur in the pagan sources. It will not do for him to say that the terminology is of little importance and that the ideas of Paul, if not the terminology, are derived from the pagan mysteries. For it is just Reitzenstein who insists upon the importance of words as the vehicle of ideas. His fundamental argument is that Paul used the terminology of the mystery religions, and with the terminology received also the ideas. It is therefore important to observe that Reitzenstein's lexical parallel utterly breaks down.

But if the Pauline doctrine of the Spirit was not derived from the pagan mystery religions, whence was it derived? The answer is perfectly plain. It was derived ultimately from the Old Testament.[1] Unquestionably, indeed, it goes far beyond the Old Testament, and the enrichment of its content may conceivably be explained in various ways. The Gospels and Acts explain the enrichment as due partly to the teaching of Jesus Himself and to the coming of the Spirit on the day of Pentecost. This explanation will be rejected for the most part by naturalistic criticism. Paul explains the enrichment as due partly to the experience which he had of the presence of Christ. This explanation is regarded as no explanation at all by the school of comparative religion. But it is not necessary in the present connection to discuss these matters. All that needs to be observed now is that the basis for the Pauline doctrine of the Spirit is found in the Old Testament.

In the Old Testament, the Spirit of God is represented as distinct from man and higher than man; there is no question in the Old Testament of a usage by which the Spirit is degraded, as in Hermes Trismegistus, below the soul. In the Old Testament, moreover, the Spirit is regarded as bestowing supernatural gifts such as prophecy and producing supernatural experiences—exactly as in Paul. But the fruit of the Spirit according to the Old Testament is something more than prophecy or any momentary experience; it is also a permanent possession of the soul. "Take not thy holy Spirit from me," says the

[1] Bousset (*op. cit.*, p. 141, Anm. 2) admits that the terminology of Paul, especially his use of the term "Spirit" instead of "mind" and his use of the terms in the contrast between "Spirit" and "flesh" may possibly be due partly to the Old Testament, but insists that such terminological influence does not touch the fundamentals of the thought. Such admissions are important, despite the way in which Bousset qualifies them.

Psalmist. (Ps. li. 11.) Let the student first examine the labored arguments of Reitzenstein, let him examine the few faint approaches to the Pauline terminology which have been gleaned from pagan sources, mostly late and of uncertain origin, let him observe that just where Greek usage approaches Paul most closely in form (as in the "divine Spirit" of Menander),[1] it is most diametrically opposed in content, let him reflect that the influence of pagan usage is contrary to Paul's own consciousness. And then let him turn to the Old Testament! Let him remember that the Pauline use of the Old Testament is no matter of conjecture, but is attested everywhere in the Epistles. And let him examine the Old Testament usage in detail. The Pauline terminology—"the Holy Spirit," the "Spirit of God" —so signally lacking in early pagan sources,[2] appears here in all its richness; and with the terminology go the depths of life. In turning from Hermes to the Hebrew Scriptures, the student has turned away from Stoic pantheism, away from the polytheism of the mystery religions, away from the fantastic speculations of a decadent philosophy, to the presence of the personal God. And, in doing so, he has found the origin of the religion of Paul.

Thus the lexical argument of Reitzenstein breaks down at the decisive points. It would indeed be rash to assert that Paul never uses a term derived from the pagan mysteries. For example, in Phil. iv. 12 he uses the verb that means "to be initiated." "In everything and in all things I have been initiated," he says, "both to be filled and to suffer hunger, both to abound and to be in want." But this example shows clearly how little importance is sometimes to be attributed to the ultimate derivation of a word. The word "initiate" is here used in a purely figurative way. It is doubtful whether there is the slightest thought of its original significance. The word has been worn down by repeated use almost as much as, for example, the word which means "supply" in Gal. iii. 5. Etymologically that word means "to be the leader of a chorus." It referred originally to the Athenian custom by which a wealthy citizen undertook to defray the cost of the chorus at one of the dramatic festivals. But later it was used to designate any act of bountiful supplying. And when it was used by

---

[1] See Burton, *op. cit.*, pp. 114–116.
[2] Burton, *op. cit.*, pp. 173–175, 187f.

Paul, its origin was entirely forgotten. It would be ridiculous to make Paul say that in bestowing the Spirit upon the Galatian Christians God acted as the leader of a chorus. It is not essentially different with the verb meaning "to be initiated" in Philippians. In both cases, an institution of ancient Hellenic life—in the former case, the religious festivals, in the latter case, the mysteries—has given rise to the use of a word, which found its way into the Greek world-language of the Hellenistic age, and continued to be used even where there was no thought of its ultimate origin.

This example is instructive because the context in the Philippians passage is plainly free from all mystical associations. Plainly, therefore, the use of a word derived from the mysteries does not necessarily indicate any agreement with the mystical point of view. Indeed, it may perhaps indicate the exact opposite. If the idea "to initiate" had associations connected with the center of Paul's religious life, it is perhaps doubtful whether Paul could have used the word in so purely figurative a way, just as he would not have used the word meaning "to be the leader of a chorus" in referring to God's bestowal of the Spirit, if he had had the slightest thought of the Athenian festivals.

If, then, it should appear that Paul uses a vocabulary derived from the mysteries, the fact would not necessarily be of any significance whatever in determining the origin of his religion. Every missionary is obliged to take the words which have been used in the religion from which converts are to be won in order to express the new ideas. Translators of the Bible in the modern mission fields are obliged to proceed in this way. Yet the procedure does not necessarily involve any modification of Christian ideas. The old words are given loftier meanings in order to become the vehicle of Christian truth; the original meanings provide merely a starting-point for the new teaching. Conceivably, the apostle Paul might have proceeded in this way; conceivably he might have used words connected with the mystery religions in order to proclaim the gospel of Christ.

As a matter of fact, the evidence for such an employment of a mystery terminology in the Pauline Epistles is very slight. In 1 Cor. ii. 6, 7, Paul uses the terms "mystery" and "perfect" or "full-grown." [1] The former word was sometimes used to

---

[1] μυστήριον and τέλειος.

designate the "mysteries" in the technical, religious sense. But
it is also used in Greek in a very much more general way. And
certainly as it is used in Paul it is very remote from the
technical meaning. The Christian "mystery" according to
Paul is not something that is to be kept secret on principle,
like the mysteries of Eleusis, but it is something which, though
it was formerly hidden in the counsels of God, is now to be
made known to all. Some, it is true, may never be able to
receive it. But that which is necessary in order that it may
be received is not "gnosis" or an initiation. It is rather acceptance of a message and the holy life that follows. "If
you would know the deep things of God," Paul says to the Corinthians, "then stop your quarreling." We find ourselves here
in a circle of ideas quite different from that of the mystery
religions. As for the word "teleios," it seems not to have
been discovered in pagan sources in the sense of "initiated,"
which is sometimes attributed to it in 1 Corinthians. Apparently it means simply "full-grown"; Paul contrasts the full-
grown man with the babes in Christ.

On the whole, it seems improbable that the converts of Paul,
in any great numbers, had lived in the atmosphere of the mystery religions.[1] At any rate, Paul certainly does not use
the technical vocabulary of the mysteries. That fact has been
amply demonstrated by Von Harnack in the illuminating study
which he has devoted to the "terminology of the new birth." [2]
The earliest genuine technical term in the vocabulary of the
early Church, Von Harnack believes, is "illumination," as
Justin Martyr uses it to designate baptism. Certainly in the
earlier period, there is not the slightest evidence of any such
fixity in the use of terms as would have appeared if the New
Testament writers had adopted a technical vocabulary.

Therefore, if the dependence of Paul upon the mystery
religions is to be demonstrated, the lexical method of Reitzenstein must be abandoned. The terminology of Paul is not
derived from the terminology of the mysteries. But possibly,
it may be said, although there is no clear dependence in the
terminology, the fundamental ideas of Paul may still be shown

[1] Oepke, *Die Missionspredigt des Apostels Paulus*, 1920, p. 26.
[2] Von Harnack, "Die Terminologie der Wiedergeburt und verwandter
Erlebnisse in der ältesten Kirche," in *Texte und Untersuchungen zur Geschichte der altchristlichen Literatur*, xlii, 1918, pp. 97-143. See especially
pp. 139-143.

to have come from the surrounding paganism. It is in this more cautious form that the hypothesis is maintained by Bousset; at least Bousset is less inclined than Reitzenstein to lay stress upon verbal coincidences.[1] The entire outlook of Paul, Bousset believes, regardless of the way in which that outlook is expressed, was derived from the mystical piety of the Hellenistic age; it was from his pagan environment that Paul derived the pessimistic estimate of human nature which is at the basis of his teaching.

At this point it may be admitted very freely that Paul was convinced of the insufficiency of human nature, and that that conviction was also prevalent in the paganism of the Hellenistic age. The Hellenistic age, like Paul, recognized the need of redemption; salvation, it was believed, could not be attained by unaided human resources, but was a gift of higher powers. But this similarity is quite insufficient to establish any relationship of dependence. Both Paulinism and the Hellenistic mystery religions were religions of redemption. But there have been many religions of redemption, in many ages and among many peoples, which have been entirely independent of one another. It will probably not be maintained, for example, that early Buddhism stood in any fundamental causal relation to the piety of the Hellenistic age. Yet early Buddhism was a religion of redemption.

No attempt indeed should be made to underestimate the community of interest which binds all redemptive religions together and separates them sharply from all others. Common recognition of the fundamental evil of the world is a far closer bond of union than agreement about the details of conduct. Gautama under the tree of knowledge in India, seeking in ascetic meditation for freedom from the misery of existence, was inwardly far nearer to the apostle Paul than is many a modern liberal preacher who loves to read the sixth chapter of Ephesians in Church. But such community of interest does not indicate any relation of dependence. It might do so if the sense of human inadequacy were an abnormal thing. In that case, the appearance of a pessimistic view of human nature would require explanation. But if human nature is really hopeless and helpless in an evil world, then the independent

[1] But compare *Jesus der Herr*, 1916, pp. 80-85.

recognition of the fact by many men of many minds is no longer cause for wonder.

Historical judgments at this point, then, are apt to be influenced by the presuppositions of the investigator. To Bousset the whole notion of redemption is distasteful. It seems to him to be an abnormal, an unhealthy thing. To explain its emergence, therefore, in the course of human history he is prone to look for special causes. So he explains the Pauline doctrine of the radical evil of human nature as being due to the piety of a decadent age. But if this world is really an evil world, as Paul says it is, then recognition of the fact will appear spontaneously at many points. For a time, in an age of high achievements like the age of Pericles, the fundamental problem of life may be forgotten. But the problem is always there and will force itself ever anew into the consciousness of men.

At any rate, whether desirable or not, the longing for redemption is a fundamental fact of history, and may be shown to have emerged independently at many points. The character of Paulinism as a redemptive religion, the Pauline doctrine of human depravity, is therefore insuﬃcient to establish dependence of Paul upon the mystery religions of the Hellenistic age. Dependence could be established only by similarity in the form in which the doctrine of depravity appears. But as a matter of fact such similarity is strikingly absent. The Pauline use of the term "flesh" to denote that in which evil resides can apparently find no real parallel whatever in pagan usage. And the divergence appears not only in terminology but also in thought. At first sight there might seem to be a parallel between the Pauline doctrine of the flesh and the Greek doctrine of the evil of matter, which appears in the Orphic sects, then in Plato and in his successors. But the parallel breaks down upon closer examination. According to Plato, the body is evil because it is material; it is the prison-house of the soul. Nothing could really be more remote from the thought of Paul. According to Paul, the connection of soul and body is entirely normal, and the soul apart from the body is in a condition of nakedness. It is true, the body will be changed at the resurrection or at the coming of Christ; it will be made more adequate for the Kingdom of God. But at any rate, there is in Paul no doctrine of the inherent evil of matter. The real starting-point of the Pauline doctrine of the flesh is to be found in the Old Testament, in the passages where "flesh" denotes human nature in its frailty. Certainly the Pauline teaching is far more highly developed than the teaching of the Old Testament. But the Old Testament provides the starting-point. The "flesh" in Paul, when it is used in its developed, ethical sense, does not mean the material nature of man; it includes rather all that man receives by ordinary generation. The contrast between "flesh" and "Spirit" therefore is not the contrast between matter and spirit; it is a contrast between human nature, of which sin has taken possession, and the Spirit of God.

Certainly, at any rate, whatever solution may be found for the intricate problem of the Pauline use of the term "flesh," the Pauline pessimism with regard to human nature is totally different from the dualistic pessimism of the Hellenistic age. It is different because it does not make evil reside in matter as such. But it is different also in a far more fundamental way. It is different in its ethical character. The Hellenistic age was conscious of the need of salvation; and salvation, it was recognized, must come from outside of man. But this consciousness of need was not always, and not clearly, connected with questions of right and wrong. The Hellenistic age was conscious of inadequacy, of slavery to fate, of the futility of human life as it is actually lived upon the earth. Here and there, no doubt, there was also a recognition of existing moral evil, and a longing for a better life. But such longings were almost submerged amidst longings of a non-ethical kind. The mysteries were cherished for the most part not because they offered goodness but because they offered happiness.

In Paul, on the other hand, the consciousness of human inadequacy is essentially a consciousness of sin. And redemption is desired because it satisfies the hunger and thirst after righteousness. At this point the contrast with the Hellenistic mystery religions is profound. The religion of Paul is like the mystery religions in that it is a religion of redemption. But there the similarity ceases. There is certainly no such similarity in the conception of that from which men are to be redeemed as would raise any presumption of dependence in the presentation of the means of redemption. And it is dependence in the presentation of the means of redemption which alone would serve to explain the origin of the religion of Paul. It is unwarranted to argue that because Paul agrees with the mystery religions in a longing for redemption therefore he must have derived from the mystery religions his method of satisfying the longing—namely his conception of the redemptive work of the Lord Jesus Christ. For even in the longing for redemption—to say nothing of the way of satisfying the longing—Paul was totally different from the mysteries. The longing which was aroused in the devotees of the mysteries was a longing for a happier immortality, a freedom from the pressure of fate; the longing which Paul sought to arouse in those for whom he labored was a longing for righteousness and for acceptance by the righteous God.

This difference is intimately connected with a highly significant fact—the presence in Paul of a "forensic" view of salvation. Salvation, according to Paul, is not only salvation from the power of sin; it is also salvation from the guilt of sin. Not only regeneration is needed, if a man is to be saved, but also justification. At this point, there is apparently in the mystery religions no parallel worthy of the name. At least there is none if Reitzenstein's attempt to exhibit a parallel [1] is at all adequate; for Reitzenstein has succeeded only in setting in clearer light the enormous difference at this point between Paul and his pagan environment. The word "justify" appears, indeed, in the Hermetic corpus (xiii. 9), but as Reitzenstein himself observes, it means not "declare righteous" but "make righteous." A parallel with Paul can be set up, therefore, only if "justify" in Paul also means "make righteous." Reitzenstein actually finds such a meaning in Rom. vi. 7, and in Rom. viii. 30. But the expedient is desperate in the extreme. It will probably be unnecessary to review again the absolutely overwhelming evidence by which the word "justify" in the Pauline Epistles is shown to mean not "make righteous" but "declare righteous." Without the slightest question Paul did maintain a forensic view of salvation. The believer, according to Paul, is in himself guilty in the sight of God. But he is given a sentence of acquittal, he is "justified," because

[1] Reitzenstein, *Die hellenistischen Mysterienreligionen*, 2te Aufl., pp. 112-116.

Christ has borne on the cross the curse of the Law which rightly rested upon those whom Christ died to save.

The presence of this forensic element in the teaching of Paul is universally or generally recognized; and it is usually admitted to be not Greek but Jewish. But there is a tendency among recent scholars to minimize its importance. According to Wrede, the forensic conception of salvation, the complex of ideas centering around justification apart from the works of the Law, was merely a weapon forged by Paul in the exigencies of controversy.[1] Against the Judaizing contention for the continued validity of the Law Paul developed the doctrine that the penalty imposed by the Law upon sin was borne by Christ, so that for the believer the bondage of the Law is over. But, Wrede believes, this whole conception was of minor importance in Paul's own life; it was merely necessary in order that he might refute the Judaizers and so continue his free Gentile mission. A somewhat similar view is advocated by Bousset; Bousset believes, at least, that the forensic conception of salvation occupies a subordinate place in the thought and life of Paul.

But there could be no greater mistake. The doctrine of justification by faith alone apart from the works of the Law appears indeed in the Epistle to the Galatians as a weapon against the Judaizers. But why was Paul opposed to the Judaizers in the first place? Certainly it was not merely because the Judaizing demand that Gentile Christians should be circumcised and keep the Law would interfere in a practical way with the Gentile mission. Paul was not like some modern leaders of the Church, who are interested in mere bigness; he was not interested in the extension of the Church if such extension involved the sacrifice of principle. Nothing could be more utterly unhistorical than the representation of Paul as a practical missionary, developing the doctrine of justification by faith in order to get rid of a doctrine of the Law which would be a hindrance in the way of his Gentile mission. Such a representation reverses the real state of the case. The real reason why Paul was devoted to the doctrine of justification by faith was not that it made possible the Gentile mission, but rather that it was true. Paul was not devoted to the

---

[1] "Kampfeslehre." See Wrede, *Paulus*, 1904, pp. 72ff. (English Translation, *Paul*, 1907, pp. 122ff.).

doctrine of justification by faith because of the Gentile mission; he was devoted to the Gentile mission because of the doctrine of justification by faith. And he was opposed to the Judaizers, not merely because they constituted a hindrance in the way of the Gentile work, but because they made the cross of Christ of none effect. "If righteousness is through the law, then Christ died in vain" (Gal. ii. 21). These words are at the very heart of Paul's life; for they involve the Pauline doctrine of the grace of God.

There could be no greater error, therefore, than that of representing the Pauline doctrine of justification by faith as a mere afterthought, as a mere weapon in controversy. Paul was interested in salvation from the guilt of sin no whit less than in salvation from the power of sin, in justification no whit less than in the "new creation." Indeed, it is a great mistake to separate the two sides of his message. There lies the root error of the customary modern formula for explaining the origin of the Pauline theology. According to that formula, the forensic element in Paul's doctrine of salvation, which centers in justification, was derived from Judaism, and the vital or essential element which centers in the new creation was derived from paganism. In reality, the two elements are inextricably intertwined. The sense of guilt was always central in the longing for salvation which Paul desired to induce in his hearers, and imparted to that longing an ethical quality which was totally lacking in the mystery religions. And salvation in the Pauline churches consisted not merely in the assurance of a blessed immortality, not merely in the assurance of a present freedom from the bondage of fate, not merely even in the possession of a new power of holy living, but also, and everywhere, in the consciousness that the guilt of sin had been removed by the cross of Christ.

There is no affinity, therefore, between the Pauline doctrine of salvation and that which is found in the mystery religions. The terminology is strikingly different, and the difference is even greater in the underlying ideas. Paulinism is like the mystery religions in being a religion of redemption, but within the great category of redemptive religions tht could be no greater contrast.

This conclusion might be overthrown if certain recent contentions should prove to be correct with regard to the second of the elements in Paulinism which are being derived from pagan religion. This second element is found in the Pauline doctrine of the sacraments. In the teaching of Paul about baptism and the Lord's Supper, we are told, there is clearly to be observed the influence of the mystery religions.

This contention depends partly upon the supposed nature of these particular sacraments and partly upon the mere fact of the presence of sacraments in the religion of Paul.

With regard to the nature of these particular sacraments there might seem at first sight to be a parallel with the mystery religions. The mysteries usually had connected with them ablutions of one kind or another and some sort of partaking of sacred food. But it is singularly difficult to determine the meaning of these practices. The various ablutions which preceded the celebration of the mysteries may have been often nothing more than symbols of cleansing; and such symbolism is so natural that it might appear independently at many places. It appears, for example, highly developed among the Jews; and in the baptism of John the Baptist it assumes a form far more closely akin to Christian baptism than in the washings which were connected with the pagan mysteries. The evidence for a sacramental significance of the ablutions in the mysteries, despite confident assertions on the part of some modern writers, is really very slight. Most interesting, perhaps, of all the passages which have been cited is that which appears in Pap. Par. 47, a papyrus letter written in the second century before Christ.[1] This passage may be translated as follows: "For you are untruthful about all things and the gods who are with you likewise, because they have cast you into great matter and we are not able to die, and if you see that we are going to be saved, then let us be baptized." It is possible to understand the death that is referred to as the mystical death which would be attained in the mysteries, and to connect the baptism with that death and with the consequent salvation. There would thus be a parallel, external at least, with the sixth chapter of Romans, where Paul connects baptism with the

[1] See Reitzenstein, *op. cit.*, 2te Aufl., pp. 85f. The passage in the papyrus reads as follows (*Notices et extraits des manuscrits de la bibliothèque impériale*, xviii, 1865, p. 315): ὅτι ψεύδῃ πάντα, καὶ οἱ παρά σε θεοὶ ὁμοίως, ὅτι ἐμβεβλήκαν ὑμᾶς εἰς ὕλην μεγάλην, καὶ οὐ δυνάμεθα ἀποθανεῖν· κἂν ἴδῃς ὅτι μέλλομεν σωθῆναι, τότε βαπτιζώμεθα. The letter is also contained in Witkowski, *Epistulae privatae graecae*, 1906, pp. 63-66.

death and resurrection of Christ. But the papyrus passage is hopelessly obscure, and is capable of very different interpretations. Moulton and Milligan, for example, take the verb "to be baptized," in a purely figurative sense, as meaning simply "to be overwhelmed with calamities." [1] According to this interpretation the reference to the mysteries disappears altogether. At any rate, the passage, if it does refer to the mysteries, is altogether isolated. And in view of its extreme obscurity it should not be made the basis of far-reaching conclusions. What is now being maintained is not that the washings which were connected with the mysteries were never sacramental. It is incautious to make such sweeping negative assertions. But so far as the pre-Pauline period is concerned, the evidence which has been adduced is, to say the least, exceedingly scanty. It has by no means been proved that in the pre-Pauline mysteries, "baptism" was connected closely with the new birth. [2]

With regard to the partaking of sacred food, the evidence is in some respects more abundant. Even in the mysteries of Eleusis, a special significance seems to have been attributed to the drinking of the "kykeon"; and the initiates into the Phrygian mysteries are reported by Clement of Alexandria (similarly Firmicus Maternus) to have used a formula including the words, "I ate from the drum, I drank from the cymbal." So far as the form of the act is concerned, the similarity to the Christian Eucharist is here certainly not great; there was eating and drinking in both cases, but everything else, so far as can be seen, was different. In the mysteries of Mithras the similarity of form seems to have been greater; the initiates partook of bread and of a cup in a way which Justin Martyr regarded as a demoniac imitation of the Christian sacrament. According to Cumont, moreover, the Mithraic practice was clearly sacramental; the initiates expected from their sacred

---

[1] Moulton and Milligan, *The Vocabulary of the Greek Testament*, s. v. βαπτίζω, Part ii, [1915], p. 102. Similarly Sethe, "Sarapis," in *Abhandlungen der königlichen Gesellschaft der Wissenschaften zu Göttingen*, philologisch-historische Klasse, Neue Folge, xiv, Nro. 5, 1913, p. 51.

[2] Tertullian, *de bapt.* 5 (ed. Reifferscheid et Wissowa, 1890), it must be admitted, connects baptism in heathen religion with regeneration, and mentions the part which sacramental washings had in the mysteries of Isis and of Mithras, and in Eleusinian rites. Despite the post-Pauline date of this testimony, the passage is certainly interesting. Compare Kennedy, *op. cit.*, p. 229.

banquet a supernatural effect.[1] But it will be remembered
that considerations of date render an influence of Mithras upon
Paul exceedingly improbable. And the significance of the eating and drinking in connection with other mysteries is obscure.
Apparently these acts did not form a part of the mysteries
proper, but were only a preparation for them.

In a very savage form of religion there appears the notion that men could partake of the divine nature by actually
eating the god. For example, in the worship of Dionysus, the
worshipers in the height of religious frenzy tore in pieces the
sacred bull and devoured the raw flesh. Here the bull apparently represented the god himself. This savage practice stands
in external parallel with certain passages in the New Testament, not only with the references in John vi to the eating
of the flesh and drinking of the blood of Christ, but also
(though less clearly) with the Pauline teaching about the Lord's
Supper. In 1 Cor. x. 16 Paul speaks of the "cup of blessing"
as being communion of the blood of Christ, and of the bread
as being communion of the body of Christ. Have we not here
a sublimated form of the pagan notion of eating the god? The
supposition might seem to be strengthened by the parallel
which Paul draws a few verses further on between the cup of
the Lord and the cup of demons, and between the table of the
Lord and the table of demons (verse 21), the demons, it is
said, being regarded by Paul as identical with the heathen
gods.

But the trouble is that the savage notion of eating the
god does not seem to have survived in the Hellenistic mystery
religions. At this point, therefore, the student of comparative
religion is faced with a difficulty exactly opposite to that
which appears in most of the parallels which have been set up
between the teaching of Paul and pagan religion. In most
cases the difficulty is that the pagan parallels are too late;
here, on the contrary, they are too early. If Paul is dependent upon the pagan notion of eating the god, he must have
deserted the religious practice which prevailed in his own day
in order to have recourse to a savage custom which had long
since been abandoned. The suggestion does not seem to be very

[1] Cumont, *Textes et monuments figurés relatifs aux mystères de Mithra*,
i, 1899, p. 321. See Heitmüller, *Taufe und Abendmahl bei Paulus*, 1903,
p. 46, Anm. 3.

natural. It is generally admitted that even where Christianity is dependent upon Hellenistic religion it represents a spiritualizing modification of the pagan practice. But at this point it would have to be supposed that the Christian modification proceeded in exactly the opposite direction; far from marking a greater spiritualization of pagan practice, it meant a return to a savage stage of religion which even paganism had abandoned.

Efforts are sometimes made to overcome this objection. "We observe in the history of religion," says Heitmüller, "that tendencies connected with low stages of religious development, which in the higher stages were quiescent or extinct, suddenly spring up again—of course in a modified form adapted to the changed circumstances." [1] Such general observations, even if they are based upon fact, will hardly serve to render the present hypothesis any more plausible. Dependence of the Pauline teaching about the Lord's Supper upon the savage notion of eating the god, when even paganism had come to abandon that notion, will always seem very unnatural.

Certainly the hypothesis is not supported by the parallel which Paul draws in 1 Cor. x. 21 between the table of the Lord and the table of demons. Paul does not say that the heathen had fellowship with their gods by partaking of them in a meal; the fellowship with those gods (verse 20) could be conceived of in other ways. For example, the cult god may have been conceived of in the sacrificial meals as the host at a feast. In point of fact, such an idea was no doubt widely prevalent. It is attributed to the Phrygian mysteries, for example, by Hepding, who supposes that the eating from the drum and drinking from the cymbal meant the entrance of the initiate into the circle formed by the table-companions of the god.[2] At any rate, the savage notion of eating the god is not clearly attested for the Hellenistic period, and certainly dependence of Paul upon such a notion is unlikely in the extreme.

No close parallel, then, can be established between the Christian sacraments and the practices of the pagan cults. But the very fact that the Pauline churches had sacraments at all —irrespective of the form of the particular sacraments—may conceivably be made a ground for connecting Paulinism with

[1] Heitmüller, *Taufe und Abendmahl bei Paulus*, 1903, p. 47.
[2] Hepding, *Attis*, 1903, pp. 186f.

the Hellenistic religions. The argument depends upon one particular view of the Pauline sacraments; it depends upon the view that baptism and the Lord's Supper were conceived of as conveying blessing not in virtue of the disposition of soul with which they were administered or received but in virtue of the sacramental acts themselves. In other words (to use traditional language), the argument depends upon the view that the Pauline sacraments conveyed their blessing not *ex opere operantis* but *ex opere operato*. In the Pauline churches, it is argued, the beginning of the new life and the communion with the cult god were connected with certain ceremonial acts. So it was also in the mystery religions. Therefore Paulinism is to be understood in connection with the mysteries.

But the interpretation of the Pauline Epistles upon which this hypothesis is based is fraught with serious difficulty. Did Paul really conceive of the sacraments as conveying their blessing *ex opere operato?* The general character of the Epistles certainly points in an opposite direction. An unprejudiced reader of the Epistles as a whole certainly receives the impression that the writer laid extraordinarily little stress upon forms and ceremonies. Salvation according to Paul was dependent solely upon faith, the simple acceptance of the offer contained in the message of the Cross. Any connection of such a religion with external forms seems even to be excluded expressly by the Epistle to the Galatians. A dispensation of forms and ceremonies, according to that Epistle, belongs to the period of childish bondage from which Christ has set men free.

Yet such a writer, it is maintained, actually taught that the mere act of baptism conveyed the blessing of a new life and the mere partaking of food and drink conveyed the blessing of communion with the risen Christ. The supposition seems at first sight to be preposterous. If it is to be established, it can only be on the basis of the clearest kind of evidence.

The evidence, it should be noted at the start, is at any rate decidedly limited in extent. It is only in the First Epistle to the Corinthians that Paul mentions the Lord's Supper at all, and it is only in Rom. vi and Col. ii. 12 that baptism is connected with the death and resurrection which the believer is said to have shared with Christ. The limited extent of the evidence may in itself be significant. If Paul held the high sacramentarian view of baptism and the Lord's Supper, it seems a little strange that he should have laid so little stress upon the sacraments. High sacramentarians of all ages have preserved a very different proportion. It seems still more strange, perhaps, that Paul should have said that Christ sent him not to baptize but to preach the gospel (1 Cor. i. 17). On the *ex opere operato* view of baptism, baptism was the highest possible function. Could an apostle who held that view have attributed relatively so little importance to it? In order to appreciate how much less importance is attributed in the Epistles to baptism and the Lord's Supper than to certain other elements in Paul's teaching, it is only necessary to compare the references to the sacraments with the references to faith. The fact is perfectly plain. When Paul speaks, in the large, about the way of salvation, it never seems to occur to him to mention the sacraments; what he does think of is the message of the gospel and the simple acceptance of it through faith.

These facts are sometimes admitted even by those who attribute a high sacramentarian view of the sacraments to Paul; Paulinism when taken as a whole, it is admitted, is certainly not a sacramentarian religion. What has happened, then, it is supposed, is that Paul has retained in the doctrine of the sacraments an element derived from a lower type of religion, an unassimilated remnant of the type of religion which is represented by the mystery cults. Thus the Pauline doctrine of the sacraments is thought to introduce a glaring contradiction into the thought and life of Paul.

Can such a glaring contradiction be attributed to Paul? It could probably be attributed to Hermes Trismegistus. But can it be attributed to Paul? The writer of the Pauline Epistles was no mere compiler, receiving unassimilated materials from many sources. He was a person of highly marked characteristics. And he was a person of commanding intellect. Could such a writer have introduced a glaring contradiction into the very center of his teaching? Could a writer who in the great mass of his writing is triumphantly and even polemically anti-sacramentarian have maintained all along a crassly sacramentarian view of the way in which religious blessing was to be obtained?

An affirmative answer to these questions could be rendered only on the basis of positive evidence of the most unequivocal kind. And such positive evidence is not forthcoming. The most that can by any possibility be said for the strictly sacramentarian interpretation of Rom. vi is that it is possible. It might conceivably be adopted if Rom. vi stood alone. But as a matter of fact Rom. vi does not stand alone; it stands in the midst of a considerable body of Pauline Epistles. And it must be interpreted in the light of what Paul says elsewhere. If Rom. vi stood absolutely alone, Paul might conceivably be thought to mean that the act of baptism in itself involves a dying with Christ and a rising with Him to a new life. But the whole character of the Pauline Epistles absolutely precludes such an interpretation. And another interpretation does full justice to the words as they stand. That interpretation is the obvious one which makes the act of baptism an outward sign of an inner experience. "We were buried with him," says Paul, "through baptism unto death." These words are pressed by the modern school of comparative religion very much as Luther at the Marburg Conference pressed the Latin words of institution of the Lord's Supper. Luther wrote on the table, "This is my body" ("hoc est corpus meum"), and would not hear of anything but the most literal interpretation of the words. So the modern school of comparative religion presses the words "through baptism" in Rom. vi. 4. "We were buried with him through baptism," says Paul. Therefore, it is said, since it was through baptism, it was not through faith, or through any inner disposition of the soul; therefore the sacramentarian interpretation is correct. But if Luther's over-literalness, fraught with such disastrous consequences for the Church, is deserted by most advocates of the grammatico-historical method of exegesis, should an equally bald literalness be insisted upon in connection with Rom. vi. 4?

Interpreted in connection with the whole trend of the Epistles, the sixth chapter of Romans contains an appeal to the outward sign of an inner experience. It is perfectly natural that Paul should here appeal to the outward sign rather than to the inner experience. Paul desires to strengthen in his readers the conviction that the life which they are leading as Christians is a new life in which sin can have no place. Unquestionably he might have appealed to the faith which had been the means by which the new life had been begun. But faith is not something that can be seen. Baptism, on the other hand, was a plain and obvious fact. To use a modern term, it "visualized" faith. And it is just the visualizing of faith that Paul here desires. When the Roman Christians were baptized, they were convinced that the act meant a dying with Christ and a rising with Him, it meant the beginning of their Christian life. It was a solemn and a definite act. It was something that could be seen as well as felt. Conceivably, indeed, the act in itself might have been unaccompanied by faith. But in the early Church such cases were no doubt extremely rare. They could therefore be left out of account by Paul. Paul assumes—and no doubt he is correct—that, whatever might conceivably have been the case, as a matter of fact when any one of the Roman Christians was baptized he died and rose again with Christ. But Paul does not say that the dying and rising again was produced by the external act otherwise than as that act was an expression of faith. Here, however, it is to the external act that he appeals, because it is the external act which can be seen and can be realized. It can only be because the newness of the Christian life is not realized that Christians can think of it as permitting a continuance in sin. What enables it to be realized is that which can actually be seen, namely, the external and obvious fact of baptism. In other words, baptism is here made to discharge in typical fashion its divinely appointed function as an external sign of an inner experience, and an external sign which is made the vehicle of special blessing.

A similar interpretation may be applied to all the references to the sacraments which occur in the Pauline Epistles. What sometimes produces the impression of an *ex opere operato* conception of the sacraments is that Paul does not take into account the possibility that the sacraments might be unaccompanied by faith. So in Gal. iii. 27 he says, "All ye who were baptized into Christ did put on Christ." These words if taken alone might mean that every man, whatever the condition of his soul, who went through the external form of baptism had put on Christ. But of course as a matter of fact Paul means nothing of the kind. What he does mean is that the baptism of the Galatians, since that baptism was accompanied by faith (Gal. iii. 2), meant in that concrete case the putting on of Christ. Here again there is an appeal, in the presence of those who were in danger of forgetting spiritual facts, to the external sign which no one could forget.

This interpretation cannot be invalidated by the passages which have been appealed to as supporting a crassly *ex opere operato* conception of the sacraments. In 1 Cor. xi. 30, for example, Paul says that because of an unworthy partaking of the Lord's Supper many of the Corinthians were ill and many had died. But these words need not necessarily mean that the bread and wine, because of a dangerous magical virtue that was in them, had inflicted harm upon those who had not used them aright. They may mean at least equally well that the physical ills of the Corinthians were a chastisement which had been inflicted by God. As for 1 Cor. xv. 29 (baptism in behalf of the dead), it can be said at least that that verse is isolated and exceedingly obscure, and that it is bad historical method to allow what is obscure to color the interpretation of what is plain. Many interpretations of the verse have been proposed. And it is by no means clear that Paul lent his own support to the custom to which reference is here made.

Thus it cannot be maintained that Paulinism was like the pagan mysteries even in the general sense that both Paulinism and the mysteries connected salvation with external acts. The acts themselves were different; and the meaning of the acts was still more diverse. An element of truth does indeed underlie the sacramentarian interpretation of Paul. The element of truth consists in the protest which is here raised against the interpretation which has sometimes been favored by "liberal" scholars. According to this liberal interpretation, when Paul speaks of dying and rising with Christ he is referring to a purely ethical fact; when he says that he has died to the Law, he means that he has made a radical break with an external, legalistic type of religion; when he says that it is no longer he that lives but Christ that lives in him, he means that he has made Christ his supreme guide and example; when he says that through the Cross of Christ he has been crucified to the world, he means that the Cross has led him to renounce all worldliness of purpose. Such interpretation is exceedingly common. But it is radically false. It is false because it does away with the supernaturalism of Paul's teaching. There could be no greater mistake than that of making salvation according to Paul an affair of the human will. On the contrary, the very essence of Pauline teaching is supernaturalism. Salvation, according to Paul, is based upon a supernatural act of God—the resurrection of Jesus Christ. And equally supernatural is the application of salvation to the individual. The new creation which stands at the beginning of the Christian life is according to Paul just as little a product of natural forces, and just as little a product of the human will, as the first creation was. The modern school of comparative religion is entirely correct in insisting upon the thoroughgoing supernaturalism of the Pauline gospel. Paulinism is a redemptive religion in the most thoroughgoing sense of the word; it finds salvation, not in a decision of the human will, but in an act of God.

But the error comes in confusing supernaturalism with sacramentalism. Paul's conception of salvation is supernatural, but it is not external. It is indeed just as supernatural as if it were external. The beginning of a man's Christian life, according to Paul, is just as little a product of his own moral forces, just as little a product of any mere moral influence brought to bear upon him, as it would be if it were produced by the water into which he was dipped or the bread and wine of which he partakes. Conceivably God might have chosen to use such means. If He had done so, His action would have been not one whit more supernatural than it actually is. But as a matter of fact, He has chosen, in His mysterious wisdom, to use the means of faith. Such is the teaching of Paul. It is highly distasteful to the modern liberal Church. But even if it is to be rejected it should at least be recognized as Pauline.

Thus the interpretation of the sacraments which is proposed by the modern school of comparative religion—and indeed the whole modern radical treatment of Paulinism as a thoroughgoing religion of redemption—marks a reaction against the modernizing exegesis which was practised by the liberal school. But the reaction has at any rate gone too far. It cannot be said that the newer exegesis is any more objective than the liberal exegesis which it endeavors to replace. The liberal scholars were concerned to keep Paul as near as possible to their modern naturalistic principles, in order to continue to use him for the edification of the Church; the radical scholars of the school of comparative religion are concerned to keep him as far away as possible from modern naturalistic principles in order to bring him into connection with the crass externalism of the mystery religions. Neither group has attained the whole truth. The Pauline conception of salvation is just as spiritual as it is thought to be by the liberal scholars; but on the other hand, it is just as supernatural as it is represented as being by Reitzenstein and Bousset.

CHAPTER VIII
THE LORDSHIP OF JESUS

CHAPTER VIII

THE LORDSHIP OF JESUS

Two of the contentions of the modern school of comparative religion have so far been examined. It has been shown that neither the group of Pauline conceptions which centers around the new birth (or, as Paul calls it, the new creation) nor the Pauline teaching about the sacraments was derived from the mystery religions. The third element of Paulinism which is thought to have come from pagan religion is found in the Pauline conception of Christ and of the work of Christ in redemption. This contention is connected especially with the name of Bousset,[1] who is, however, supported in essentials by a considerable number of contemporary scholars. The hypothesis of Bousset is intimately connected with those hypotheses which have already been examined. A complete treatment of it at this point would therefore involve repetition. But it may here be set forth at least in a somewhat systematic, though still in a merely summary, way.

According to Bousset, the primitive Christian community in Jerusalem regarded Jesus chiefly as the Son of Man—the mysterious person, mentioned in the Jewish apocalypses, who was finally to come with the clouds of heaven and be the instrument in ushering in the Kingdom of God. Bousset is doubtful whether or no the title Son of Man was ever assumed by Jesus Himself, and regards the settlement of this question as lying beyond the scope of his book. But the tendency of the book is decidedly toward a radical denial of the Messianic consciousness of Jesus. And at this point the cautious investigator, even if his presuppositions are the same as Bousset's own, may well be inclined to take alarm. The method which is here pursued seems to be leading logically to the elimination from the pages of history of the whole Gospel picture of Jesus,

[1] *Kyrios Christos*, 1913; *Jesus der Herr*, 1916.

or rather to the use of that picture in the reconstruction not'
of the historical Jesus, but only of the belief of the Christian
community. Of course Bousset does not push matters to such
lengths; he is by no means inclined to follow W. B. Smith and
Drews in denying the historicity of Jesus. But the reader of
the first part of the "Kyrios Christos" has an uneasy feeling
that if any of the Gospel picture still escapes the keen edge
of Bousset's criticism, it is only by accident. Many of those
incidents in the Gospel narrative, many of those elements in
the Gospel teaching, which have been considered most characteristic of the historical Jesus have here been removed. There
seems to be no particular reason why the rest should remain;
for the elements that remain are quite similar to the elements
that have been made to go. No mark of authenticity seems
to be proof against the skepticism of this latest historian.
Bousset thus illustrates the difficulty of separating the natural
from the supernatural in the Gospel picture of Jesus. When
the process of separation begins, it is difficult to bring it to a
halt; the wheat is in danger of being rooted up with the tares.
Bousset has dealt a severe blow to the prestige of the liberal
reconstruction of Jesus. By the recent developments in his
thinking he has shown by his own example that the liberal
reconstruction is in a state of unstable equilibrium. It is always in danger of giving way to radical denial either of the
historicity of Jesus or of the historicity of the Messianic consciousness. Such radicalism is faced by insuperable difficulties.
Perhaps, then, there is something wrong with the critical
method from which the radicalism always tends to result.

But it is necessary now to examine a little more closely
the belief of the primitive Jerusalem Church. That belief,
Bousset maintains, did not involve any conception of Jesus
as "Lord." The title "Lord," he says, was not applied to
Jesus on Palestinian ground, and Jesus was not regarded by
the early Jerusalem Church as the object of faith. The piety
of the primitive Church was thus exclusively eschatological;
Jesus was expected to return in glory from heaven, but meanwhile He was regarded as separated from His disciples. He
was the heavenly "Son of Man," to come with the clouds of
heaven, not the "Lord" now present in the Church.

These momentous assertions, which lie at the very basis of
Bousset's hypothesis, are summed up in the elimination from

Jerusalem Christianity of the title "Lord" as applied to Jesus. This elimination of the title "Lord" of course involves a rejection of the testimony of Acts. The Book of Acts contains the only extant narrative of the early progress of Jerusalem Christianity. And so far as the designations of Christ are concerned, the early chapters of the book have usually been thought to produce an impression of special antiquity and authenticity. These chapters apply the title "Lord" to Jesus; the words in Acts ii. 36, "God has made him both Lord and Christ," have often been regarded as especially significant. But to Bousset, in view of his opinion about the Book of Acts as a whole, the elimination of this testimony causes no difficulty.

But how does Bousset know that the primitive Jerusalem Church did not apply the term "Lord" to Jesus? The principal argument is derived from an examination of the Synoptic Gospels. The title "Lord," as applied to Jesus, Bousset believes, appears only "on the margin" (as it were) of the Gospel tradition; it does not appear as one of the primitive elements in the tradition. But since it does not appear firmly fixed in the Gospel tradition, it could not have formed a part of Christian belief in the community where the Gospel tradition was formed. The community where the Gospel tradition was formed was the Jerusalem Church. Therefore the title Lord as applied to Jesus did not form part of the belief of the Jerusalem Church. Such, in bare outline, is the argument of Bousset.

An examination of that argument in detail would far transcend the limits of the present discussion.[1] But certain obvious remarks can be made.

In the first place, it is not perfectly clear that the title Lord appears only in secondary elements of the Gospel tradition. Certainly it must be granted to Bousset that the instances where the word "Lord" appears in the vocative case do not necessarily involve any recognition of the lofty title "Lord" as belonging to Jesus; for the word could be used in direct address in the presence of any person to whom respect was to be paid. Nevertheless, in some of the passages the word does seem to be more than a mere reverential form of address.

[1] See Vos, "The Kyrios Christos Controversy," in *The Princeton Theological Review*, xv, 1917, pp. 21-89. See also the review of Bousset's "Kyrios Christos" by the same author, *ibid.*, xii, 1914, pp. 636-645.

Bousset himself admits that such is the case at least in Matt. vii. 21, "Not every one who says unto me Lord, Lord, shall enter into the kingdom of heaven," and his opinion that this passage is secondary as compared with Lk. vi. 46 is insufficiently grounded. The cases in the Gospels where the title is used absolutely are not very numerous, and they occur chiefly in the Gospel of Luke. But the estimate of them as secondary depends of course upon certain critical conclusions about the relationships of the Synoptic Gospels. And it is doubtful whether Bousset has quite succeeded in refuting the argument which can be derived from Mk. xii. 35-37 (and parallels), the passage about David's son and David's Lord. Bousset himself uses this passage as an important testimony to the belief of the early Jerusalem Church, though he does not regard it as representing a genuine saying of Jesus. Yet here Jesus is made to call attention to the fact that David called the Messiah "Lord." If this passage represents the belief about Jesus of the primitive Jerusalem Church, what stronger testimony could there be to the use in that church of the title "Lord" as applied to Jesus? Bousset avoids the difficulty by calling attention to the fact that the Old Testament passage (Ps. cx. 1) is here quoted not according to the original but according to the Septuagint translation. In the original Hebrew, says Bousset, there was a distinction between the word "Lord" as applied to God and the word "Lord" as applied to the other person who is referred to; the Hebrew has, "Jahwe said to my Lord (adoni)." Thus that second person, according to the Hebrew, can be regarded as a human individual, and all that is meant by the term "Lord" as used of him by David is that he stood higher than David. Bousset seems to think that this explanation destroys the value of the passage as a witness to the use in the Jerusalem Church of the religious term "Lord" as applied to Jesus. But such is by no means the case. For if the Messiah (Jesus) was higher than David, so that David could call Him Lord, then Jesus must have occupied some very lofty position. . If David could call Him Lord, would the title be refused to Him by humble members of the Jerusalem Church? On Bousset's interpretation the passage may not directly attest the use of the title by the Jerusalem Church, but it does seem to presuppose it. It may also be questioned whether Bousset has succeeded in getting rid of Mk. xi. 3, as a witness to the title Lord as applied to Jesus in the Jerusalem Church.

But does the infrequency of the use of the title "Lord" in the Gospels necessarily indicate that that title was not prevalent in the primitive Jerusalem Church? It must be remembered that the title "Christ," which was of course applied to Jesus by the Jerusalem Church, is also very infrequent in the Gospels. Why should the infrequency in the Gospel use of one title be regarded as an argument against the use of that title in the Jerusalem Church, when in the case of the other title no such argument can possibly be set up? Bousset is ready with his answer. But the answer is entirely inadequate. The title "Christ," Bousset says, was an eschatological title; it referred to a dignity which in the belief of the Jerusalem Church Jesus was not to attain until His coming in glory. Therefore it could not readily be applied to Jesus in the accounts of His earthly ministry. Hence in the case of that title there was a special obstacle which hindered the intrusion of the title into the Gospel tradition. But in the case of the title "Lord," there was no such obstacle; therefore the non-intrusion of that title into the Gospel tradition requires a special explanation; and the only possible explanation is that the title was not used in the Jerusalem Church.

It would be difficult to crowd into brief compass so many highly debatable assertions as are crowded together in this argument. Was the title "Christ" a purely eschatological title? It is not a purely eschatological title in Paul. It is not really a purely eschatological title anywhere in the New Testament. At any rate, Bousset is here adopting a conception of the Messiahship of Jesus which is at best problematical and is rejected by men of the most widely divergent points of view. And did the title "Lord" designate Jesus especially as the present Lord of the Church, rather than as the one who was finally to usher in the Kingdom? Was Jesus in the belief of the early Church the "coming" Christ any more than He was the "coming" Lord; and was He the present Lord any more than He was the present Christ? These questions cannot be answered with absolute certainty. At any rate, even if Bousset can point to a larger proportion of eschatological interest in the one title than that which appears in the other, yet such a distinction is relative only. And it still remains true that if the infrequency of the title "Christ" in the Gospels does not indicate the non-existence of that title in the Jerusalem Church, the infrequency of the title "Lord" in the Gospels is not any more significant.

With regard to the title "Son of Man," Bousset makes a remark somewhat similar to that which he makes about the title "Christ." The title "Son of Man," he says, was eschatological; therefore it could not be introduced into the narrative part of the Gospels. But it will always remain one of the paradoxes of Bousset's theory that according to Bousset the title "Son of Man," which (except in Acts vii. 56) appears in the tradition only in the words of Jesus, and never as the title used when men spoke about Jesus, should be supposed to have been the characteristic title used in speaking about Jesus in the Jerusalem Church. If the belief of the Jerusalem Church about Jesus was so exclusively a Son-of-Man dogma, as Bousset supposes it was, and if that church was so little concerned with historical fact, it seems somewhat strange that the title, "Son of Man," has not been allowed, despite its eschatological character, to intrude into the Gospel narrative. Another hypothesis will always suggest itself—the hypothesis that Jesus really used the title, "Son of Man," in a somewhat mysterious way, in speaking about Himself, and that the memory of the fact that it was His own special designation of Himself has been preserved in the curious limitaticn of the use of the title in the New Testament. In that case, in view of the accuracy thus established with regard to one title, the testimony of the Gospels with regard to the other title, "Lord," cannot lightly be rejected.

But the evidence for the use of the title "Lord" in the primitive Jerusalem Church is not contained merely in the Gospels. Other evidence appears in the Pauline Epistles.

The most obvious fact is that Paul himself uses the term as the characteristic title of Jesus. And it is equally evident that he did not invent this usage. Evidently it was a continuation of a usage which prevailed before he began his work. So much is fully admitted by Bousset. But whence did Paul derive the usage? Or rather, supposing that he began his own use of the title at the moment of the conversion, in accordance with the representation in Acts ("Who art thou, Lord?"), whence did he derive his assumption that the title was already in use? The most obvious view is that he assumed the title to be already known because it was in use in the early Jerusalem Church. The matter-of-course way in which Paul applies the title "Lord" to Jesus has always, until recently, been taken as indicating that the title had been prevalent from the very beginning of the Church's life.

But at this point appears one of the most important features of Bousset's theory. Paul derived the title "Lord," Bousset believes, from those who had been Christians before him; but he derived it, not from the Jerusalem Church, but from the Christian communities in such cities as Antioch, Tarsus, and perhaps Damascus. It is in these communities, therefore, that the genesis of the title "Lord," as applied to Jesus, is to be placed.

Attention has already been called to the difficulties which beset this interposition of an extra link between Paul and the Jerusalem Church. It has been shown that what Paul "received" he received not from the churches at Antioch and Tarsus but from the original disciples at Jerusalem. But in addition to the general considerations which connect the whole of Paulinism with the Jerusalem tradition about Jesus, there are certain special indications of a Jerusalem origin of the title "Lord."

One such indication may be found, perhaps, in Gal. i. 19. When, in connection with a visit to Jerusalem which occurred three years after the conversion, Paul speaks of "James the brother of the Lord," the natural inference is that "the brother of the Lord" was a designation which was applied to James in Jerusalem; and if so, then the title "Lord" was current in the Jerusalem Church.[1] Of course, the inference is not absolutely certain; Paul might have designated James as "the brother of the Lord" because that was the designation of James in the Galatian Churches and the designation which Paul himself commonly used, even if it was not current in Jerusalem. But the natural impression which the passage will always make upon an unsophisticated reader is that Paul is using a terminology which was already fixed among James' associates at the time and place to which the narrative refers. It should be observed that in speaking of Peter, Paul actually uses the Aramaic form and not the Greek form of the name.

[1] Knowling, *The Witness of the Epistles*, 1892, p. 15.

The indications are that with regard to the leaders of the Jerusalem Church Paul is accustomed generally to follow the Jerusalem usage. And the evidence of such a passage as Gal. i. 18, 19, where Jerusalem conditions are mentioned, is doubly strong. The use in this passage of the title "brother of the Lord" would indeed not be absolutely decisive if it stood alone. But taken in connection with the other evidence, it does point strongly to the prevalence in the early Jerusalem Church of the title "Lord" as applied to Jesus.

More stress is usually laid upon the occurrence of "Maranatha" in 1 Cor. xvi. 22. "Maranatha" is Aramaic, and it means "Our Lord, come!" Why was the Aramaic word "Our Lord" included, as a designation of Jesus, in a Greek letter? The natural supposition is that it had been hallowed by its use in the Aramaic-speaking church at Jerusalem. Accordingly it pushes the use of the title "Lord" back to the primitive Christian community; the title cannot, therefore, be regarded as a product of the Hellenistic churches in Antioch and Tarsus.

This argument has been met in various ways. According to Böhlig, the passage does attest the application of the Aramaic title "Lord" to Jesus, but that application, Böhlig believes, was made not in Palestine but in Syria, not in Jerusalem but in Antioch. Syria, indeed, with Cilicia, was, Böhlig insists, the special home of the designation "Lord" as applied to the gods; the word "Baal," the common Semitic title of the Syrian gods, means "Lord." And Böhlig also points to the appearance of the title Mar along with Baal as a title of divinity.[1]

But why was the Semitic title retained in a Greek letter? In answer to this question the bilingual condition of Syria may be appealed to. But what particular sanctity could be attached to the Semitic usage of Syria; why should Paul follow that usage in writing to a church that was situated, not in the East, but in Greece proper? If, on the other hand, the title "Mar" had been hallowed by the use of the original disciples of Jesus, then the retention of the original word without translation is perfectly natural.

Bousset now proposes another hypothesis.[2] The phrase

[1] See Böhlig, "Zum Begriff Kyrios bei Paulus," in *Zeitschrift für die neutestamentliche Wissenschaft*, xiv, 1913, pp. 23-37.
[2] Bousset, *Jesus der Herr*, 1916, pp. 22f. Compare *Kyrios Christos*, 1913, p. 103.

"Maranatha," he says, probably had nothing to do with Jesus; it constitutes merely a formula of cursing like the "anathema" which immediately precedes in 1 Cor. xvi. 22; the Maran (or Marana) refers not to Jesus, but to God; the formula means, "Our Lord (God) shall come and judge." But Bousset adduces no real evidence in support of his explanation. No such formula of cursing seems to have been found in Semitic sources. And why should Paul introduce such a Semitic curse in writing to Corinth? The latest hypothesis of Bousset is certainly a desperate expedient.

"Marana" in 1 Cor. xvi. 22, therefore, certainly refers to Jesus, and the strong presumption is that it was derived from Palestine. The passage constitutes a real testimony to the use of the title "Lord" as a designation of Jesus in the Palestinian Church.

Possibly, moreover, this passage may also serve to fix the original Aramaic form of the title. Bousset and certain other scholars have been inclined to detect a linguistic difficulty in the way of attributing the title "Lord" to the Aramaic-speaking Church. The absolute "Mara," it is said, does not seem to have been current in Aramaic; only "Mari" ("my Lord") and "Maran" ("our Lord") seem to have been commonly used. But it is just in the absolute form, "the Lord," that the title appears most frequently in the Greek New Testament. Therefore, it is concluded, this New Testament Greek usage cannot go back to the usage of the Aramaic-speaking Church. It will perhaps be unnecessary to enter upon the linguistic side of this argument. Various possibilities might be suggested for examination to the students of Aramaic—among others, the possibility that "Mari," "Maran," had come to be used absolutely, like "Rabbi," "Rabban," the original meaning of the possessive suffix having been obscured.[1] But in general it can probably be said that if persons of Aramaic speech had desired to designate Jesus, absolutely, as "Lord" or "the Lord," the language was presumably not so poor but that the essential idea could have been expressed. And it is the essential idea, not the word, which is really important. The important thing is that the attitude toward Jesus which is expressed by the Greek word "Kyrios," was, unless all indications fail, also the attitude of the Jerusalem Church.

But may not the Greek title itself have originated in

[1] Compare Bousset, *Kyrios Christos*, 1913, p. 99, Anm. 3.

Jerusalem? This possibility has been neglected in recent discussions of the subject. But it is worthy of the most careful consideration. It should be remembered that Palestine in the first century after Christ was a bilingual country.[1] No doubt Aramaic was in common use among the great body of the people, and no doubt it was the language of Jesus' teaching. But Greek was also in use, and it is by no means beyond the bounds of possibility that even Jesus spoke Greek when occasion demanded. At any rate, the early Jerusalem Church included a large body of Greek-speaking persons; the "Hellenists" are mentioned in Acts vi. 1 in a way to which high historical importance is usually attributed. It is altogether probable, therefore, that the terminology current in the Jerusalem Church from the very beginning, or almost from the very beginning, was Greek as well as Aramaic. From this Greek-speaking part of the Church the original apostles could hardly have held themselves aloof. Total ignorance of Greek on the part of Galileans is improbable in view of what is known in general about linguistic conditions in Palestine; and in the capital, with its foreign connections, and its hosts of Hellenists, the opportunity for the use of Greek would be enormously increased. It is altogether improbable, therefore, that the Greek terminology of the Hellenists resident in Jerusalem was formed without the approval of the original disciples of Jesus. When the apostle Paul, therefore, assumes everywhere that the term "Lord" as applied to Jesus was no peculiarity of his own, but was familiar to all his readers, the phenomenon can be best explained if not only the sense of the title, but also its Greek form, was due to the mother Church. In other words, the transition from Aramaic to Greek, as the language of the disciples of Jesus, did not occur at Antioch or Tarsus, as Bousset seems to think. In all probability it occurred at Jerusalem, and occurred under the supervision of the immediate friends of Jesus. It could not possibly, therefore, have involved a transformation of the original faith.

But the linguistic considerations just adduced are only supplementary. Even if the use of Greek in Jerusalem was less important than has here been suggested, the state of the

---

[1] Zahn, *Einleitung in das Neue Testament*, 3te Aufl., i, 1906, pp. 24-32, 39-47 (English Translation, *Introduction to the New Testament*, 2nd Ed., 1917, i, pp. 34-46, 57-67).

case is not essentially altered. Every attempt at separating the religion of Paul sharply from the religion of the Jerusalem Church has resulted in failure. Whatever may have been the linguistic facts, the divine Lord of the Epistles was also the Lord of those who had been intimate friends of Jesus of Nazareth.

Bousset of course rejects this conclusion. But he does so on insufficient grounds. His theory, it may well be maintained, has already broken down at the most decisive point. It is not really possible to interpose the Christianity of Antioch and Tarsus between the Jerusalem Church and Paul; it is not really possible to suppose that that Christianity of Antioch was essentially different from the Jerusalem Christianity which had given it birth; in particular it is not possible to deny the use of the title "Lord," and the religious attitude toward Jesus which the title represents, to the original friends of Jesus. Examination of the further elements of Bousset's theory, therefore, can be undertaken only under protest. But such examination is important. For it will confirm the unfavorable impression which has already been received.

If, as Bousset says, the title "Lord," as a designation of Jesus, originated not at Jerusalem but at Antioch, in what way did it originate? It orginated, Bousset believes, in the meetings of the Church, and it originated in dependence upon the surrounding pagan cults. At Jerusalem, according to Bousset, the piety of the disciples was purely eschatological; Jesus was awaited with eagerness, He was to come in glory, but meanwhile He was absent. There was no thought of communion with Him. At Antioch, however, a different attitude began to be assumed. As the little community of disciples was united for comfort and prayer and the reception of the ecstatic gifts of the Spirit, it came to be felt that Jesus was actually present; the wonderful experiences of the meetings came to be attributed to Him. But if He was actually present in the meetings of the Church, a new title was required to express what He meant to those who belonged to Him. And one title lay ready to hand. It was the title "Lord." That title was used by the pagans to designate their own false gods. Surely no lower title could be used by the Christians to designate their Jesus. The title "Lord," moreover, was especially a cult-title; it was used to designate those gods who presided especially over the worship, over the "cult," of the pagan religions. But it was just in the "cult," in the meetings of the Church, that the new attitude toward Jesus had arisen. The experience of Jesus' presence, therefore, and the title which would give expression to it, were naturally joined together. In the rapture of a meeting of the group of worshipers, in the midst of wonderful ecstatic experiences, some member of the Church at Antioch or Tarsus, or perhaps many members simultaneously, uttered the momentous words, "Lord Jesus."

Thus occurred, according to the theory of Bousset, the most momentous event in the history of Christianity, one of the most momentous events in the whole religious history of the race. Christianity ceased to be merely faith in God like the faith which Jesus had; it became faith in Jesus. Jesus was now no longer merely an example for faith; He had become the object of faith. The prophet of Nazareth had become an object of worship; the Messiah had given way to the "Lord." Jesus had taken a place which before had been assigned only to God.

This estimate of the event of course depends upon Bousset's critical conclusions about the New Testament literature. And those conclusions are open to serious objections. The objections have already been considered so far as the title "Lord" is concerned; that title cannot really be denied to the original disciples of Jesus. Equally serious are the objections against what Bousset says about "faith in Jesus." A consideration of these objections lies beyond the scope of the present discussion. The ground has been covered in masterly fashion by James Denney, who has shown that even in the earliest strata of the Gospel literature, as they are distinguished by modern criticism of sources, Jesus appears not merely as an example for faith but as the object of faith—indeed, that Jesus actually so presented Himself.[1] Christianity was never a mere imitation of the faith which Jesus reposed in God. But it is now necessary to return to the examination of the Antioch Church.

The title "Lord," as applied to Jesus, Bousset believes, originated in the meetings of the Antioch disciples—in what may be called, for want of a better term, the "public worship" of the Church. This assertion constitutes an important step

[1] Denney, *Jesus and the Gospel*, 1908.

in Bousset's reconstruction. But the evidence adduced in support of it is insufficient. The passages cited from the Pauline Epistles show, indeed, that great importance was attributed to the meetings of the Church; they show perhaps that the custom of holding such meetings prevailed from the very beginning. But they do not show that the whole of the Church's devotion to Christ and the whole of Paul's religion were derived, by way of development, from the cult. It is not necessary to suppose either that the individual relation to Christ was derived from the cult, or that the cult was derived from the individual relation. There is also a third possibility—that individual piety and the cult were both practised from the very beginning side by side. At any rate, Bousset has vastly underestimated the importance of the conversion as determining the character of Paul's religious life. The Damascus experience lay at the very foundation of all of Paul's thinking and all of his actions. Yet that experience had nothing to do with the cult.

But even if, in accordance with Bousset's reconstruction, the title "Lord" was applied to Jesus under the influence of the ecstatic conditions that prevailed in the meetings of the Church, the origin of the title is not yet explained. How did the Christians at Antioch come to think that their ecstatic experiences were due to the fact that Jesus was presiding over their meetings? And if they did come to think so, why did they choose just the title "Lord" in order to express the dignity that they desired to attribute to Him?

At this point, Bousset has recourse to a comparison with the surrounding paganism. The term "Lord," he says, was common in the Hellenistic age as a title of the cult-gods of the various forms of worship. And the material which Bousset has collected in proof of this assertion is entirely convincing. Not only in the worship of the Emperors and other rulers, but also in the Hellenized religions of the East, the title "Lord" was well known as a designation of divinity. Indeed, Paul himself refers plainly to the currency of the title. "For though there be," he says, "that are called gods, whether in heaven or on earth; as there are gods many, and lords many; yet to us there is one God, the Father, of whom are all things, and we unto him; and one Lord, Jesus Christ, through whom are all things, and we through him" (1 Cor. viii. 5, 6). In this passage, the "lords many" are of course heathen gods, and it is clearly implied that the term "lord" was the title which was given them by their own worshipers. Bousset is entirely correct, therefore, when he says that the title "Lord," at Antioch, at Tarsus, and everywhere in the Greco-Roman world, was clearly a title of divinity. Indeed, it may be added, the word "lord" was no whit inferior in dignity to the term "god." [1] When the early Christian missionaries, therefore, called Jesus "Lord," it was perfectly plain to their pagan hearers everywhere that they meant to ascribe divinity to Him and desired to worship Him.

Thus the currency of the title in pagan religion was of great importance for the early Christian mission. But that does not necessarily mean that the title was applied to Jesus in the first place because of the pagan usage, or that the ascription of divine dignity to Jesus was first ventured upon because the Christians desired to place the one whom they revered in a position at least equal to that of the pagan cult-gods. It is these assertions which have not been proved. Indeed, they are improbable in the extreme. They are rendered improbable, for example, by the sturdy monotheism of the Christian communities. That monotheism was not at all impaired by the honor which was paid to Jesus; the Christian communities were just as intolerant of other gods as had been the ancient Hebrew prophets. This intolerance and exclusiveness of the early Church constitutes a stupendous difference between the Christian "Jesus-cult" and the cults of the other "Lords." The pagan cults were entirely tolerant; worship of one Lord did not mean the relinquishment of another. But to the Christians there was one Lord and one only. It is very difficult to see how in an atmosphere of such monotheism the influence of the pagan cults could have been allowed to intrude. Any thought of the analogy which an application of the title "Lord" to Jesus would set up between the meetings of the Church at Antioch and the worship of the heathen gods would have hindered, rather than have actually caused, the use of the title. Evidently the title, and especially the divine dignity of Jesus which the title expressed, were quite independent of the pagan usage.

[1] Warfield, "'God our Father and the Lord Jesus Christ,'" in *The Princeton Theological Review*, xv, 1917, p. 18.

Certainly the mere fact that the Christians used a title which was also used in the pagan cults does not establish any dependence upon paganism. For the title "Lord"[1] was almost as well established as a designation of divinity as was the term "God." [2] Whatever had been the origin of the religious use of the word, that use had become a part of the Greek language. A missionary who desired to proclaim the one true God was obliged, if he spoke in Greek, to use the term "God," which of course had been used in pagan religion. So if he desired to designate Jesus as God, by some word which at the same time would distinguish Him from God the Father, he was obliged to use the word "Lord," though that word also had been used in paganism. Neither in the one case nor in the other did the use of a Greek word involve the slightest influence of the conceptions which had been attached to the word in a polytheistic religion.

But there was a far stronger reason for the application of the Greek term "Lord" to Jesus than that which was found in its general currency among Greek-speaking peoples. The religious use of the term was not limited to the pagan cults, but appears also, and if anything even more firmly established, in the Greek Old Testament. The word "Lord" is used by the Septuagint to translate the "Jahwe" of the Hebrew text. It would be quite irrelevant to discuss the reasons which governed the translators in their choice of this particular word. No doubt some word for "Lord" was required by the associations which had already clustered around the Hebrew word. And various reasons may be suggested for the choice of "kyrios" rather than some other Greek word meaning "lord." [3] Possibly the root meaning of "kyrios" better expressed the idea which was intended; perhaps, also, a religious meaning had already been attached to "kyrios," which the other words did not possess. At any rate, whatever may have been the reason, "kyrios" was the word which was chosen. And the fact is of capital importance. For it was among the readers of the Septuagint that Christianity first made its way. The Septuagint was the Bible of the Jewish synagogues, and in the synagogues the reading of it was heard not only

---

[1] κύριος.
[2] θεός.
[3] As, for example, δεσπότης

by Jews but also by hosts of Gentiles, the "God-fearers" of the Book of Acts. It was with the "God-fearers" that the Gentile mission began. And even where there were Gentile converts who had not passed at all through the school of the synagogue—in the very earliest period perhaps such converts were few—even then the Septuagint was at once used in their instruction. Thus when the Christian missionaries used the word "Lord" of Jesus, their hearers knew at once what they meant. They knew at once that Jesus occupied a place which is occupied only by God. For the word "Lord" is used countless times in the Greek scriptures as the holiest name of the covenant God of Israel, and these passages were applied freely to Jesus.

This Septuagint use of the term "Lord," with the application of the Septuagint passages to Jesus, which appears as a matter of course in the Epistles of Paul, was of vastly more importance for the early Christian mission than the use of the term in the pagan cults. And it sheds vastly more light upon the original significance of the term as applied to Jesus. But the pagan usage is interesting, and the exhibition of it by Bousset and others should be thankfully received. An important fact has been established more and more firmly by modern research—the fact that the Greek word "kyrios" in the first century of our era was, wherever the Greek language extended, distinctly a designation of divinity. The common usage of the word indeed persisted; the word still expressed the relation which a master sustained toward his slaves. But the word had come to be a characteristically religious term, and it is in the religious sense, especially as fixed by the Septuagint, that it appears in the New Testament.

Thus it is not in accordance with New Testament usage when Jesus is called, by certain persons in the modern Church, "the Master," rather than "the Lord." Sometimes, perhaps, this usage is adopted in conscious protest against the New Testament conception of the deity of Christ; Jesus is spoken of as "the Master," in very much the way in which the leader of a school of artists is spoken of as "the Master" by his followers. Or else the word means merely the one whose commands are to be obeyed. But sometimes the modern fashion is adopted by devout men and women with the notion that the

English word "Lord" has been worn down and that the use of the word "Master" is a closer approach to the meaning of the Greek Testament. This notion is false. In translating the New Testament designation of Jesus, one should not desire to get back to the original meaning of the word "kyrios." For the Greek word had already undergone a development, and as applied to Jesus in the New Testament it was clearly a religious term. It had exactly the religious associations which are now possessed by our English word "Lord." And for very much the same reason. The religious associations of the English word "Lord" are due to Bible usage; and the religious associations of the New Testament word "kyrios" were also due to Bible usage—the usage of the Septuagint. The Christian, then, should remember that "a little learning is a dangerous thing." The uniform substitution of "the Master" for "the Lord" in speaking of Jesus has only a false appearance of freshness and originality. In reality it sometimes means a departure from the spirit of the New Testament usage.

Accordingly, Bousset has performed a service in setting in clear relief the religious meaning of the word "Lord." But he has not succeeded in explaining the application of that word to Jesus.

Further difficulties, moreover, beset Bousset's theory. The term "Lord" as applied to Jesus, and the religious attitude toward Jesus expressed by the term, arose, according to Bousset, in the meetings of such communities as the one at Antioch, and under the influence of pagan conceptions. But of course Bousset's explanation of the origin of Paulinism has not yet been completely set forth. Paulinism is something far more than an ecstatic worship of a cult-god; the personal relation to Christ dominates every department of the apostle's life.

Bousset recognizes this fact. The religion of Paul, he admits, is something far more than the religion which was expressed in the meetings of the Antioch Church. But he supposes that the other elements of Paul's religion, far-reaching as they are, had at least their starting-point in the cult. Here is to be found one of the least plausible elements in the whole construction. Bousset has underestimated the individualistic character of Paul's religion. At least he has not succeeded in showing that the Pauline life "in Christ" or "in the Lord" was produced by development from ecstatic experiences in the meetings of the Antioch Church.

But if the individualistic religion of Paul was developed from the "cult," how was it developed? How shall the introduction of the new elements be explained? Bousset has attacked this problem with great earnestness. And he tries to show that the religion of Paul as it appears in the Epistles was developed from the cult religion of Antioch by the identification of "the Lord" with "the Spirit," and by the generalizing and ethicizing of the conception of the Spirit's activity.

The Pauline doctrine of the Spirit, Bousset believes, was derived from the pagan mystical religion of the Hellenistic age. Quite aside from the matter of terminology—though the contentions of Reitzenstein are thought by Bousset to be essentially correct—the fundamental pessimistic dualism of Paul was based, according to Bousset, upon that widespread type of thought and life which appears in the mystery religions and in the Hermetic writings. According to this pessimistic way of thinking, salvation could never be attained by human nature, even with divine aid, but only by an entirely new beginning, produced by the substitution of the divine nature for the old man. By the apostle Paul, Bousset continues, this supernaturalism, this conception of the dominance of divine power in the new life, was extended far beyond the limits of the cult or of visionary experiences; the Spirit was made to be the ruling principle of the Christian's life; not only prophecy, tongues, healing, and the like, were now regarded as the fruit of the Spirit, but also love, joy, peace, longsuffering, kindness, goodness, faithfulness, meekness, self-control. But this Pauline extension of the Spirit's activity, Bousset insists, did not involve the slightest weakening of the supernaturalism which was characteristic of the original conception; the Spirit that produced love, joy, peace, had just as little to do with the human spirit as the Spirit that caused men to speak with tongues. And the supernaturalism which here appears in glorified form was derived, Bousset concludes, from the mystical pagan religion of the Hellenistic age.

This contention has already been discussed, and the weakness of it has been pointed out. The Pauline doctrine of the Spirit was not derived from contemporary paganism. But the exposition of Bousset's theory has not yet been finished. The Spirit whose activities were extended by Paul into the innermost recesses of the Christian's life was identified, Bousset says, with "the Lord" (2 Cor. iii. 17). This identification exerted an important influence upon both the elements that were brought together; it exerted an important influence upon the conception both of "the Lord" and of "the Spirit." If "the Lord" was identified, or brought into very close relation, with the Spirit, and if the Spirit's activity extended into the whole of life, then "the Lord" could no longer be for Paul merely the cult-god who was present in the meetings of the Church. On the contrary, He would have to be present everywhere where the Spirit was present—that is, He would have to be that in which the Christian lived and moved and had his being. Thus Paul could form the astonishing phrase "in Christ" or "in the Lord," for which Bousset admits that no analogy is to be found in pagan religion. On the other hand, the conception of the Spirit, Bousset believes, was necessarily modified by its connection with "the Lord." By the identification with an actual person who had lived but a few years before, "the Spirit" was given a personal quality which otherwise it did not possess. Or, to put the same thing in other words, the Pauline phrase "in the Lord" is not exactly the same in meaning as the phrase "in the Spirit"; for it possesses a peculiar personal character. "This remarkable mingling of abstraction and personality," says Bousset, "this connection of a religious principle with a person who had walked here on the earth and had here suffered death, is a phenomenon of peculiar power and originality."

At this point, Bousset is in danger of being untrue to the fundamental principles of his reconstruction; he is in danger of bringing the religion of Paul into connection with the concrete person of Jesus. But he detects the danger and avoids it. It must not be supposed, he says, that Paul had any very clear impression of the characteristics of the historical Jesus. For if he had had such an impression, he never could have connected Jesus with an abstraction like the Spirit. All that he was interested in, then, was the fact that Jesus had lived and especially that He had died.

Yet these bare facts are thought to have been sufficient to impart to Paul's notion of the Spirit-Lord that peculiar personal quality which arouses the admiration of Bousset! The truth is, Bousset finds himself at this point face to face with the difficulty which besets every naturalistic explanation of the genesis of Paul's religion. The trouble is that a close connection of Paul with the historical Jesus is imperatively required by the historian in order to impart to Paul's relation to Christ that warm, personal quality which shines out from every page of the Epistles; whereas, on the other hand, a wide separation of Paul from the historical Jesus is just as imperatively required in order that Paul might not be hampered by historical tradition in raising Jesus to divine dignity and in bringing Him into connection with the Spirit of God.

Modern criticism has wavered between the two requirements; it tries to preserve the rights of each. Bousset is more impressed by the second requirement; Wernle, his opponent, is more impressed by the former.[1] But both are equally wrong. There is really only one way out of the difficulty. It is an old way and a radical way. But the world of scholarship may come back to it in the end. The fundamental difficulty in explaining the origin of Paulinism will never disappear by being ignored; it will never yield to compromises of any kind. It will disappear only when Jesus is recognized as being really what Paul presupposes Him to be and what all the Gospels represent Him as being—the eternal Son of God, come to earth for the redemption of man, now seated once more on the throne of His glory, and working in the hearts of His disciples through His Spirit, as only God can work. Such a solution was never so unpopular as it is to-day. Acceptance of it will involve a Copernican revolution in many departments of human thought and life. But refusal of such acceptance has left an historical problem which so far has not been solved.

At one point, Bousset admits, the religion of Paul was based upon an historical fact. It was based upon the death of Jesus. But the Pauline interpretation of the death of Jesus was derived, Bousset believes, in important particulars from contemporary pagan religion; the Pauline notion of dying and rising with Christ was formed under the influence of the widespread pagan conception of the dying and rising god. This assertion has become quite common among recent

[1] Wernle, "Jesus and Paulus. Antithesen zu Boussets Kyrios Christos," in *Zeitschrift für Theologie und Kirche*, xxv, 1915, pp. 1-92.

scholars; material in support of it has been collected in convenient form by M. Brückner.[1] But as a matter of fact, the evidence in support of the assertion is of the feeblest kind.

The review of Hellenistic religion which was attempted in Chapter VI revealed, indeed, the fact that certain gods, especially Attis, Adonis, and Osiris, were represented first as dying and then as being resuscitated. The similarity of these figures to one another may perhaps be explained by the hypothesis that all of them were originally vegetation gods, whose death and resuscitation represented the withering of vegetation in the autumn and its renewal in the spring. At first sight, the parallel between these gods and Jesus may seem striking. Jesus also was represented as dying and as coming back to life again. But what is the significance of the parallel? Can it mean that the entire New Testament story of the death and resurrection of Jesus was derived from these vegetation myths? Such has been the conclusion of certain modern scholars. But of course this conclusion is absurd, and it is not favored by Bousset. The essential historicity of the crucifixion of Jesus under Pontius Pilate and of the rise of the belief in His resurrection among His intimate friends stands too firm to be shaken by any theory of dependence upon pagan myth. Thus the argument drawn from the parallel between the New Testament story and the pagan myth of the dying and rising god proves too much. If it proves anything, it proves that the New Testament story of the resurrection was derived from the pagan myth. But such a view has not been held by any serious historians. Therefore it will have to be admitted that the parallel between the belief that Adonis and Osiris and Attis died and rose again, and the belief that Jesus died and rose again was not produced by dependence of one story upon the other. It will have to be recognized, therefore, that a parallel does not always mean a relationship of dependence. And if it does not do so at one point, perhaps it does not do so at others.

But Bousset will insist that although the New Testament story of the death and resurrection of Jesus was not originally produced by the pagan myth, yet the influence of the pagan conception made itself felt in the interpretation which Paul placed upon the story. Paul believed that the Christian shared

[1] *Der sterbende und auferstehende Gottheiland*, 1908.

the fate of Christ—died with Christ and rose with Christ. But a similar conception appears in the pagan religions. The classical expression of this idea appears in the oft-quoted words reported by Firmicus Maternus, "Be of good courage, ye initiates, since the god is saved; for to us there shall be salvation out of troubles."

But it must be remembered that the testimony of Firmicus Maternus is very late, and that the evidence for the prevalence of the conception in the early period is somewhat scanty. The confident assertions of recent writers with regard to these matters are nothing short of astonishing. Lay readers are likely to receive the impression that the investigator can reconstruct the conception of a dying and rising god, and of the share which the worshipers have in the death and resurrection, on the basis of some vast store of information in the extant sources. As a matter of fact, nothing of the sort is the case. The extant information about the conception in question is scanty in the extreme, and for the most part dates from long after the time of Paul.

It would be going too far, indeed, to assert that the conception of the dying and rising god, with its religious significance, was not in existence before the Pauline period. An ancient Egyptian text, for example, has been quoted by Erman, which makes the welfare of the worshiper depend upon that of Osiris: "Even as Osiris lives, he also shall live." [1] Very likely some such conceptions were connected also with the mourning and subsequent rejoicing for Attis and Adonis. But if the conception was existent in the pre-Pauline period, it by no means follows that it was common. Certainly its prevalence has been enormously exaggerated in recent years. Against such exaggerations, J. Weiss—who surely cannot be accused of any lack of sympathy with the methods of comparative religion as applied to the New Testament—has pertinently called attention to 1 Cor. i. 23. Christ crucified, Paul says, was "to the Gentiles foolishness." [2] That does not look as though the Gentiles among whom Paul labored were very

[1] Erman, "A Handbook of Egyptian Religion" (published in the original German edition as a handbook, by the *Generalverwaltung* of the Berlin Imperial Museum), 1907, p. 95.
[2] J. Weiss, "Das Problem der Entstehung des Christentums," in *Archiv für Religionswissenschaft*, xvi, 1913, p. 490.

familiar with the notion of a dying god. If the contentions of Brückner were correct, if the conception of the dying god were as common in Paul's day as Brückner supposes, the Cross would not have been "to the Gentiles foolishness"; on the contrary, it would have seemed to the Gentiles to be the most natural thing in the world.

But even if the early prevalence of the conception of a dying and rising god, with its religious significance, were better established than it is, the dependence of Paul upon that conception would by no means be proved. For the Pauline conception is totally different. One difference, of course, is perfectly obvious and is indeed generally recognized—the Pauline Christ is represented as dying voluntarily, and dying for the sake of men. He "loved me," says Paul, "and gave himself for me." There is absolutely nothing like that conception in the case of the pagan religions. Osiris, Adonis, and Attis were overtaken by their fate; Jesus gave His life freely away. The difference is stupendous; it involves the very heart of the religion of Paul. How was the difference caused? Whence was derived the Pauline conception of the grace of Christ? Was it derived from Jesus Himself? Was it derived from the knowledge which Paul had of the character of Jesus? The supposition might seem to be natural. But unfortunately, from the point of view of Bousset, it must be rejected. For if Paul had had any knowledge of Jesus' real character, how could he ever have supposed that Jesus, a mere man, was the heavenly Lord?

Another difference is even more fundamental. The death and resurrection of the pagan gods was a matter of the cult; the death and resurrection of the Pauline Christ was a fact of history. It has been observed in the review of Hellenistic religion that the cults in the pagan religions were much more firmly fixed than the myths, in the opinion of modern scholars, the myths were derived from the cults rather than vice versa. So in the case of the "dying and rising gods," one is struck above all things with the totally fluid character of the myths. The story of Attis, for example, is told in many divergent forms, and there does not seem to have been the slightest interest among the Attis worshipers for the establishment of any authentic account of the death and resurrection of the god. Particularly the "resurrection" of the god appears in the myths of Attis, Adonis, and Osiris scarcely at all. The real death and resurrection occurred only in the cult. Every year in March, the Attis-worshipers at Rome first saw the god lying dead as he was represented by the fir-tree, and then rejoiced in his resurrection. The death and resurrection were hardly conceived of as events which had happened once for all long ago. They were rather thought of as happening at every celebration of the festival.

The Pauline treatment of the death and resurrection of Christ is entirely different. By Bousset, indeed, the difference is partly obscured; Bousset tries to show that the Pauline conception of the dying and rising of the believer with Christ was derived from the celebration of the sacraments. But there could be no more radical error. What is plainest of all in the Epistles is the historical character of the Pauline message. The religion of Paul was rooted in an event, and the sacraments were one way of setting forth the significance of the event. The event was the redemptive work of Christ in His death and resurrection.

Here lies the profoundest of all differences between Paul and contemporary religion. Paulinism was not a philosophy; it was not a set of directions for escape from the misery of the world; it was not an account of what had always been true. On the contrary, it was an account of something that had happened. The thing that had happened, moreover, was not hidden in the dim and distant past. The account of it was not evolved as a justification for existing religious forms. On the contrary, the death and resurrection of Jesus, upon which Paul's gospel was based, had happened only a few years before. And the facts could be established by adequate testimony; the eyewitnesses could be questioned, and Paul appeals to the eyewitnesses in detail. The single passage, 1 Cor. xv. 1-8, is sufficient to place a stupendous gulf between the Pauline Christ and the pagan saviour-gods. But the character of Paulinism does not depend upon one passage. Everywhere in the Epistles Paul stakes all his life upon the truth of what he says about the death and resurrection of Jesus. The gospel which Paul preached was an account of something that had happened. If the account was true, the origin of Paulinism is explained; if it was not true, the Church is based upon an inexplicable error.

This latter alternative has been examined in the preceding

discussion. If Jesus was not the divine Redeemer that Paul says He was, how did the Pauline religion of redemption arise? Three great hypotheses have been examined and have been found wanting. Paulinism, it has been shown, was not based upon the Jesus of modern naturalism; if Jesus was only what He is represented by modern naturalistic historians as being, then what is really distinctive of Paul was not derived from Jesus. The establishment of that fact has been a notable achievement of Wrede and Bousset. But if what is essential in Paulinism was not derived from Jesus, whence was it derived? It was not derived, as Wrede believed, from the pre-Christian apocalyptic notions of the Messiah; for the apocalyptic Messiah was not an object of worship, and not a living person to be loved. It was not derived from pagan religion, in accordance with the brilliant hypothesis of Bousset; for pagan influence is excluded by the self-testimony of Paul, and the pagan parallels utterly break down. But even if the parallels were ten times closer than they are, the heart of the problem would not even have been touched. The heart of the problem is found in the Pauline relation to Christ. That relation cannot be described by mere enumeration of details; it cannot be reduced to lower terms; it is an absolutely simple and indivisible thing. The relation of Paul to Christ is a relation of love; and love exists only between persons. It is not a group of ideas that is to be explained, if Paulinism is to be accounted for, but the love of Paul for his Saviour. And that love is rooted, not in what Christ had said, but in what Christ had done. He "loved me and gave Himself for me." There lies the basis of the religion of Paul; there lies the basis of all of Christianity. That basis is confirmed by the account of Jesus which is given in the Gospels, and given, indeed, in all the sources. It is opposed only by modern reconstructions. And those reconstructions are all breaking down. The religion of Paul was not founded upon a complex of ideas derived from Judaism or from paganism. It was founded upon the historical Jesus. But the historical Jesus upon whom it was founded was not the Jesus of modern reconstruction, but the Jesus of the whole New Testament and of Christian faith; not a teacher who survived only in the memory of His disciples, but the Saviour who after His redeeming work was done still lived and could still be loved.

INDEX

I NAMES AND SUBJECTS

II BIBLICAL PASSAGES

OLD TESTAMENT

NEW TESTAMENT